Click - Connecting you with Jesus and His Word

Published by: Mesoamerica Region Discipleship Ministries

www.discipleship.MesoamericaRegion.org

www.SdmiResources.MesoamericaRegion.org

Copyright © 2018 - All rights reserved

ISBN: 978-1-63580-079-1

All of the scripture verses quoted are from the NIV Bible unless otherwise stated.

Translated into English from Spanish by:
Noel Smallish (Lessons 1-11), Abdiel Jiménez (Lessons 12-25), Dr. Dorothy Bullón (Lessons 26-52)

Printed in the United States

Table of Contents

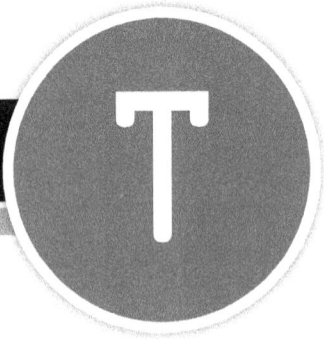

Unit 4 • Christians and modern beliefs

Unit 5 • Emotions

Unit 6 • Life Project

Presentation

Congratulations for getting this book of Christian education lessons for youth and young adults.

As a teacher of adolescents and young adults, it will help you to know that the material you have in your hands is 100% biblical, and prepared especially for teenagers and young adults. An international team of people trained in various disciplines, and knowledgeable about today's adolescents and young adults, prepared each lesson.

On the following pages, you will find 52 lessons divided into six thematic units. They don't have the same number of lessons, but vary according to the importance and sub-themes selected.

Understanding the characteristics and needs of the stages of adolescence/youth and young adults, the book is designed for two age groups: One for adolescents/youth from 12-17 years and one for young adults from 18 to 23 years. In any case, you are free to adapt it according to the needs and facilities you have in your local church.

In each lesson, you will find the following sections:

- The objective that will guide you throughout the lesson.
- The Connect section, which is the introduction to the topic where activities for each age group are suggested.
- The Navigate section where the theme of the lesson is developed.
- The Review/Application section where the lesson is wrapped up and applied to life.

We hope that this material is used to the maximum in your local church, and that through it, you can train adolescents and young adults about what God's Word says about health, cults, stewardship and spiritual life, among other topics contained in this book.

Patricia Picavea
Editor in Chief, Ministries Publications

Helps (H)

for the Teacher

Teaching the Bible is a privilege that God has given us, but it entails a great responsibility, since the teaching must be based on the Word of God. Therefore, we should be very careful to search the Scripture. We must seek the purpose that God wishes to communicate through the biblical writers.

In this labor, certainly, you will be the one who learns most as you study and impart each lesson. Therefore, be grateful for the privilege that you have to draw close to the Scriptures in order to then teach it to others. Make each encounter with the Bible an intimate time with the Lord. Think how the Lord himself is teaching you with love and patience so that you will grow and become one to pass on to others the things that He has taught you (Matthew 28:20).

Following, we have included for you various suggestions that we hope will help you to prepare and better present each lesson.

Preparing the lesson

1. Before preparing each lesson, pray, asking God for wisdom and discernment to understand the biblical study passages and to apply it to your life. Additionally, pray for your students so that they may be receptive to the teaching of the Word of God, so that in the midst of the particular situations in which they are living, the Word of God would be of help, strength, and guidance.

2. Prepare a place free from distractions to study the lesson, where there is a table or desk. It's important to have some materials available such as paper, pens, pencils, and erasers, among others.

3. In addition to the Click teacher book, you will need a Bible, and it would be of much help if you have on hand different versions. Also, try to have a language dictionary, a biblical dictionary and a good biblical commentary related to the lesson on hand.

4. Read the objective for the lesson multiple times. Knowing where you want to take the lesson will make the path much easier.

5. Memorize the Bible verse. You should be an example of what you are going to teach.

6. Read the lesson thoroughly as many times as necessary. Knowing the topic deeply will help you to develop the class time.

7. The book is designed for two groups of youth (ages 12-17, and ages 18-23). Therefore, read the introductory activity for the group which is under your care. Practice it to be sure that it's feasible. Check to see if it will be necessary to take any additional material to the class.

8. Look in the Bible and read each biblical reference as indicated. Practice the reading, especially of those passages that have difficult words to pronounce.

9. Make your own summary of the lesson to guide yourself in the class. Write on a sheet of paper, or electronically on a tablet or phone, the name of the lesson, the principal points and develop a summary as you study the lesson, point by point. Write out and highlight the biblical references that will be read during the class.

10. Look for the meaning of unknown words so that you may better understand the lesson.

Presenting the Lesson

1. Be the first one to arrive at the class room and arrange the area in the best way possible. For each new unit, you can change the arrangement of the chairs, the board, etc. Look for ways to create a comfortable environment for the development of the class. Remember that a good environment will help create good attitudes from people.

2. Always begin at the scheduled time.

3. Start by welcoming your students. This allows you to create a comfortable study environment. Know the name of each student, looking for ways to remember the names of new students.

4. Begin class with prayer, asking the Lord to help all to understand His Word and to give everyone the desire to obey it.

5. Begin with the introductory activity; this will help to enter into the topic.

6. Write the title of point 1 and begin to explain it. Use the board and the flip chart as a teaching resource to note explanations. When you finish point 1, write the title of point 2 and continue in this way. Highlight important aspects of the topic.

7. Encourage the participation of each person in the class. Form work groups to develop each point. Ask your students to look up the biblical references, read them, and comment on them. Allow them to give their points of view. Ask for the participation of those who for any reason don't participate. Don't criticize any suggestion, be polite and don't avoid difficult discussions. Rather, guide them with the council of the Word of God.

8. Dedicate a few minutes to comment on how to apply the biblical truths learned in class to our daily lives.

9. Motivate the students to invite other youth to the next class. In a creative way, give them an idea of what the next lesson will deal with. Create anticipation in the youth.

10. Finish the class with prayer. Do it in different ways each day.

Other suggestions

1. Goals and prizes: You can offer a simple prize for the students that, during each class:
   - Memorize all the biblical texts.
   - Punctually attend all the classes of the unit.

2. Memorization. An important aspect of learning the Bible is memorization. You should keep in mind that when something is memorized, it's typically understood better and for a longer time. Therefore, help your students understand each biblical text that they are going to memorize. In order to do so, you can help by reading or writing it from different versions of the Bible, explaining to the students the meaning of difficult words, and helping them apply the text to a real situation in their lives. The following are some activities that we hope will help in the task of memorizing and helping others memorize the Word of God. Of course, you should choose the activity that works best in your situation. Keep in mind the number of people in each class, the characteristics of the class, and the class area and resources available.
   - Write the text on the board, and as you develop the lesson, begin to erase words as the students memorize them. Give some sort of prize to the first person that says the verse correctly.
   - Form teams of no more than four people. Give each team cards with words from the memory verse (one word per card). Allow one or two minutes so that, without looking at the Bible, the students put the verse together correctly and all the members of the team memorize it. Give a prize to the winning team.
   - Hide the text somewhere inside the classroom. Allow some time for students to look for it and memorize it. The one who achieves this first will be the winner. Don't forget a prize!
   - Make stations in different places in the classroom. At each one, present part of the lesson. Before beginning each point, they must memorize part of the verse. The hope is that by the end of the lesson, all will have the verse memorized.
   - Make two groups and ask each one to memorize the verse by creating hand motions. After a few minutes, when all members of the teams have the verse and the respective hand motions memorized, they will present it to the other group.
   - Divide the class into multiple groups to memorize the text. The group that memorizes it first and can say it without any mistakes will be the winner. Give some sort of recognition to the winning group.

How much is money worth?

> **Objective:** That the students would discover the true value of money in the life of Christians.
> **To memorize:** "Jesus answered, 'If you want to be perfect, go, sell your possessions and give to the poor, and you will have treasure in heaven. Then come, follow me.'" (Matthew 19:21)

Connect | Navigate

Introductory activity (12-17 years)
- Materials: Paper and pencil.
- Instructions: Write on the board the following affirmation and the question: If you had such amount of money (give a specific amount, depending on the country), what would you spend it on? This exercise serves to reflect on what each student gives relevance or worth to and introduces the topic.

Introductory activity (18-23 years)
- Material: Cards and pencil
- Instructions: Write on the board or on a card the following affirmation and the question: If you had such amount of money (give a specific amount, depending on the country), what would you spend it on? Clarify that students may only write one thing on which they would spend the money. When they have written their answer, they must each read it out loud and those with similar responses must form a team to discuss their answer and explain their response as a team. Those whose answers don't match any other person's answer will reflect individually.

Did you know that a person can become blinded by money? It's true! Because of money, a person can become blind to their relatives, unable to see the people that surround them, unable to see a world in need that grows more in need each day and is right next to them. But overall, they are unable to see the Word of God, and as a consequence, they stray far away from the Kingdom.

Connect | Navigate

Money has been and continues to be something important in the daily life of people. One works, among many other reasons, for money, with which one is able to buy and sell. There exists a popular saying that goes: "almost all can be bought with money". Money came to solve the complications that were generated by trade (exchange of things or services), which was used to be able to sell goods or services within society. Money is used to buy, to pay for services and when our economy permits, to be saved. But, have you ever asked yourself, "What is money?" Yes, they are pieces of paper and of metal. Esthetically speaking, they are not necessarily beautiful pieces. However, it would be difficult to find anyone in this world that doesn't desire to have it, and who, regardless of how much money he or she comes to have, won't always want more.

In the Bible, we find Jesus in a conversation with a rich young man. By the attitude that the young man demonstrated, we can understand the value that money had for him. It's necessary to discover the correct way to understand the true value of money so that it may serve us, rather than for us to serve it. The love of money and the desire to have many possessions are not recent matters, but rather ancient, which is why the Bible discusses it.

1. The value of money

Money is a means created by man which should be earned in an honorable way and used with wisdom. Scripture indicates that money is a protection from poverty and the problems that come with it, and money allows people to acquire the fundamental basics for life. It's not to be treasured, since we'll take absolutely nothing with us upon death.

In our daily life, it's common to hear commentaries related to money, principally about the lack of it. Some years ago in a university class, they gave us a very interesting book "Consumerism and New Poor People," the title already having much to tell us. This book mentions the great problem that the economic politics which govern the world lead us to. The key point of the topic is that in the overvaluing of brands, today it doesn't matter so much how you dress but rather what brand you are wearing. It's no longer enough to provide for needs, but rather the interests which mark a society of consumerism. In a few words, it would appear that money, more than being used for basic necessities (food, housing, clothing), exists to cater to vanity. What would happen if we stopped to look at our possessions, and being honest with ourselves asked ourselves, "How much of what we have really is necessary and how much is simply for pleasure?" What would our response be?

One of the problems that we see is that money becomes more and more insufficient. On one hand, this is fact; without understanding much about economics, we can see that the economic situation of the world is going through difficult times, and monetary values seem to drop each day. Combined with that, there is also an invisible problem: money is insufficient because the market offers us more and more unnecessary products, which call for our attention and we falsely believe that they will give us an added value if we possess them.

The Bible says in 1 Timothy 6:9, "Those who want to get rich fall into temptation and a trap and into many foolish and harmful desires that plunge people into ruin and destruction." People work and work as if, by buying the most recent product being sold, they will receive eternal happiness. What's more, we buy it and nothing changes, but the following week the same product comes out "improved", and we come to desire it, falling into a vicious cycle. This is what God calls in His Word "foolish ambitions." Therefore, we cannot say that money is good or bad, or that it's of the devil. Money is a great tool for people, and we Christians cannot exclude ourselves, saying "We don't need money." But the value that we should give to it's totally different than the value which the world gives it. Ask your students: "What value do you believe that we as Christians should give to money?"

2. The usefulness of money

Begin by asking the students: What is money useful for? What problems can the love of money bring you? Suggest that they look up the following passages: 1 Timothy 6:7-10, 17, 18.

Money has the capacity to satisfy our basic needs, such as food, education, clothing and housing; all the rest is pure vanity. "But if we have food and clothing, we'll be content with that." (1 Timothy 6:8)

How do we use the money that we earn or that we have? We as Christians know that money serves to cover our needs, and we should recognize that it also covers many wants that are not necessary. We shouldn't be anxious to get more and more money, but rather we should be happy with what we have. We should understand that we're not valuable for what we have or what we earn, but for who we are as people.

What should we use the money for that we earn? In various biblical passages, we can find a good use for money. For example, in Ephesians 4:28, it speaks of working and earning money in order to share. In 2 Thessalonians 3:7-12, it speaks of working and earning money so as to support ourselves. So we see money from a new perspective: not to satisfy ourselves or to accumulate it, but rather to serve God, for personal sustenance and to do good. This is the teaching that God had for the young rich man in Matthew 19:21. Money is not good or bad in and of itself; what is good or bad is the way we use it.

3. Stewardship of money

Begin by asking students: What problem do we encounter in these passages with respect to not sharing what we have? What benefits will we obtain if we share what we have with others? Suggest that they look at the following passages: Matthew 19:21-22 and 2 Corinthians 9:6-8.

As children of God, we should demonstrate who our Father is, even in the stewardship of money. We must be conscious of the fact that money is provided by God and it's from Him; it doesn't belong to us, but we should administrate it.

People try to fill their lives with money and possessions because they are in a consumerist society. Instead, we Christians understand that God has supplied absolutely everything, and we still have so much to give. As Christians, if we seek the kingdom of God, we're not going to lack any of our basic needs, as promised in Matthew 6:32-33. The Christian sees money as a provision of God for their life, and this becomes an act of faith: trusting that God will supply all our needs.

Money is a blessing, and as a blessing, we should ask for wisdom in administering it correctly, being willing to give to our neighbors and to the service of the Lord. We should take into consideration the advice of John Wesley: "Gain all that you can, save all that you can, so that you can give all that you can."

We should think about how to distribute our money in such a way that we can put aside what is for God, and have what we need for our basic needs, so that there is still some left to share with others and to save. This is possible if we see money not as an end in itself, but rather as a means of blessing that God gives us to bless others. In 2 Corinthians 9:6-8, we're encouraged to be generous Christians, who think not only of our own needs, but also of the needs of others.

Let's put to the test our ability to give. On how many occasions have we given away something or money for our needy neighbor or for the work of God in our church? We as students and some as workers perhaps don't have a large or constant income, but we all have something that we can give. Let's give generously.

Review/Application:

Discuss as a group.

1. What is the difference between vanity and what is a necessity? (Vanity is something superficial, a want, a style that marks society. A necessity is something basic/required for life.)
2. According to Ephesians 4:28, what should we do with our money? (Share with those in need.)
3. What advice does Wesley give us? (Earn all that we can, save all that we can, so we can give all that we can.)
4. What is the use and the value of money? (Money is useful for basic needs. Insofar as value, money is not good or bad. Its value is determined by how we use it.)

Work ... what a bother!

Objective: That the students would understand the responsibility that we have to God for our work.
To memorize: "Whatever you do, work at it with all your heart, as working for the Lord, not for human masters." Colossians 3:23

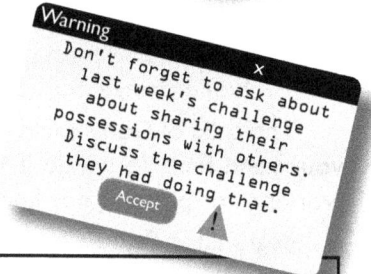

Warning
Don't forget to ask about last week's challenge about sharing their possessions with others. Discuss the challenge they had doing that.
Accept

Connect | Navigate

Introductory activity (12-17 years)

- Materials: Each one receives paper and a pencil.

- Instructions: Have the students form a circle. Pass out a small piece of paper and a pencil to each student. Then, ask them to write the name of a job or profession that they would like to have (construction worker, painter, architect, doctor, cook, administrator, etc.), without letting anyone see. Then, ask each student to ask another person which the job they wrote down. They should then begin to form groups with those who have written the same job, and share with each other why they like that job. If some students end up by themselves, they can share with the group why they like that job so that everyone can participate.

Introductory activity (18-23 years)

- Materials: Each one receives paper and a pencil.

- Instructions: Ask each student to mention on their paper characteristics that they think the ideal job should have, and then share what they have written with the group.

Connect | Navigate

Generally, together with work comes discontentment, be it due to inadequate salaries, excessive responsibilities or innumerable pressures, and the fear of losing their job. Work is a part of the human life. Our work occupies most of our time and requires that we use our capacities to carry it out. To be satisfied with our work, Scripture teaches us that we should do everything, including work, as doing it for the Lord.

Nowadays, it would be difficult for many people to imagine a work week of more than 8 hour days, or without resting Saturday and Sunday, or one of the two, or whichever day during the week, or other rights which we depend on today such as vacation time, bonuses, medical insurance, etc. In the 16th century, work conditions were very different. Work days could last up to 16 hours, with jobs beginning at 4 in the morning and ending at 8 at night. However, although in many cases conditions have improved, there still exits much inconformity. Today, "fun at work" is being promoted, but not all work places can install things in the workplace like relaxation areas, gyms, pool tables, etc. What is wanted is good attitudes among workers to increase efficiency.

1. Who invented work?

The Word of God teaches us that work was instituted by God before the fall. Let's read Genesis 2:15. The first thing that God did with Adam was to put him to work (Genesis 2:19). Work was created for the benefit of humans, although some people don't believe it to be so. Work is not a consequence of sin. It's not a curse. After the fall, work became more difficult (Genesis 3:17-19), but it was not the punishment for sin. On the contrary, work gives people dignity, which is why in Exodus 20:9, God declares, "Six days you shall labor and do all your work..." In Exodus 20:11, we see that God himself worked.

2. Why do we work?

Work is a activity that comes from God, and through Him, our needs are provided. Ecclesiastes 5:18 says, "This is what I have observed to be good: that it's appropriate for a person to eat, to drink and to find satisfaction in their toilsome labor under the sun during the few days of life God has given them—for this is their lot." This passage teaches us that we should enjoy work and the fruits that it brings, and we shouldn't be irritated or annoyed by it.

In the Bible, we find the following:

- If we're faithful, God is the one who makes our work prosper. This truth should be our motivation in our efforts as employees. Many don't prosper in their jobs and they see their lives frustrated because they don't understand this truth. (Genesis 39:2-3)

- God gives us our abilities. Exodus 36:1 demonstrates this truth. God gives us unique abilities. There doesn't exist one person who is better than another, but rather each one is given different abilities. It's our job to develop these abilities and to use them to the fullest.

- God controls promotions. Psalms 75:6-7 shows us that promotions don't depend on our boss, but on God. This should change our attitude at work.

The child of God should do all that is placed in his hands in the best possible way. Ecclesiastes 9:10 says, "Whatever your hand finds to do, do it with all your might, for in the realm of the dead, where you are going, there is neither working nor planning nor knowledge nor wisdom." When it says all, that includes work as well.

Years later, Paul refers to servants in Colossians 3:22-25, commanding them to obey their earthly masters, not serving only when they are seen, but serving correctly even when they are not being controlled or when they are not seen. All that is done at work should be done with a heart understanding that one is serving God, and that it's part of one's testimony, without worrying about whether the work is secular or Christian, or if the boss is good or bad. According to the apostle, absolutely all that is done is seen by God whom we say that we love and serve. For that reason, the apostle motivates us to do everything with all our hearts.

3. Why should I work?

The Bible motivates us to do everything with diligence and excellence. A Christian should never be connected to laziness or mediocrity. In 2 Thessalonians 3:8-9, the apostle writes a phrase that was common among the Hebrews: "nor did we eat anyone's food without paying for it"; this involves the idea of earning one's living. The apostle affirms that they didn't accept a room or food without paying for it. The apostle was referring to the fact that no one should be maintained or live at the expense of others.

In 2 Thessalonians 3:10, it goes on to say, "For even when we were with you, we gave you this rule, 'The one who is unwilling to work shall not eat.'" This verse clearly shows us an exhortation for people who didn't desire to work. It's possible that idle people were asking for food from the church, and Paul commands them to work, as is honorable for people, and so receive their daily provisions. It was a general rule for the poor that they work each day to earn their provisions and have food to eat.

When it comes to work, we as Christians should be careful. In no way should work be an impediment to the service of God, because if it's so, one demonstrates by their actions that work is first in life and not God. (Matthew 6:33)

It's important to keep the day of rest. This commandment is still very useful today. The body is like a machine that needs its time of rest. This can be difficult when one is under pressure from work or economic or academic pressure, but it's important to apply faith by working hard and conscientiously for six days and pray that the Lord would make our time bear fruit in what we do. The Lord himself instituted a day of rest in Exodus 20:8-11 for the physical, mental and spiritual wellbeing. We shouldn't fail to take care of our health, which has also been given by the Lord.

Work is very important for sustaining ourselves, but it's also important because it helps to develop the worker's character. Work can create discipline, diligence, skill, restraint, responsibility and leadership.

Review/Application:

Discuss as a group.

1. Who invented work and for what purpose? (God did, in order to administer creation, to sustain us, and to develop us.)

2. What does 2 Thessalonians 3:6-12 teach us about work? (No Christian should be connected to laziness or mediocrity. Each one should work to support him or herself.)

3. What principles for success in work do we find in the testimony of Joseph in Genesis 39:1-5; 21-23; 41:39? (If we obey God and we behave correctly in our work, He will be with us and all will work for good.)

4. According to Colossians 3:22-24, even in our work, we serve God. Is this true in your life? In what way?

5. What does Ecclesiastes 9:10 teach us? (While we have life, we should give our greatest effort in all the we do.)

Challenge the class to commit themselves to work hard and do their best in all that they do. They can even talk to their parents or others to help them grow in this area.

Administrators or owners?

Objective: That the students would understand that what he or she has is of the Lord and that he or she is an administrator of those possessions.
To memorize: "Whoever can be trusted with very little can also be trusted with much, and whoever is dishonest with very little will also be dishonest with much." Luke 16:10

Warning
Don't forget to ask about last week's challenge to work hard and do their best in everyting they do. Allow them to discuss what they did, and how it went.
Accept

Connect / Navigate

Introductory Activity (12-17 years)
- Materials: Pass out paper and pencils
- Instructions: Ask each student to write a list of 10 things that they own that they love a lot. In front of each one, they should write the pronoun 'my'; for example: my cell phone, my computer, my wallet, my rings, etc.

    Then, ask them to reflect on Psalm 24:1 "The earth is the Lord's, and everything in it, the world, and all who live in it" and help them to think how all they have is the Lord's, not only in theory but also in practice.

Once they finish, tell them that none of the things they wrote are totally theirs and to write the list anew, this time write 'your'. For example: your cell phone, your computer, your wallet, your rings, etc.

Introductory activity (18-23 years)
- Instructions: Ask them to make a list of everything that is theirs personally.
- Ask them to explain the difference between administrator and owner.
- Together, write a definition of each of the words in a sentence. Then, begin the topic and use these definitions at the end.

Connect / Navigate

When born again as Christians, people encounter an endless number of challenges and new skills that require action and practice in daily life. The challenge of giving up the "I" to do the will of God is perhaps the greatest conflict that the Christian will have to deal with in life. It will be a challenge to face each day; Jesus himself did so when he said, "Whoever wants to be my disciple must deny themselves and take up their cross daily and follow me" (Luke 9:23).

The human being, by nature, is selfish, tending to think of "me" and nothing but that. One of the times in which this can be seen best is in children between 4 and 5 years old, who demand things for themselves and declare ownership of absolutely everything around them, including their parents', guardians' or friends' attention at play.

Although over time there is a process of maturity, the tendency to think "only of me" persists throughout life. When born in Christ, the conflict with this aspect begins, since the goal, in the words of Paul, should be that "I no longer live, but Christ lives in me" (Galatians 2:20). This dilemma takes on another dimension when confronted with the biblical idea that all things that humans claim to possess, even life itself, don't really belong to them, but are of God, and that the person, on the contrary, is simple the administrator. As Psalm 24:1 says, "The earth is the Lord's, and everything in it, the world, and all who live in it."

1. Of what are we administrators (Stewards)?

The truth that the Bible communicates to us is that while God is the owner of all things, he puts everything in the hands of his creation, i.e., humanity, so that we could be administrators (not owners) of these resources and take care of them as good administrators.

What do we administer?

It would be very important at this time to be reminded of what God has given to us to care for as administrators, according to Genesis 1:26, 28. List with your students the things of which we're administrators, and write the ideas on the board. These can be some of the answers.

God has trusted us to administer:
- Our soul, the spirit made in the image of God, with the understanding, imagination, memory, will and emotions that encompass the human being.
- Our bodies, will all their power, members, organs, and senses.
- The goods of this world: food, clothing, homes, and money.

- The talents and spiritual gifts that allow us to develop ourselves in our life in this world.

2. How can I be a good administrator?

Although we saw some of this in Lesson 1, now we'll look in closer detail. Wesley gives three points which summarize how we should manage God's resources that he has entrusted to us:

a. "Earn all that you can"
- Without doing so at the expense of our lives, health, and bodies. It shouldn't lead to an unmeasured and harmful lifestyle, for life should be balanced and integrally healthy.
- Without damaging our minds; keeping a healthy mind.
- Without it leading to anything sinful or illegal.
- Without it being harmful to our neighbors: not to themselves, to their bodies or to their possessions, and without charging them unjustly.

b. "Save all that you can"
- Without spending it on something that will only gratify the desires of the flesh or the pleasures of our senses: unnecessary foods, expensive or unnecessary decoration or ornamentation.
- Without spending it on things solely to be recognized or admired by others.
- Without spending it on things for others that are not of benefit to them; rather, giving them only what is necessary and what, with certainty, will edify their lives.

c. "Give all that you can"
- First: Provide for what you need for yourself: food, dress, health.
- Second: Provide all that is necessary for your family and those who live under your roof.
- With what's left: Do good for the family of faith.
- If there's still some left: Do good for all people.

3. The parable of the administrator

Suggestion for studying the parable:
- The parable of the astute administrator can be read together by all. Then, you can divide up into groups to analyze and reflect on the teaching of the parable for our lives today.

Concerning stewardship or administration, speak about the parable of the astute administrator as found in Luke 16:1-13 which, as a forewarning, is not an easy passage to interpret. In this parable, according to the commentator Barclay, we're given an example of the slyness that can be found very well in real life more than in literature. This parable was directed, according to the passage, to the disciples, but it included all the sympathizers and even the Pharisees that were listening to him, according to verse 14.

This steward was as unfaithful as one could be toward a master or supporter, but in verse 9 we read the words of Jesus and they seem to confuse us.

Was Jesus approving dishonesty in stewardship? No, not at all; rather, what he was teaching them was:
- That as stewards, they should use earthly riches in such a way that by their good use, they store up heavenly and everlasting treasures. The disciples needed to use diligence, sagacity, and prudence to ensure a place in eternity, just as the steward uses his employment to ensure a future on earth.
- Jesus was teaching them that Christians would be more genuine if they were as interested in living and serving Christ no matter the consequences, as those of the world are interested in possessing money and all that can be had with it.
- Our Christian life will begin to be sincere and will bear fruit when we dedicate as much time and interest to the gospel as we dedicate to pleasure, business, boyfriends and girlfriends, sports, or studies.

Without a doubt, being a Christian and being one fully, demands that we're conscientious as stewards or administrators of our role before God, before oneself, and before our neighbor. A correct relationship with the Owner and Creator of all things leads to a proper completion of the functions delegated to his creation, humanity in this case; it leads to a correct administration (stewardship) of all things in this world that have been given to humanity.

Review/Application- Answer individually and then discuss as a class:

1. How do I feel when I consider the things which I wrote in the list of "my possessions" are not really mine, but rather than I'm administering them temporarily?
2. In the great ways that I'm called to administer, in which do I need to pay more attention to be able to administer in a better way? Why?
3. Being honest with myself, if I had to give myself a grade from 10 to 100 to judge the way that I'm administering my possessions, what grade would I give myself? Why?
4. What changes should be made in my life in light of what I have learned in this lesson?

Challenge your students to take the role of administrators seriously. Help them in their weak areas.

Who can help me?

Lesson 4
David González • Mexico

Warning
Remember to begin class today by asking the students about last week's challenge. Encourage them to share their experiences about their roles as administrators.
Accept

Objective: That the students would value the importance of asking for advice in order to make wise decisions.
To memorize: "Listen to advice and accept discipline, and at the end you will be counted among the wise." Proverbs 19:20

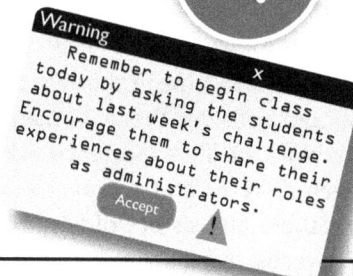

Connect | Navigate

Introductory Activity (12-17 years)
- Materials: A circle with a bull's-eye drawn on it and darts with glue or tape on the points.
- Instructions: Form two or three groups. Set up the bull's-eye on the wall where the darts should be aimed. Each group will select one representative who will have their eyes covered. The representative from each group will walk with eyes covered from the place where their group is to the place where the bull's-eye is set up. Once there, each representative will have an opportunity to try to put the dart in the center of the bull's-eye. The members of his or her team will be able to guide their representative by giving oral instructions from their places, but never using physical contact. The winning team will be the one whose representative manages to place their dart closest to the center of the bull's-eye. One variation of the activity is that members from other teams can be of distraction for opposing representatives by giving incorrect instructions. If you cannot find a bull's-eye set for this activity, you could instead use small balls that need to be put into a basket with eyes closed.

After the activity, tell students that many times, making wise decisions becomes like playing bull's-eye with eyes closed, where one doesn't know whether or not they will be on target. For this reason, it's necessary to have the help of others who show us things that we cannot see; in other words, others who counsel us.

Introductory Activity (18-23 years)
- Materials: Paper and pencil for all participants.
- Instructions: Today we'll talk about listening to advice in order to make wise decisions, so please respond to the following question: Who should we go to in order to receive good advice?
- Guide the youth in a brief discussion, without giving a definite answer to the question; then, begin the development of the lesson.

Connect | Navigate

Today, adolescents and youth live surrounded by means of communication that bombards them with all types of products, programs, games, etc. The daily use of Internet, friends from school and work, the accelerated life, parents that work all day, minimal church attendance, loss of moral values, etc. cause youth to encounter difficult situations each day in which they need to make wise decisions. For this reason, it's necessary that they can count on suitable people to counsel them. Today we want the students to realize that they need to seek out the correct people from which they can receive good advice and not be led away from the correct path.

1. In search of good counselors

In Psalms 1:1, we find two pieces of advice regarding counselors.

a. Avoid the advice of bad advisers:

The first is that if you want to be happy, you should avoid living in the counsel of the wicked; in other words, from the people that don't have the fear of the Lord, who don't care about going against the will of God in order to satisfy their own desires. It's very important, then, to decide from whom we'll seek advice. Let's analyze two youth who followed bad advice and how it turned out for them. You can divide the class into two groups and ask each group to read one short story and come up with the teaching point. Then, each group should choose a representative who will explain the passage and the teaching with the other group. In this way, all the class will be familiar with the examples and the application.

- Amnon (2 Samuel 13:1-29): As a consequence, his brother ordered that he be killed.
- Rehoboam (1 Kings 12:1-20): He lost the kingdom and the support of the people.

b. Look for good advisers:

On the contrary, one must look for the advice of people who fear the Lord, who keep his Word, whose lives are a reflection of a relationship with Him, people that love us, who speak truth to us, in whom we trust, who commit to praying with and for us. It would be good if these people have gone through similar experiences to our own because they will share with us from their experience, but this is not a requirement.

Does this mean that we shouldn't seek advice from those who are not Christian? Of course we may, but first we should consider those whose advice we're seeking. Try to look for someone who, be it through academic preparation or work or life experience, will share new knowledge, or will help to analyze the situation in a clearer way. However, even if we listen to expert advice on the topic from non-Christians, we should always ask for help from family and brothers and sisters of faith to be sure that the decision reflects love for and a desire to please God. In the book of Proverbs, there are many principles concerning the importance of good advisers: "Plans fail for lack of counsel, but with many advisers they succeed" (Proverbs 15:22); "but victory is won through many advisers" (Proverbs 11:14b); "Surely you need guidance to wage war, and victory is won through many advisers" (Proverbs 24:6).

One of the great benefits of having advisers is that they will help to interpret the situation and to see details that we're probably not considering. An adviser can also help to maintain a balanced position, thus avoiding the possibility that criteria will be manipulated when analyzing alternative positions.

2. Let's seek the counsel of God

The second piece of advice (although, in order of importance, it's the first) that can be found in Psalms 1 is the following: "Surrender your will in obedience to the Word of God." Verse 2 invites us to meditate on Scripture day and night; in other words, it says how at all times, in all circumstances, in every place, regardless of the consequences, there must be a commitment and connection to God and his Word.

As we learn more of the Word, we'll have more understanding of His advice. When King David passed through a time of trial and emotional crisis in which he fell into despair, he went to the temple and there found the counsel of God through prayer (Psalms 73:1-28). In verse 24, David exclaims: "You guide me with your counsel…" There, David realizes that his hope is God and nothing else has value.

Other passages also support the idea of seeking the counsel of God in his Word. Proverbs 3:1, 21 read, "My son, don't forget my teaching, but keep my commands in your heart… preserve sound judgment and discretion," and the prophet exclaims in Isaiah 25:1, "Lord, you are my God; I will exalt you and praise your name, for in perfect faithfulness you have done wonderful things, things planned long ago." God gives advice in his Word for each need or decision that you must make. You only need to look for that advice through prayer and through his Word.

3. Situations in which we should seek advice

Christian youth encounter the need to make multiple decisions each day. Some are short-term, such as: what clothing I will wear, which team will I root for, if I will go to school or not, if I will go out with this or that boy/girl, if I will do my homework or not, etc…

But some decisions that we make are long-term and can change our lives. For example, who will I marry, what major will I study, if I will try drugs and alcohol or not, if I will be a good Christian or not, what will I invest my earned money in, what will I do for work, etc.

It's important that as Christian youth, we're willing to not make decisions lightly, but rather to make wise decisions. Read His Word, seek God and people who love you; they will be able to give you good advice.

Review/Application

Answer individually and then discuss as a group if people are comfortable:
- How can you distinguish between good and bad advisers, according to Psalms 1:1-2?
- Are you listening to bad advisors? Who? Why?
- Do you believe that God can counsel you? How?
- Why is it often difficult to ask advice of God?
- What kind of an advisor are you being for others?
- Name the areas in your life in which you could use counsel right now:

Save for tomorrow ... today

Tabitha González • Brazil

Objective: That the students would understand the importance of saving, and would know how to save according to biblical principles.
To memorize: "The plans of the diligent lead to profit as surely as haste leads to poverty." Proverbs 21:5

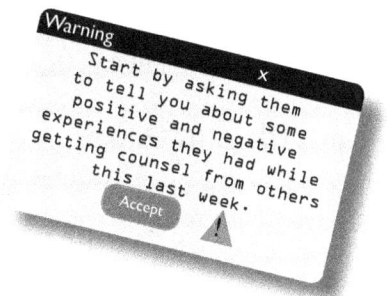

Warning
Start by asking them to tell you about some positive and negative experiences they had while getting counsel from others this last week.
Accept

Connect | Navigate

Introductory Activity (12-17 years)
- Materials: It will be necessary to have a board to write on, paper, pencil, and six chocolate coins or real coins, or play bills for each student.
- Instructions: Before beginning the class, write the following articles on the board in list form (or cut the products from newspaper and place them on the board or on a table): clothes that are in style, a professional development course*, flat-screen TVs, a university course*, music devices, video and audio systems, a video game, a house*, a trip, a language course*, and imported perfume [On the list, you can include things that you know the youth are interested in].

At the start of the class, distribute paper, pencils, and three chocolate coins (or real coins or toy bills) to each student. Tell them that the value of each one can only buy one of the items listed on the board; this means they may buy three of the items. Ask them to choose which items they'd like to buy. After they have made their choices, discuss with them the reasons why the decided to buy those items. Those students who chose the items with a * will be able to receive three more coins, in reward for their good purchase. At the end of the activity, talk with the students about how much they would need to save for each of these things. The objective of the activity is to allow the students to reflect on the importance of saving and spending wisely in order to be able to enjoy their purchases in the long run.

Introductory Activity (18-23 years)
- Materials: You will need paper and pencils for each student.
- Instructions: The teacher should read the following to the class: "A distant uncle of the family who is very rich thought of you today and decided to give you a special gift as compensation for all the years in which he didn't give you a gift for your birthday. Since he doesn't know you very well and doesn't know what to get for you, he decided to send a sum of money equivalent to 1,000 dollars (change the sum according to the country, or give a significant sum). Then, ask them to make a list of what they would do with the money.

After reading the above, give time for the students to make their lists. Once the students have their lists, ask some volunteers to share what they have written.

Then, ask the following questions: Thinking about your future, what are some of your goals and what will be necessary to achieve them? How would the money that your uncle gave you help you to achieve those objectives?

Then, help them recognize the connection between what they have received and what they long to achieve in the future.

his generation is known for their search for momentary satisfaction, without concern of what will happen in the future. What matters is the moment, what you feel and what you enjoy. This thought, together with the consumerist system in which we live, has moved many youth to waste what they receive or earn on trivial things (that are unnecessary), ignoring future challenges.

To save is a matter of wisdom. Saving prepares youth for the challenges to come. There are many advantages to saving, but only when we do so according to biblical principles.

1. Why save?

a. Because we honor God when we save

Concerning the wise man, Proverbs 21:20 says, "There is treasure to be desired and oil in the dwelling of the wise; but a foolish man spendeth it up" (KJV). To have treasures in that time was a way of saving, and oil represented provision. In other words, the verse can be understood in the following way: "The wise man saves and in his house he lacks nothing, but the fool uses everything foolishly." God's desire is that we honor Him with all that we have (Proverbs 3:9). One of the ways in which we honor Him is to wisely care for all that we have received from Him. When we save, we honor God, obey His Word, and are stewards that wisely care for what we have received (Ecclesiastes 7:12).

b. Because it helps us in difficult times

One of the advantages of saving is that we have provisions for difficult times. After Joseph interpreted Pharaoh's dream, telling him all that would happen in Egypt (the seven years of abundance and the seven years of famine), with wisdom he told him, "Save!" (Genesis 41:34-36). Through Joseph's story, we can see how God takes care of his people, and his provision in difficult times. If we take good care of what we receive and save wisely, these resources can be part of God's provision for us in times of difficulty and need. God gave Joseph wisdom, and, due to saving for seven years, God's people and many other people survived the time of scarcity.

c. Because it helps us to invest better and frees us from debt

Saving is the opposite of having debt. When we save, we're providing for the future; on the contrary, when we incur debt, we're taking away from the future. Many times when we invest in something to pay over time, with interest, we diminish our potential to buy since we lose what must go to pay interest: be wary of credit cards and making small payments! These become a real trap if we don't know how to use them. Many economists say that the best way to buy something is with cash. We can receive discounts when we buy this way, and we also don't lose anything to interest. When we make saving a habit, we diminish the chance of getting in debt and we strengthen our good example before men (Proverbs 21:5).

2. Save for the right reasons

a. Not for love of riches

I Timothy 6:9-10 speaks about the temptation of the man who wants to become rich, and at the end affirms, "For the love of money is a root of all kinds of evil." Many people, for love of riches, end up neglecting to tithe, to pay what is due to the government, and to taking advantage of others by not paying what is just. As a result of this love for riches, they wander from the faith. The objective of saving shouldn't be the desire to become rich, but rather exclusively to administer well what we have received from God and in this way, to honor Him. To keep what we have only in order to get rich has its root in greed, and it creates in us attitudes that separate us from God and from His purpose for our lives (Matthew 6:24).

b. Without forgetting our responsibilities

When we have something extra, it makes it much easier for us to help others who are in need. In Galatians 6:10, we're encouraged to do good to all, especially to those from the family of faith. If we have a life in which debts consume all that we have, we don't have the capacity to help others. However, if we take care of what we have and we save wisely, we can help others with what we have, especially those from our own home.

c. Without forgetting what is important

In Luke 12:13-21, we encounter the parable of the man who, after his great harvest, planned to build barns to keep all he had, and his soul rested in this idea.

The first mistake the man in this parable made was to keep all that he had for himself. This man didn't give over to God all that belonged to Him, and he didn't share what he had received. He simply kept it for himself and gave greed a place in his life.

The second mistake the man made was that afterwards, according to this passage, his soul rested and rejoiced in this fact. There is only one place where our soul should rest, and that place is in God. Our joy comes from Him, not from what we have, but what we are in God. In the end, all that we are and have comes from Him (John 3:27).

Finally, this man did the opposite of what Jesus taught in Matthew 6:20; he accumulated treasures for himself and he forgot to store his treasures in heaven (Matthew 6:33).

3. Practical advice for saving

"Four things on earth are small, yet they are extremely wise: Ants are creatures of little strength, yet they store up their food in the summer" (Proverbs 30:24-25).

Many might say that, because you are youth, it's difficult for you to save. It's a fact that youth often don't have many resources; the majority have not finished their studies and don't have a job. But it's important to save, especially for youth, because soon they will become independent, leave their parents' home, start a family, etc. This requires a strong effort of saving and wisdom in the use of your finances. So saving, especially for youth, is a task like that of the ants. Perhaps you already work and receive a salary or you study and your parents give you your spending money or allowance. With what you receive, you can already begin to learn the good habit of saving.

Following are some practical pieces of advice that will help you to save as soon and as much as you can.

a. Keep your accounts under control. Keeping account sunder control will help you not to fall into unnecessary or uncontrolled spending and, at the same time, will help you to have a better idea of what truly can be saved. Make a budget of your earnings and spending that you'll use for the month or the pay period.

b. After tithing, separate what you have planned to save. If we don't separate what we can save from the beginning, you will certainly be tempted to use what is God's: first the tithe, then, the savings.

c. Start with something, even if it's small. You might think, "What I can save isn't much, just a few coins a month, so there's no point." But the amount isn't what matter most; what is important is creating a habit of saving, and even though you start with a small amount, as time passes, it could become something of great worth that will help you in the future.

d. Keeping your savings under your pillow is not the best option. Keeping our savings somewhere within our reach is not the best option. We should, as soon as possible, start a savings account; in this way, we don't lose out with the devaluation of money and we maintain it in a place free from the temptation to use it. If someone is not old enough to open a bank account, his or her parents could open one for him or her; many banks offer the option of opening savings account without fees or commission, or they have accounts for minors.

e. Take advantage of extra earnings. Wages that we were not expecting or counting on in our budget are an excellent sum to save!

Review/Application

Answer individually and then discuss as a group if people are comfortable:

Think about how you are using your resources, and some changes that you might need to make from now on to save. Remember, it's not about quantity, it's about having a concrete plan to invest and save your income adequately to do what God wants you to do with it.

Loaned or given?

Objective: That the students would be motivated to pay attention to the need to take their commitments seriously.

To memorize: "All these blessings will come on you and accompany you if you obey the Lord your God." Deuteronomy 28:2

Warning

Don't forget to ask how they did with their plan for income, expenses and savings last week.

Accept

Connect | Navigate

Introductory activity (12-17 years)
- Materials: A measuring tape and a surface area on which to work (it could be on the floor or on a table).
- Instructions: Divide the students into groups of three or more people depending on the number of students; try to make no more than four teams. Tell them they will build a tower with the things they bring (wallet, purse, book, watch, planner, music player, coins, CD, shoes, etc.). They may not use the Bible, move objects from their place, borrow from another team, or remove clothing. They should build it with whatever they already have. The tallest tower will win. They have three minutes!

At the end, ask them, "Would you have liked to be able to borrow from another team or use things from the room or other people in the church? How did you feel not being able to borrow from others? Then, have them consider the idea that it's not always possible nor good to borrow things.

Introductory activity (18-23 years)
- Materials: Paper and pencil
- Instructions: Divide the students in groups of four or five people, depending on the number of students. Then, ask them to write three reasons why they consider loans good and three reasons why they consider loans bad.

Then, ask each group to read their responses and begin the class.

Connect | Navigate

When I studied in high school, I had a friend whose name I don't remember; I only remember that his last name was Pérez and we called him "Big Hands".

Big Hands was always forgetting something. One day it was a pen, the next day a photocopy, then it was the calculator. There was always someone to lend him supplies so that he wouldn't be in a pinch.

One day, we arrived at school half an hour before an important exam. In that moment, Big Hands realized that to be able to do the test, he had to turn in a required assignment. Quickly he asked Mark for blank paper, Mary for a folder, me for a ruler, and he asked Ben to read off the answers to the assignment so that he could copy it! In a mocking tone, Ben answered, "If you want, go to breakfast and we'll take the exam for you, too!"

1. What is a loan?

According to the Ocean Dictionary, a loan is "An obligation that one must pay or payback something, or completion of an obligation. Sin." What an interesting definition, coming from a secular dictionary. When we talk about debts, that includes what is owed to credit card companies, bank loans, loans from parents or friends, mortgages and taxes.

Each day, people around the world focus more on satisfying their own needs, regardless of whether or not they are basic needs or not. Marketing creates in us an anxiety to possess certain items, and the more we want them, the more they become a "need." The philosophy that is currently talked about everywhere is based on how to stand out. It would appear that we live in a constant competition, and the idea of being better and having more separates us from biblical truths and causes us to incur debt to stay ahead as if it were something normal.

In addition to monetary debt, we also become debtors of another type of debt For example: How many times a day do you say the phrase "Lend me..."? How many times in a week? How many times in a month? How many times do you remember to return something that you've borrowed? Generally, we lend something or it's lent to us (a pencil, a piece of paper, a book, a CD, a notebook, even a favor), and when it's received, the response is "I owe you one."

When someone asks for something, he or she becomes a debtor of that which they have borrowed. For that reason, if you ask to borrow a book from a friend and it gets lost, what will you do? You must buy a new one and return it because when you asked for it, you acquired a debt in which you promised to return what was lent to you, except in cases of debt from the bank or another entity in which interest is charged. Then you have to pay back the original plus extra. In Exodus 22:14, God commanded that if an animal was lent and then it was hurt or it died, it should be paid for; this can also be applied to anything that is borrowed today. That is why we must think before we ask to borrow something.

There exists a saying in some places which goes: "Foolish is the one who lends, and more foolish is the one who returns the borrowed item." What do you think about this? Does this saying apply to Christians?

Lending is not necessarily foolish, because one does so out of love and conviction that the other person needs what he or she asks for and is committed to returning it, since he or she asks to borrow and not to keep. In the Sermon on the Mount, Jesus said, "Give to the one who asks you, and don't turn away from the one who wants to borrow from you" (Matthew 5:42). On the other hand, the one who returns the borrowed item is not foolish either, because Scripture says in Romans 13:7-8, "Give to everyone what you owe them: If you owe taxes, pay taxes; if revenue, then revenue; if respect, then respect; if honor, then honor. Let no debt remain outstanding, except the continuing debt to love one another, for whoever loves others has fulfilled the law."

2.   The fulfillment of our obligations

Another characteristic of our world currently is the ease with which we can communicate with people in other places. This becomes simpler when we all speak the same language, although some words change meaning in different places (for example, the word "carriage," in some places is used to discuss automobiles, while in other places it means a something that people ride in that is pulled by horses).

But, when did the meaning of the word loan change? Never. Although some people around us confuse it with a gift or donation.

- Loan: To give something to someone so that they may use it during a given time and then make restitution for it or return it in the same conditions in which it was received.
- Gift: Something given to someone, without receiving anything in exchange, something as a sign of affection or consideration or for some other reason.

Those who confuse these ideas obtain objects that have been loaned and never return them and don't consider themselves debtors. It would appear that they use the word lend as a diplomatic way of asking for something for free.

It very common that among friends we feel free to ask to borrow things, sometimes clothes, a CD, a book, etc. But in that friendship, we should always be diligent in returning what we have borrowed. There is a popular saying, "Clear accounts, long friendships." Even if there is a lot of trust among friends, we should be very clear when we take on a loan, and we should be responsible for returning what we have asked to borrow.

Where money is involved, the matter is more complex. I once read in a book, "If a friend asks you to lend him some money, think carefully about which you want to lose: the friend or the money." It seems that lending money to a friend is a mistake, because in one way or another, you will lose something. Be it that the friend is the type who confuses the terms and never returns the money to you or that, due to the concern with recovering the debt, the friendship between the two is damaged. Yes, perhaps you get back what was lent, but the trust might never be regained. How terrible to live like that. If a friend asks you to lend him or her money, and your friendship is important but you know they won't return it, it would be better to give it as a gift, though if you can't give all they want, give what you can.

The Bible commands that one fulfills what has been promised. If you owe something, it's right to pay it, without delay, as soon as possible, because, "The wicked borrow and don't repay, but the righteous give generously." (Psalm 37:21) In this way, we avoid endangering the name of Jesus before a world that is attentive to our actions.

3. Free or slaves

Proverbs 22:7 says, "The rich rule over the poor, and the borrower is slave to the lender." When we have economic debts, we are slaves to our creditor. And the more we become indebted, the more we become slaves and don't have total freedom nor discretion to decide on what we'll spend our money. This puts us in a dilemma to get out of debt.

In ancient times, it was common that when a kingdom submitted to the dominion of another kingdom, the would receive an economic punishment (Deuteronomy 15:6). This might be in the form of tributes or taxes that the subjugated nation would have to pay punctually to the conqueror. This tax had many purposes:

a. To enrich the conquering nation.

b. To maintain the fallen nation as slaves, limiting their economic growth.

c. To create a dependency.

The way in which finances are managed can rob the heart of peace and compromise freedom. In Deuteronomy 28:1-2,12, it says that if the people were obedient to God, they wouldn't have to borrow from other nations. This would free them from becoming the slaves of nations that lent to them. But if they disobeyed the commandments of God, they would have to borrow from other nations, becoming the tail instead of the head (Deuteronomy 28:15, 43-44).

The danger for Christian youth is getting used to living by always borrowing from others, because they have not learned to live and be happy with what they have (Philippians 4:12). This poor way of living with debt can turn them into slaves their whole life, and can cause sad consequences such as being pointed out for not paying back their debts, in a time of need no one wants to lend to them, or worse, they lose their friends. Therefore, now is the time to make good decisions and learn not to be slaves to debt. And if by necessity, we acquire some sort of debt, we should be responsible in taking care of it in the amount of time that we have promised.

Review/Application

Answer individually and/or as a group and then discuss as a group if people are comfortable.

Do you agree?

Following, you will find a list of ten phrases. Read each one and answer whether or not you agree with what each one says. (You may consult the biblical references for help) Then, compare your responses with the rest of the group and discuss any differences.

Do you agree?

1. If a friend asks you to lend him some money, you will lose the friend, or the money.
2. Elijah was the prophet who made a borrowed axe float. (2 Kings 6:5)
3. When friendship is true, a friend can take from another without letting the owner know.
4. When we ask for a loan, we're compromising our future. (Deuteronomy 15:6)
5. If I ask to borrow a CD from a friend and it gets scratched, I don't need to replace it since my friend knows that that happens normally. (Exodus 22:14)
6. In Matthew 5:42, Jesus teaches that if someone asks to borrow something from us, it's best to just give it to them.
7. The Bible teaches that people who don't pay their debts are those who neither fear God nor honor His Name. (Psalm 37:21)
8. If you have debt, then you are not free. (Proverbs 22:7)
9. In Nehemiah 5:2, we find that the people had borrowed grain due to extreme need.
10. As Christians, we have a greater responsibility in the administration of our things because we know that everything is from God and of God.

Help your students think about what they have borrowed ... even very small things which may seem unimportant. Direct them to make a written list and - if necessary - find a way to help them go and return the items.

Learn to give

Odily Díaz • El Salvador

Objective: That the students would understand the importance of giving, and be motivated to action.
To memorize: "And God is able to bless you abundantly, so that in all things at all times, having all that you need, you will abound in every good work." 2 Corinthians 9:8

Warning
Start by checking with your students on how they did with returning items that they had borrowed.
Accept

Connect | Navigate

Those who give, sleep well!

"It was two in the morning when my father woke me up because he had heard sounds in the back yard of the house. We went out and we found a neighbor with a machete in hand who was cutting plantains from the tree that fed our family. In spite of the risk that the man could have killed my father, my father said, "Give me the machete." Then my father cut off one bunch of plantains and gave it to the neighbor. Then he said, "Everything you need from my yard from here on out, just come through the main door and don't ask us for it. Remember to leave something for my children." The compassionate way in which my father handled the situation with that man was one of the ways that he influenced my life. That night, he taught me that those who take, eat well, but those who give, sleep well."

Paul W. Powell

Introductory activity (12-17 years)
- Materials: Paper and pencil
- Instructions: Organize students into pairs, sitting face to face, and give them each a piece of paper and a pencil. Then, ask each one to write five things that they would ask their partner for. Next, ask them to exchange papers and read what was requested of them, and let their partner know whether or not they can give each thing. At the end, gather everyone back together and discuss which things would be easy to give and which things would be hard to give.

Introductory activity (18-23 years)
- Materials: Paper and pencil
- Instructions: Ask the students to write three things on their paper that they willingly gave to someone this week, and three things that they didn't want to give when someone asked it of them. Each student will share what they wrote with the group and will describe how it felt when they did or didn't give each thing.

Connect | Navigate

"Will you allow me to ask you how much you are worth?" a reporter asked a rich man. He responded, "400,000 dollars." "But according to my information, you have millions of dollars," replied the journalist. "That's true," the man said, "but you asked me how much I'm worth. I believe my price is what I give and not what I possess. Last year I gave $400,000 for charity work and for me, that is the barometer of my true worth."

If your price was based on your giving, more than on your resources, what would be your true worth?

1. The principle of giving

In Matthew 5:42, Jesus gives rules of coexistence about sharing, calling attention and being specific in saying, "Give to the one who asks you, and don't turn away from the one who wants to borrow from you." The Jewish law had specific commandments about giving, and we can read them in Deuteronomy 15:7-11. For that reason, what Jesus was saying was not something new, but rather something that was not being carried out.

The law referred to the seventh year (v.9), because every seven years, debts were canceled and someone who was very stingy could refuse to lend money because the seventh year was close and debts would be forgiven.

Obsessions with things that are possessed cause people to back away from the idea of giving what is theirs. Many times, when someone approaches us to ask us for something, we ask what they need it for, or at least wonder what it's for. Sometimes, homeless people approach us to ask for money and we don't give it to them because we think that they want it to continue using drugs, alcohol, or something of the sort. But we don't seek to help

21

them in other ways by giving them, for example: food, clothing, shoes, etc. Jesus was teaching in the passage of Matthew that we need to have a generous and compassionate spirit for the needy. Perhaps if we would focus more on treasures in heaven and being content with the food and clothing that we have, it would be less difficult for us to share.

According to the commentator Barclay, the rabbis had some principles that should govern giving.

1. No one may be denied.
2. One must give what is necessary for survival.
3. Giving should be done secretly, not for recognition.
4. Giving is a privilege and an obligation.

2. Giving versus love

In 1 Corinthians 13:3, the apostle expresses that the act of giving doesn't make me a compassionate or loving person; sometimes one gives simply for pity or so people will go away. That is not good! The passage says that it's worthless to give all one possesses if one doesn't have love. The type of giving that Paul refers to is not charity of giving just to give, or giving to be done with it. The apostle is referring to giving with profound feeling, with affection, understanding what the other feels, making it so the one who receives what we give them doesn't feel humiliated by what they receive, but rather feels loved.

Giving is not limited only to material things, but also to sharing the great salvation that we have. There are people who perhaps don't have physical or material needs, but who do need to fill a heart that is empty and without peace. When Jesus sent the twelve, he told them, "Freely you have received; freely give" (Matthew 10:8). Generosity is like a tide that lifts and carries the boats; everything benefits from it." For the Jews, this was not something unfamiliar to their culture, since the rabies knew that they had received the teachings from God freely and that they should give in the same way.

3. God loves the cheerful giver

In 2 Corinthians 9:6-9, the God Speaks Today version of the Bible says, "Remember this—a farmer who plants only a few seeds will get a small crop. But the one who plants generously will get a generous crop." (v.6). "You must each decide in your heart how much to give. And don't give reluctantly or in response to pressure. For God loves a person who gives cheerfully. And God will generously provide all you need. Then you will always have everything you need and plenty left over to share with others. As the Scriptures say, "They share freely and give generously to the poor. Their good deeds will be remembered forever." (v.9).

The decision to give before receiving produces a new perspective on life. In the words of a wise man: "We earn our way in life with what we give." That allows us to fulfill what God commands us to do and it brings reward. "And if anyone gives even a cup of cold water to one of these little ones who is my disciple, truly I tell you, that person will certainly not lose their reward." (Matthew 10:42)

When we experience a genuine spiritual conversion, it's not difficult give. This work of God in us makes us new creatures; it transforms us from selfish beings that only look to receive, into generous and cheerful givers, moved and inspired by the gift of grace and salvation that are offered to us in Christ Jesus. "They also will answer, 'Lord, when did we see you hungry or thirsty or a stranger or needing clothes or sick or in prison, and didn't help you?' He will reply, 'Truly I tell you, whatever you didn't do for one of the least of these, you didn't do for me.' Then they will go away to eternal punishment, but the righteous to eternal life." (Matthew 25:44-46)

Review/Application

Organize the class into teams of three or four members and have each team analyze the following passages, noting the consequences that we receive for not giving and the blessings that we receive when we give.

- Deuteronomy 15:7-11

- 2 Corinthians 9:6-9

Make a list of things that could be included in a "basket of love" (sugar, coffee, flour, butter, cookies, or something prepared for them, etc.). Take time at the end of the lesson to ask the students to sign up for something on the list and to bring food items the following Sunday. The following week, set a box or basket (you can decorate it if you desire) in the class where the students can place the food they bring. As a class, give it to a family who needs it at the end of the church service (it could be a family from the church or neighborhood). Be careful to do this in a way that doesn't cause embarrassment to the family you're helping.

Our house

Objective: That the students would understand the responsibility that we have before God for our environment.
To memorize: "The Lord God took the man and put him in the Garden of Eden to work it and take care of it." Genesis 2:15

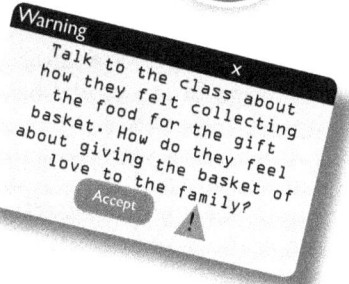

Warning
Talk to the class about how they felt collecting the food for the gift basket. How do they feel about giving the basket of love to the family?
Accept

Connect · Navigate

The story of creation is known by many youth, and it reminds us that God is a Creator and Sustainer and that He is interested in us and in our lives here on this planet. He himself designed the world to be our home.

The difficulty appears when we as human beings forget our responsibility to respect and care for the environment that God has provided for us. God has given us the privilege of taking care of His creation! He wants to help us do a good job!

Introductory Activity (12-17 years)
- Materials: Trash (boxes, empty bottles, fruit peels, paper, batteries, dry leaves, etc.) and two plastic bags of different colors (white and black).
- Instructions: Arrive early to the classroom and toss the trash that you brought throughout the room, over the tables, chairs, etc. When the students arrive to the classroom, greet them and ask them if they like how the room looks today. After listening to various reactions, ask them what they can do to fix the problem. Invite them to pick up the trash, placing it in the plastic bags: the organic trash in the white bag and the inorganic in the black bag.

  At the end of the activity, give the students the opportunity to share how they felt while carrying out the activity. Motivate them to think about our planet like the classroom they had just cleaned.

Introductory Activity (18-23 years)
- Materials: A large piece of paper and pencil, or a white board.
- Instructions: Divide the paper or the board in two parts, making a straight line in the middle. On one side, write the title "Ways in which we take care of the environment" and on the other side "Ways in which we don't take care of the environment." Together, think about, share, and write some examples on each side of the line. For example: "Ways in which we take care of the environment": saving paper and reusing sheets (we protect the trees) or "Ways in which we don't take care of the environment": Throwing trash in the street.

Connect · Navigate

Throughout the history of humanity, there have been people that have been interested in a detailed study of planet Earth and the beings who inhabit it. There are people dedicated to studying mountains and their heights or the sun and the planets; there are people dedicated to classifying animals and studying their way of life, and there are people who love to observe and learn more about human beings.

In the same way, there have been people who are not that interested in the environment in which they live. Their attitude and way of life have brought destruction to planet Earth, the animals, and even the people who inhabit it. This problem arises when we think that planet Earth is "ours" and we can do "what we want with it." However, in the Bible God says that the planet is His, because He designed it and created it. Even to this very day, God sustains it with his mighty hand. What's most incredible of all is that He give us the privilege of living on planet Earth and of caring for the environment, the plants, and the animals. What a marvelous opportunity! To think that God leaves us in charge of his precious creation! Remember that we're not alone in this task; He helps us do it.

1. God designed and created planet Earth

In the first verse of the Bible, we read that "God created the heavens and the earth." In the rest of the first chapter, we read the amazing account of how God also created each living being: the plants, the animals, and even the human being. Imagine the powerful and amazing work that God did during the time of creation. Imagine what you would have felt if you could somehow have been witness to that display of power.

Think about how God "spoke" and there appeared fruits trees and pine trees, flowers, the grass, as well as every type of animal: the birds, the animals that live in the jungle, in the desert, domestic animals, like cats and dogs, even bacteria. What amazing variety! When we stop to study the planet which God has given us to live in and care for, we realize that it's an amazing place and that it has been designed with complete care, delicacy, and precision.

Think about a project that you have done for school or your work or the university. When we create something with our own hands, we generally feel very proud of our work, we admire what we created, and we take care of it responsibly. These feelings are greater if the work came out well.

Have students read verses 10, 18, 21, 25 and especially verse 31 of the first chapter of Genesis, then ask them, "What is it that is repeated in each one of these verses?" We read that God saw that what he had made was good. Genesis 1:31 says in this way, "God saw all that he had made, and it was very good." That is to say, God didn't only design and create our planet, but He also did a good job. Planet Earth is amazing!

In the same way that we like others to respect the things that we create or that belong to us, God instructs us to take care of the planet that He created. When we're conscientious of the fact that God is the creator of our planet, we're able to have a correct perspective that will help us to respect His creation.

2. God chose humans to care for planet Earth

Introduce the following exercise and ask them to write their responses on a piece of paper:

- Think of one person that you consider responsible. What makes that person responsible?

- Think of a person that you consider irresponsible. What is it that makes that person irresponsible?

- Think of a person who cares for what they have. What behaviors about that person make you believe that he or she is a person who is good at caring for their belongings and those of others?

- Finally, have them share their responses with the group. Help them think about how God considered that we can be responsible, and for that reason He gave us the world to administer. But, how do we respond to that request from God?

In Genesis 1:28-31, we read that God, out of his love for people, considered us responsible enough to take care of creation and make good use out of it. He put animals and plants at our disposal so that they would serve for food. Plants are not only for food, but they also provide shade and wood for us to build houses. The animals also help with work in the fields and transportation, and domestic animals provide great company.

The interdependence of humans with the environment in which they live is demonstrated clearly in Genesis 2:15. In this verse, God instructs humans to work the Earth, which is to say that they work it and plant it in order to yield fruit. Finally, God also tells people to "keep" the Earth.

It's good to know and trust that God provides for our needs. When we take care of planet Earth, we ourselves benefit. For example, if we care for and plant trees, we'll have wood, paper, and other things in the future. Creation itself is a testimony of the greatness of God's power and love, as we saw in the previous point of this lesson. Knowing that God created the Earth and that he has given it to us to enjoy, our response in thankfulness should be to always care for the Earth and protect the beings that live on it. As Christians, our behavior should be an example to the everyone. We were not only created by God, but He has given us the special mission of caring for his creation.

3. God will redeem planet Earth

The destruction of creation that man has caused is not a coincidence ... it's a consequence of sin. Since Adam and Eve disobeyed God in the garden of Eden, sin in the hearts of mankind has caused people to live separated from God and to not carry out the responsibility that God gave them for caring for the environment (Genesis 3:7-21).

Finally, in Romans 8:20-22, we read that not only we as human beings, but also creation itself is suffering and waits with great expectation for the second coming of Jesus. This is due to that fact that, although God has given us the privilege of caring for His creation, this creation needs God to come in His power and restore what has been damaged. Until Christ comes, we as Christians, since we have been set free from our sins and have been restored to a new relationship with the Creator, should be the first ones responsible for caring for His creation and encouraging others to do the same. It's interesting that the greatest movements in the world which promote the care of the environment with Green Peace and others have not come out of Christian churches, but rather are movements from New Age, agnostics, and Buddhists, among others.

During our time here on Earth, we as Christians have at times not taken seriously our responsibility to care for creation. Think about a time when your mom gave you a responsibility that you didn't follow through with, such as the day the trash collector comes, she asked you to take out the trash and you forget. What happened? If at some point you have forgotten to do this, as has happened in my house, the trash sits around until the next time that the garbage truck comes, and this causes bad odors and attracts flies. In the same way, our decisions to complete or not complete our responsibilities bring consequences. When we don't take care of the Earth as we should, there exist consequences for which the plants, the animals, the atmosphere, and even we ourselves in physical, mental and spiritual health will suffer.

While we're here on planet Earth, we have the responsibility of caring for God's creation, and we should take our job seriously. Not only that, but promoting care for the environment is a good way to speak to our friends about Christ, hope, and His second coming, and that those who are saved will be able to enjoy a restored environment.

Some of the things that we can do are to be careful of our use of water, use plastic and other disposable materials as little as possible, watch out for emissions of harmful gasses in our modes of transportation or use public transport, protect the trees, respect the habitats of the different animals, and finally, donate our time and money to organizations whose objective it's to care for our planet.

Despite all the effort that we can make, there is so much damage that has already been done and that we ourselves cannot restore. The hope that this verse in Romans give us is that God still is very interested in His creation. We can fully trust that, although the situation is not ideal, we along with creation wait for God to come again to redeem us, restore us, and make us new!

In the meanwhile, there are things that we can do so the destruction doesn't advance.

What are some of these things? Allow students to share practical ways in which they can contribute to caring for the environment. For example: use plastic bottles less often (plastic takes years to be destroyed in natural form), don't use disposable plates, cups, or silverware, don't buy water bottles but rather carry around your own water container, etc.

Review/Application

Individually and/or as a group, come up with definitions for the following words/phrases:

- To care for
- To appreciate
- To guard
- To prosper
- To respect
- To bless
- To make

Discuss as a class the possibilities that you have to help with the care of the environment in your community. Take time and help your students make a commitment to God to change their habits of life and help in the care of the environment.

Control Yourself

Lesson 9

Díaz Odily • El Salvador

Objective: That the students would comprehend the importance of good management of economic resources and would develop a financial budget.
To memorize: "In the same way, those of you who don't give up everything you have cannot be my disciples." Luke 14:33

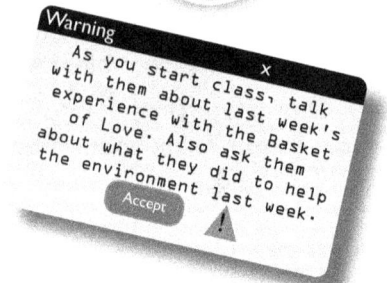

Warning
As you start class, talk with them about last week's experience with the Basket of Love. Also ask them about what they did to help the environment last week.
Accept

Connect | Navigate

Introductory activity (12-17 years)

- Materials: A dark bag, cookies and spaghetti noodles.
- Instructions:

  Place the materials in a dark bag or a box so that no one can see what's inside. Form two groups. Then, explain to them that they must build a tower with the materials that are given to them.

  When the groups are formed, give one group the spaghetti noodles and the other group the cookies. Then, give a considerable amount of time for the groups to form their towers.

  When the allotted time is up, ask the following questions:

- What did you expect when you saw the bag/box?
- What did you think when you saw your materials?
- How much time did you take to plan how to make the tower and evaluate if the material would be sufficient?
- How many ate the resources without thinking about using them later?
- How many let the materials fall down and didn't pay any attention to them?

  Reflect with them and explain to them the importance of knowing what materials one is working with before planning something, and of taking care of the resources that one has.

Introductory activity (18-23 years)

- Instructions:

  Place different objects in a bag (toy cars, toy houses, money, a Barbie doll, CDs, jewelry, a computer, balls, clothing, shoes, medicine, notebooks, etc.). Then, take the objects out of the bag one at a time and ask the students to tell what they relate the object to that is being shown. They have five seconds to reflect for each object and to arrive at a conclusion, which they can write on the board.

  For example: the Barbie doll represents the obsession for beauty; the notebooks are related to studies; the clothing, to fashion, etc.

  When finished, reflect with them on what is really valuable and what is an unnecessary expense.

Connect | Navigate

To be a disciple of Jesus, we should learn about some important aspects. By way of his Word, Jesus teaches us the importance of planning, budgeting, and thinking about our finances. A miner in West Virginia once said, "When your expenses exceed your income, nothing can prevent your bankruptcy." (Book: The Principle of Interpersonal Relationships by Stan Toler), which is why it's important to pay attention to the following. We're aware of the fact that we receive spiritual and material blessings from God. God uses distinct ways for us to obtain all that we need to live.

We live in a world that is driven by consumerism. The majority of people spend or desire to spend more than what they receive or earn. What's more, advertising is constantly telling people to change their clothes, shoes, accessories, furniture, cars, etc. Fashions pass very quickly and no one wants to be left behind. This causes one to spend on unnecessary things and not think about what is the best use of the money they have.

1. Good management of resources

In Luke 14:25-33, Jesus is teaching about aspects of following Him or what it costs to follow Him. Jesus was on his way to Jerusalem and he knew that the cross waited for him. Verse 25 reads, "Large crowds were traveling with Jesus, and turning to them he said…" These people were possibly following him because they thought he was going to take the throne. For that reason, Jesus spoke to them in the clearest way possible. He knew that what was waiting for him would be difficult, and only his love for God and for humanity would help him complete it.

It's interesting that in verse 26, Jesus refers to the question: What is it that those who wanted to be his disciples should hate? "If anyone comes to me and doesn't hate father and mother, wife and children, brothers and sisters—yes, even their own life—such a person cannot be my disciple." The word "hate" shouldn't be understood literally; what Jesus was teaching was that no love of this world can compare to the love that we should have for God.

In verse 28, perhaps Jesus changed his tone of voice and asked a question that he himself answered. The Modern English Version of the Bible says it in this way: "For who among you, intending to build a tower, doesn't sit down first and count the cost to see whether he has resources to complete it?"

For Jesus, it was important to know how to administer money, and one part of good administration is planning and budgeting. Planning means to establish how to do things and in how much time. Budgeting is making calculations of how much one has and how much it will cost to carry out what is desired.

Big businesses develop rigid strategies for planning and budgeting, the majority of them being long-term. That is to say, they plan their incomes and expenditures for at least five years.

Jesus taught the importance of planning and budgeting in all that one does so that everything turns out correctly and so people won't mock. Though Jesus was talking about calculating the cost of following him, the example demonstrates that sensible people make calculations for what they wish to undertake.

Perhaps in this moment you are young and you don't earn much money, or you depend on the money that your parents give you to be able to go to school. Regardless, it's important that even with that money you learn to administer it adequately. Have you ever asked yourself, "How much money do I receive each month from my parents or work, and how do I spend it?" Sometimes we aren't even aware of the money we receive, and we haven't stopped to think how to make better use of that money.

2. God is first in the management of my resources

God teaches us that we receive our money from Him, and He gives us strategic ideas to be able to use it in the best way. In Ecclesiastes 5:19, we read, "Moreover, when God gives someone wealth and possessions, and the ability to enjoy them, to accept their lot and be happy in their toil—this is a gift of God."

One of the secrets of good planning and of a good budget is in understanding that everything comes from God. For this reason, it's important to put God in first place when budgeting, and to give Him all that is due to Him—a minimum of 10% of all our income, without worrying if we receive much or little, and not forgetting offerings. God says in Malachi 3:10, "'Bring the whole tithe into the storehouse, that there may be food in my house. Test me in this,' says the Lord Almighty, 'and see if I won't throw open the floodgates of heaven and pour out so much blessing that there won't be room enough to store it.'" If God is given what is due Him, He will pour out abundant blessings over our lives. These blessings won't necessarily be money; God gives us blessings when He gives us work, health, friends, etc. So when budgeting, the first thing that should be written should be the tithe, even if it's very little. If youth learn from an early age to set apart the Lord's tithe, it won't be difficult for him or her to do it when they earn a greater sum of money. It shouldn't be forgotten!

3. Simple practices for the use of resources

In Matthew 14:13-21, we read the account of the feeding of the five thousand. Verse 20 reads, "They all ate and were satisfied, and the disciples picked up twelve basketfuls of broken pieces that were left over." We see here that nothing was wasted, nor was it handed out again, nor were the leftovers forgotten on the ground, but rather the disciples gathered what was left over, giving value to the food. Have you thought about this detail? The same thing happens in the feeding of the 4,000 in Matthew 15:32-39.

Jesus teaches us that after passing out the food and covering the basic needs, it's important to keep what is left over and not waste or squander it.

This teaches us that whenever we receive a salary or money is given to us for spending, we should cover basic needs and if there is any left over, it should be cared for. In accounting, this is called a balance and one relies on this until the next reception of money.

It's important that to be a good disciple of Jesus, we should be responsible even with finances. Pray to God, asking Him to help you recognize what things are necessary, and to make good use of the blessings that He gives you.

Review/Application

Challenge your students to begin a budgeting system, even if they don't have a regular income

Here is an example of a budget. Each student should make their own budget, using actual figures from their own jobs, or starting with a figure that you give them.

Sample:

Income	$100
Tithe (10%)	$10
Savings (10% minimum)	$10
Spendable Income	**$80**

House & utilities	$30
Debt	$5
Food	$15
Car/gas/transport	$10
Clothes	$10
Entertainment	$5
Phone	$5
Total expenses	**$80**

Created by God?

Objective: That the students would understand the importance of technology, its benefits and its risks.

To memorize: "For wisdom is more precious than rubies, and nothing you desire can compare with her." Proverbs 8:11

> **Warning**
> You asked your class last week to put together and follow a budget. Ask them to talk about the process and ask them how it has gone in following a budget.
> Accept

Connect | Navigate

Introductory activity (12-17 years)
- Instructions: Have each student remain in complete silence and still, without talking, whistling, singing, laughing, crying, making noise with their body, answering cell phones, sending text messages, or anything else for two minutes. Simply being completely silent and still.

  During this time, observe the attitudes of each student. Note that some can't be still. When you finish, ask them how they felt.

  Then, explain to them that we're in the age of technology, in which everything has a sound, color, noise, a light, or a movement. If it's not this way, it's not entertaining, attractive, and doesn't call for one's attention. According to studies, this generation has the ability to do various things at one time. They talk on the cell phone while they watch television, listen to music devices, use a digital camera and pet their favorite pet, all at the same time. And they still have the capacity to listen to you if you speak to them in that moment. This is something that for past generations is incomprehensible.

Introduction activity (18-23 years)
- Materials: Sheet of paper and pencil.
- Instructions: Ask them to write a list of all the names of electronic devices they can think of in 30 seconds. Then, find out who listed the most in that time.

  Next, explain to them that we're in an age in which technology is much more accessible than in previous times. It's even accessible to people of all ages around the world. What's more, because of the variety of brands and prices, technology is available to people of different socioeconomic levels.

Connect | Navigate

The Bible teaches us that everything was created by Him and for Him, and technology is not exempt from this truth. For some time, the church was using technology very little since it was costly and hard to access. However in this age, the costs are much more accessible and there are a variety of resources to use in teaching, preaching, worship, etc. Simply put, technology is a tool. God is the creator of all things, and He put everything in our hands to be used to accomplish His mission. The problem is that many people are using it for incorrect or destructive purposes. For this reason, many Christians today fear its use in Christian liturgy. The truth is that we can use it fully for productive purposes, given the creativity that our Creator put in us.

1. The benefits of technology

The majority of youth in churches use technology daily. The use of the smart phone, computer and the Internet have generated a massive means of communication in which youth can express themselves by way of chat rooms and apps such as Facebook, Instagram, WhatsApp, etc. It's also very common to see youth using cellphones with great skill, not only to communicate, but also to listen to music, take pictures and videos, play games, etc.

The use of technology is amoral, neither good nor bad in and of itself; the important thing is the way in which we use it.

1. What do the following passages recommend regarding the use of technology?

   - Philippians 4:8

   - 1 Corinthians 6:12; 10:23

2. How can we use technology for our own benefit?

As Christians, we must not lose our foundation that is found in reading the Word of God and in prayer, and we should meditate on all that helps us to grow in our faith.

2. Dangers in the use of technology

Technology is a tool, and as for every other created thing, God put it into our hands and we should manage it well. This has a double purpose. It can be used for benefit, such as making communication faster, more effective and more economical; but it can also be used badly, for things such as pornography, bullying, etc...

One of the most serious problems generated by this type of technology is that youth have become more closed in their communication with their parents, and many have stopped relating to others in a personal way. The use of personal items, such as music devices, cell phones and personal computers, have provoked the loss of growth and development of their interpersonal relationships.

Youth need to learn that everything has a time and a place to be used, and that it shouldn't be something that creates problems for us, especially when it involves obedience to God and to their parents. Many will usually spend a lot of time chatting or talking on their cell phone or sending text messages, but when it comes to reading the Bible, they get bored or it doesn't hold their attention.

Following are some dangers into which youth may fall by using technology indiscriminately:

a. Technology can become like a drug

The more it's used, the more addicting it becomes, and this can take partial or total attention away from what God wants for your life and what your parents ask of you.

One of the most serious problems generated by this type of technology is that youth have become more closed in their communication with their parents and many have stopped relating to others in a personal way. The use of personal items, such as music devices, cell phones and personal computers, have provoked the loss of growth and development of their interpersonal relationships.

Youth need to learn that everything has a time and a place to be used and that it shouldn't be something that creates problems for us, especially when it involves obedience to God and to their parents. Many will usually spend a lot of time chatting or talking on their cell phone or sending text messages, but when it comes to reading the Bible, they get bored or it doesn't hold their attention.

b. Technology can contaminate the mind

For example, by way of pornography in video, photos, stories, or in animated drawings, many youth are drawn in. Something that begins as simple curiosity ends up poisoning their minds. The enemy knows that. Thus, he uses advertisers and marketers who know that one of the most attractive things on the internet is pornography.

The human eye is not satisfied easily; the writer of Proverbs says. "Death and Destruction are never satisfied, and neither are human eyes." (Proverbs 27:20)

The human eye is not easily satisfied. Keeping this in mind, on the internet there exists a system of connections between different sites. So, when one is opened which has explicit sexual content, when the youth tries to close it, automatically three or four more pages are opened. And the more they see, the more their curiosity to see more is awakened. Not only this, but they also begin to seek stronger experiences that lead to the incorrect use of their bodies and minds.

c. Technology also brings physical consequences

According to studies done, the current generations are suffering a variety of sicknesses that before were only generated by old age. Some of these sicknesses are deterioration of sight due to the exaggerated exposure of the eyes to screens, strong headaches, deafness caused by the high volume of music devices and the use of headphones, wrist problems due to the use of the mouse and keyboard, back problems due to the long time spent sitting down, negative reactions, such as responding inappropriately to parents, etc...

d. Technology gives away confidential information

It can be seen on the news that recently tools such as Facebook, Instagram, WhatsApp, Twitter, etc., have been used to gather information about people, such as where they travel, gifts they receive, what they buy, cars they use and many other types of information, which is used for identity theft, kidnapping and blackmail. For this reason, it's important to ask youth to be prudent with the information they publish since, "The fish dies by his own mouth."

e. Technology produces a need for consumerism

We live in a world where technology is being updated day after day. This causes youth each day to need to spend more money on the purchase of these products, which bring serious problems for family finances. Many feel badly when they see that a friend has a better or more expensive device than their own. This has caused problems between youth and their parents, even leading to extremes like robbery, simply for the need to have. Some youth believe what advertising tells them about the use of different devices, and they feel badly if they don't have one or if one of their friends has one that is better or more expensive. Hebrews 13:5 tells us:, "Keep your lives free from the love of money and be content with what you have, because God has said, 'Never will I leave you; never will I forsake you.'" However, technology is one of the weapons that the enemy uses to lead us astray from the correct path.

3. How to use technology with wisdom from God

So we can learn that:

a. God designed us with a creative mind. God has put wisdom in mankind so that he will be creative for his own good, for the good of humanity, and for his work (Exodus 28:3; 31:3, 6). We thank God for what people have created and for the access that we have to new technology and its uses for various purposes that are of benefit.

b. God made us good administrators of resources and tools. If God has given us the freedom to use technology, let's use it for correct uses within His will. Be careful not to become youth who are dependent on technology, when the Word of God indicates clearly that we were called to freedom and not slavery (Galatians 5:1).

c. We should glorify God with all that we do. The use of technology should be in a way that is responsible and healthy, since it's also part of our lives, and as we know, we should glorify God with all that we do, as the apostle tells us in 1 Peter 4:11. Nothing that we do in public or private should dishonor the name of our God (2 Thessalonians 1:12).

d. God considers us capable to use technology. We're in the world but we're not of the world (John 17:16). This affirmation confirms for us that we can and should use what exists, but always with honorable goals. Additionally, we should have dominion over its use. Respectively, the Bible tells us that "There is a time for everything, and a season for every activity under the heavens" (Ecclesiastes 3:1), but many youth don't live in this way, and technology is consuming much of their time.

Review/Application

Divide the students into two groups. Have each group write down 10 examples of how they can use technology to evangelize and disciple others, and then explain their reasoning. They can use movies, music, TV programs, messages, apps, internet, etc. Discuss the answers as a group.

Also discuss as a group:

• What dangers or problems are youth encountering in their daily use of technology?

• How do you apply Philippians 4:8 to your life personally, regarding the wise use of technology?

This week have each person keep a diary of the electronic activities they do. Guide them in the way they should do this, and ask them to commit themselves to God to be honest and careful in recording activities.

Live Life!

Objective: That the students would know what bioethics is and what the Bible says about it.

To memorize: "God blessed them and said to them, "Be fruitful and increase in number; fill the earth and subdue it. Rule over the fish in the sea and the birds in the sky and over every living creature that moves on the ground." Genesis 1:28.

Warning
Ask volunteers to share the results of their evangelistic activity through electronic means. Also, don't forget to ask about their journal of their time on electronics.
Accept

Connect | Navigate

To introduce the topic, it's good to define the following words:

- To be fruitful: concerning a plant: to bear fruit. Concerning a thing: to yield results
- Subjugate: To conquer.

We can know that when the story of the creation of the heavens and the Earth is narrated in the book of Genesis, God gave mankind the order to rule, increase, and subdue the created things. This means that we should recognize the value of the life that God gave man, animals, and plants, and work to conserve it in the best way.

Introduction Activity (12-17 years)

- Instructions: Pass out paper and pencils to students. They will be asked to write a letter to God in which they should tell Him how they have treated animals and plants throughout their life. When finished, some students will be asked to share their letter with the class. The teacher can take a letter that he or she has written during the week to read to the students.

Introductory Activity (18-23 years)

- Instructions: Form two groups in order to carry out a debate. Before beginning, the following rules should be read:
  - Respect other people's opinions.
  - Don't be violent.

- Always be polite.
- Be sincere when there are disagreements.
- Try to discern how many of the differences are of ethic, scientific, or simply personal nature.
- Agree when possible without compromising your convictions.

Read the following case: "A girl was raped, and as a result, she became pregnant. She just found out that the baby has problems of deformity. In her city, abortion is permitted. What should this girl do?"

Ask one group to defend the position in favor of the abortion and the other to defend the position against abortion. This activity shouldn't last more than 10 minutes.

Connect | Navigate

Bioethics deals with specific dilemmas, both within the medical field, as well as referring to the political and social fields: sanitary assistance models and distribution of resources, the relationship between the health professional and the sick person, prenatal medical practices, abortion, genetic engineering, eugenics, euthanasia, transplants, experiments on human beings, etc.

1. The scope of bioethics

Humanity more and more desires to have more control over life in general. There exist organizations that try to legalize abortion, euthanasia, cloning, and other manipulations of life. It's for that reason that as Christians we shouldn't only be informed about these topics, but also know what our position should be as children of God seeking to do His will.

We should be good administrators of God's creation, not only with people, but also with the animals and plants. We're responsible for our environment and for respecting life in general.

In the first two chapters of the book of Genesis, we're told of God creating the heavens and the Earth. We can read how God cared for each detail of His creation and He gave man the wonderful responsibility of looking out for His creation. Sadly, humans have not always done their job well. Various species of animals and plants are endangered or extinct. Our grandparents were familiar with various plants that don't exist anymore. Many animals are only known through old stories or photographs.

In the same way, man now often wishes to be creator, not recognizing that the only giver of life is God. Today a mother "decides" if her child will be born or not, and in many countries, they don't have to hide anymore since it's legal. What's more, it's considered to be a woman's right, without considering the rights of the fetus or the father (who in some cases are against the abortion).

On the other hand, some medical professionals are making genetic manipulations so that the children are born with certain physical characteristics (color of eyes, hair, etc.), as if God's creation needs to be "improved" by man.

These types of cases are becoming more and more common. We hear the news and it no longer affects us since we're accustomed to this happening.

2. Bioethics and the human being

God asked us to care for His creation, not because He couldn't do it, but as a sign of His trust in us, since He believed we could do it.

When Jesus was on the Earth completing His mission, he showed concern for the life of people; in fact, there are many stories told to us about how He took his time to heal the sick. In 3 John 1:2, the desire for us to have health appears: "Dear friend, I pray that you may enjoy good health and that all may go well with you, even as your soul is getting along well."

Life is of worth in and of itself. This worth constitutes the base, support and foundation for any other moral value to be developed in its personal and social projection.

Life is of sacred worth. The Christian understand that life is a gift, because he knows that it's God's creation. Your life and the life of others is not private property but a loan from God. In this way, as children of God we should consider ourselves as mere administrators of what God has given us.

Jesus said in Matthew 10:39, "Whoever finds their life will lose it, and whoever loses their life for my sake will find it." This doesn't mean taking life lightly, nor does it mean desiring to commit suicide. Rather, this highlights the centrality of our faith in following Christ. In Christianity, life on earth is a constant surrender to the Lord.

Life is a concept and a reality which is personal, communal, and environmental. Human life is not only a personal reality, but also a collective and ecological reality.

Human life includes the concept of quality. With human life, we don't mean only the fact of existence as opposed to death, but also a life that has the quality and the dignity of being called human.

It's necessary that man obtains all that is necessary to live a life truly human, such as food, clothing, housing, health, the right to free choice of place and of having a family, education, work, a good reputation, respect, adequate information, to work according to the standards of their conscience, the protection of private life and religious freedom.

God wants us to have "life and life in abundance" (John 10:10b). This should be the desire for ourselves and for others, since in this way we'll respect the right to life of every being.

3. Some principle points about bioethics

Abortion

Permissive option - Liberal posture of "pro-abortion" which gives absolute rights to the woman for her body, including unborn babies.

Normative option - "Pro-life" posture, which morally condemns abortion and only allows it in cases of imminent risk of death for the mother. It gives moral rights to the fetus, as a person, from conception.

Contextual option - It accepts the moral value of the fetus, but considers circumstances and extenuating circumstances that could justify the abortion (e.g. incest, rape, genetic deformities of mother or child, social situations such as extreme poverty, psychosis).

Galatians 1:15 reads, "But when God, who set me apart from my mother's womb and called me by his grace..." and Jeremiah 1:4-5 says, "The word of the Lord came to me, saying, 'Before I formed you in the womb I knew you, before you were born I set you apart; I appointed you as a prophet to the nations.'" God recognizes us as people from the time we're in our mother's womb.

Assisted reproduction and Eugenics
- Artificial insemination is the use of means other than natural to implant semen in a woman in order to fertilize the egg and become pregnant. It can be done through the spouse or a donor.
- In vitro fertilization. Fertilization of the egg outside the female body in a controlled, artificial environment.

- Transference of gametes to the fallopian tubes. This occurs within the body just as in natural fertilization. The gametes are injected into the fallopian tubes through surgery, previous to hormonal treatment of the woman. In this case there exists a relatively high possibility that it will result in twins.
- Substitute maternity (surrogate mother). The two types are:
  - In gestation - the substitute only provides the womb.
  - Single substitution - the substitute provides both the egg and the womb.
- Eugenics or "good birth" is the predeterminations of which fetuses should live and which should not. It's closely tied to the topic of assisted reproduction.

If we're in God's hands, He has control of all things that happen. Psalm 139:13-16 says, "For you created my inmost being; you knit me together in my mother's womb. I praise you because I'm fearfully and wonderfully made; your works are wonderful, I know that full well. My frame was not hidden from you when I was made in the secret place, when I was woven together in the depths of the earth. Your eyes saw my unformed body; all the days ordained for me were written in your book before one of them came to be." We should rest in Him to work, and wait on His will.

Euthanasia

It means "good death" or "smooth death, without paint" (eu=good; tánatos=death). It can be voluntary or involuntary, depending on the role that the patient plays. There exist various classes and classifications of euthanasia.
- Passive - The doctor decides not to treat a secondary disease of a terminal patient.
- Semi-passive - The doctor withdraws all treatment—clinical, nutritional, etc., of a patient in a coma.
- Semi-active - The doctor disconnects the artificial respirator of a patient in vegetative state (cerebral death).
- Accidental or "double effect" - When narcotics are given as pain therapy to a terminal patient and the result is a reduced ability to breathe, to the point of death.
- Suicide - When the terminal patient decides for himself to take his life by ingesting medication or other things.
- Active - When the doctor administers and mortal overdoses of morphine or potassium to a terminal patient.

Scripture

Euthanasia is a way in which man tries to usurp the authority of God by wanting to decide when we die. The Bible teaches that human beings are created in the image of God (Genesis 1:26), and for that reason, humans have dignity and value. Human life is sacred and shouldn't be ended simply because it's difficult or inconvenient. Psalm 139 teaches that humans have been made as an admirable creation, as a wonderful work. Society shouldn't focus on an arbitrary standard of quality above the absolute standard of God regarding worth. This doesn't mean that people won't need to make difficult decisions about treatment and care, but it does mean that these decisions will be guided by an objective and absolute standard of human worth.

The Bible also teaches that God is sovereign over life and death. Christians can agree with Job when he said, "The Lord gave and the Lord has taken away; may the name of the Lord be praised" (Job 1:21). The Lord said, "See now that I myself am he! There is no god besides me. I put to death and I bring to life, I have wounded and I will heal, and no one can deliver out of my hand" (Deuteronomy 32:39). God has ordained our days (Psalm 139:16) and He is in control of our life.

Another fundamental principle involves a biblical vision of taking away life. The Bible specifically condemns murder (Exodus 20:14), and this includes active forms of euthanasia in which another person (doctor, nurse, or friend) accelerates the death of the patient.

Though the Bible doesn't specifically speak about the topic of euthanasia, the history of the death of King Saul (2 Samuel 1:9-16) is instructive. Saul asked a soldier to kill him while he lie dying on the battlefield. When David found out about this act, he ordered the soldier to die for "destroying the Lord's anointed." Although the context is not euthanasia exactly, it does show the respect that we should show toward human life, even in such tragic circumstances.

Christians should also reject the attempt of the modern euthanasia movement in promoting the "right to die." Secular society's attempt to establish this "right" is wrong for two reasons. First, to give a person the right to die is the same as promoting suicide, and suicide is condemned in the Bible. Man is prohibited from killing, and this includes the killing of one's self.

Review/Application

Bioethics should be a topic of interest for Christian families. This week, have your students take time to talk with their parents about this lesson. Have them find out if there are laws in your country regarding abortion, euthanasia, etc., and ask their parents what they think of them.

Fulfilling the promise

Objective: That the students, through Caleb's example, learn how to wait for the promises of God for his/her life.

To memorize: "But because my servant Caleb has a different spirit and follows me wholeheartedly, I will bring him into the land he went to, and his descendants will inherit it." Numbers 14:24

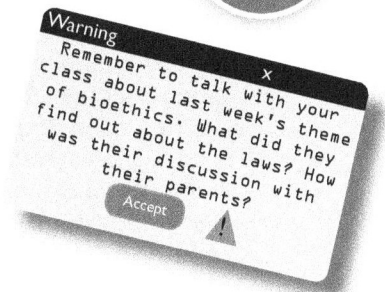

Warning
Remember to talk with your class about last week's theme of bioethics. What did they find out about the laws? How was their discussion with their parents?
Accept

Connect | Navigate

Caleb, whose name means reckless, impetuous, was one of the 12 people sent to explore the land of Canaan. Trusting in God's power, he gave a hopeful report. Regardlessly, the people of Israel didn't believe in the promise of conquering the land. God rewarded him and Joshua for trusting in His promise by being the only people from their generation to enter Canaan. The Lord promised to Caleb, when Israel was still traveling through the desert, that he and his descendants would inherit the lands he explored along with the other 11 spies 45 years before. These lands were the lands of Hebron, where the "giants," the sons of Anak, lived.

Introductory activity (12-17 years)
- Resources: Landscape picture and a cloth to cover the eyes.
- Instructions: Ask two or three students to cover their eyes with the cloths. Ask the rest of the group to describe the landscape picture to those with their eyes covered.

  Finally, have them uncover their eyes and look at the image. Ask them if that was how they imagined it when it was being described. Explain how things change from hearing a description to seeing things, since everyone has different ways of perceiving and appreciating things.

Introductory activity (18-23 years)
- Instructions: Dialogue with your students about impatience. Ask them how impatient they are, and which situations they have experienced that made them wait a long time for something they wanted.

Connect | Navigate

For forty days, 12 men explored Canaan (Numbers 13). Ten out of the twelve saw the difficulties and were filled with fear and terror. We can read in verses 31-33 that they saw themselves as grasshoppers before their enemies. On the other hand, Joshua and Caleb spoke about a land that they could conquer because God had already prepared it for them. It's important to have the correct attitude when we're facing our difficulties, to have the correct attitude before the challenges God allows in our way. It's so important to know that to avoid murmuring and negative expressions, just as Caleb did (Numbers 13:30) when he trusted God's love, His power and protection (Numbers 14:7-9).

In Caleb's life, we can observe how he had the correct spirit. As a man of faith, he knew how to look at the difficulties as opportunities where God's love could be manifested. Caleb was a man who knew how to keep his faith for 45 years, and he was able to claim his inheritance. When he was 85 years old, he said to Joshua, my strength is the same, I still have faith, neither my trust nor my faith in God has become smaller. He will make my enemies fly away before me, no matter their size, no matter they strength, for God is with me. God rewarded his faith and his attitude. And because he had the right attitude, God gave him the best of Canaan's lands (Joshua 14:6-15). Caleb, a man with character, a man with dreams that came true because he knew how to keep his faithfulness to his God.

1. Caleb's life stages

A. The suffering Caleb

- He was 40 years old when they were in Kadesh-barnea (Joshua 14:7), so he must have been born in Egypt, where the Jewish people endured great suffering.
- He was born a slave, but he died a leader.

This means that the conditions of one's birth may influence someone's future, but doesn't determine it. Caleb was born a slave but he never had a slave's mind-set. He trusted God to fulfill the promise to be transformed from a slave to the owner of an inheritance from God.

B. The brave Caleb

- While in the desert, 12 spies were sent to explore Canaan. Caleb was among the 12 chosen, and while 10 spies saw the problems of the land, Joshua and Caleb rejoiced in it.
- The nation wanted to retreat, but two men of faith wanted to move forward. While others thought of giants, they thought of the benefits and the great promise given by the Lord.
- The majority were walking by sight, the minority by faith. As Christians, we're called to ignore giants and trust the Almighty God, to believe He has the power to defeat obstacles and give us what He has promised. The rebel nation only saw obstacles, while Caleb saw the opportunities. What was the outcome of Caleb's faith?
- Ten spies died wandering in the desert.
- Joshua and Caleb entered into the Promised Land.
- Caleb faced the whole nation and God honored him for that. While the people yelled against the idea, he and Joshua spoke of trust. The nation even threatened them, but God protected them, giving Caleb a rewarding promise for trusting Him.

C. The pilgrim Caleb

- Caleb didn't die in the desert, but he had to travel for 40 years with the unfaithful nation. Perhaps he had to suffer the constant complaining and gossiping.
- How was he able to keep a healthy spirit when surrounded by all that carnality? It's simple. His body was in the desert, but his heart was in Canaan, the inheritance, God's promise.
- Don't give up when you are in the desert. You may have to go through many trials while you wait to receive your promise, but don't forget to fix your eyes upon the One who gives the promises and keeps them to the end.

D. The conquering Caleb

- Someone with faith is someone with strength. Caleb was 85 years old and he still was looking forward to taking possession of his inheritance from the Lord.
- When we think about ourselves, and if we imagine ourselves at the age of 85, most of us would think of our weaknesses and our need to retire. Scripture gives us Caleb's example - he didn't surrender to his old age. We tend to believe that our days follow a schedule, and being weak and ill is unavoidable. But young people also grow weak and ill. Every day of our lives is a gift of grace and mercy. Today, because of God's grace, we have a path before us, and we're called to work doing His purpose. How far we go on this path isn't dictated by a calendar, but by God's will and our obedience.
- If the mission God gave us is still unfinished, we must not focus on how weak or ill we are, and how hard our circumstances may be. Even at 85 years old, Caleb's responsibility wasn't finished because God gave him Hebron –the richest land of Canaan. When the spies returned from doing their reconnaissance, they said "This land flows milk and honey" (Numbers 13:27). Only one grapes cluster from Escol valley required two people to carry it. The richness was obvious. Escol valley was in Hebron and its soil produced the best of Canaan. And Caleb, for his unconditional faithfulness, received this land as his reward.
- We all can agree that Canaan was extremely good. In Canaan we have our legacy as well - life. Christians who love God will receive this inheritance, but only Caleb received it as a reward. The promise land that God has for you is yours, but you have to set your foot on it to receive it as an inheritance. Here's why Caleb wasn't retiring yet, because he hadn't received his reward. Caleb had the spirit of a young man. Despite his old age, he was able to fight, and that's why God protected them. Not every tribe received an inheritance, because they didn't set foot on the land. Caleb received from his Lord the best of Canaan. Even if we reach our Canaan, if we don't have yet the Crown of life and righteousness, we need to say as Caleb did, "Now give me this hill country that the Lord promised me that day" (Joshua 14:12).
- Caleb's wish when he was 85 was the most dangerous territory - land that devoured those living in it and inhabited by people of great size. At 40 years old, Caleb wasn't afraid; at 85 he was a brave man. The expression "give me this hill country" indicates he was ready to take possession of the land. Thanks to God, Caleb received the land.
- He had vision and vitality. There were "giants" and 10 spies were afraid, but Caleb defeated them with his attitude. Disbelief sees giants, but faith sees God. Joshua and Caleb conquered with physical weapons and took possession of material inheritance. We conquer with spiritual weapons (2 Corinthians 10:3-5) to receive a spiritual inheritance. It's expected that Christians will be triumphant through faith in Christ (1 John 5:4). We must overcome the world (1 John 5:5). We must overcome false teachings (1 John 4:1-4). And we must overcome the evil one (1 John 2:13-14). Let's have faith in Christ; He has overcome the world (John 16:33).

Review/Application

Individually, have your students identify each stage of Caleb's life with some stage of their own lives, write them down, and then share those situations with the group if they are comfortable doing so

A healing miracle

Objective: That the students become aware of the challenge of a thankful life towards God for His miracles in their life.

To memorize: "He touched her hand and the fever left her, and she got up and began to wait on him" Matthew 8:15.

Warning
Ask your students about their attitudes about this last week concerning the Promised Land that God has for them, and the obstacles they had to overcome this week.

Accept

Connect | Navigate

Introductory Activity (12-17 years)
- Resources: Whiteboard and enough markers
- Instructions: Divide the whiteboard in two sections and write with the students a list of good or useful things to do when someone is ill, and another list of not-so-good things to do. The list can include things from they own experiences with illness. Example: "when I was sick, it made me very happy when my friends brought me flowers" or "when someone is sick, it doesn't help to tell that person that he or she is sick because they probably did something wrong."

Introductory Activity (18-23 years)
- Resources: Paper and markers.
- Instructions: Ask every student to write three illness he or she has experimented, at which age, how that made them feel and how the healing process happened. Each student will briefly share the experiences with the group. Give conclusions about the importance of support and company of friends and family and divine intervention during illness.

Have you experienced sickness during your lifetime? Maybe a cold or chickenpox? Some people may say getting sick is fun since you can skip school, be looked after by your parents, and watch TV. But after a few days, staying in bed doesn't seem fun anymore. When we think about the consequences, we can realize that skipping classes means more work when returning (to catch up with the missed assignments). For adults, it's even more complicated because they can get reductions on their salary. In today's story, we'll read the experience of an ill woman.

Connect | Navigate

One of the things that most affects our life as human beings is sickness, either physically (a disease in our bodies), or emotionally and mentally (when we're sad or our minds aren't working properly). The wonderful truth behind these difficulties is that God is here to help us, and it's through these circumstances that we can pay more attention to see how He works miracles and changes things that are impossible for us. In today's story, we'll closely study one of Jesus' miracles in the life of a woman (Matthew 8:14-17).

1. The woman's need

In the first verse of the text that we're studying this lesson, we see Jesus spending time with his disciples; they were close friends so he was able to visit them in their own homes. Even today, Jesus is interested in all parts of our life. Since Jesus was a good friend of Peter's, He visited him and saw the need of Peter's family. This shows that Jesus was paying attention to his friends' needs, "…he saw Peter's mother-in-law lying in bed with a fever." (v.14)

Today, having a fever and spending days resting is not a big deal, especially if we can home, skip school and receive care and company from our parents. However, in the time of Peter and his mother-in-law, the situation was completely different. The first consideration we must have is that women in those times were under-appreciated. Even today, there are regrettably disrespected and mistreated women.

Generally, being a woman wasn't a thing to be happy for, since they weren't appreciated very much. Women in those times weren't allowed to study, and they were expected to simply stay at home and serve others. Women had no academic preparation and no work training. They depended completely on their husbands, older sons or sons-in-law for a place to live and food to eat.

The second consideration is that Peter's mother-in-law was a woman and she was sick; therefore, she was even less "important" or even "invalid" for the society where she lived. This was because she couldn't do her responsibilities in the house, which was her "reason for being." Imagine how she would feel in this situation. There is no doubt she felt frustrated, worried, tired and sad, longing to be healthy.

Knowing this, it's fascinating seeing Jesus consider and look at Peter's mother-in-law. Here we see how different Jesus was. Anyone would have thought that this mother-in-law was the least important person in the house. Jesus took time to see her and think of her. We can see how Jesus will never ignore us, no matter how "small" or "insignificant" we may feel in the eyes of the people, or even in our own eyes. We can rest assured that Jesus cares and loves us.

2. Jesus' response

In verse 15, we read about the healing Jesus did for Peter's mother-in-law. It's wonderful how Jesus not only saw the woman in need, but he did something to help her. In this passage, we can see God's amazing love for us, love that wants to help and transform our situation. Jesus wasn't only compassionate about Peter's mother-in-law, but he also "touched her hand," that is, he was with her, by her side during her illness.

Verse 15 states that "the fever left her," which is a reminder of God's power. The most wonderful thing is to be reminded of our assurance in God, for He is able to help us in any difficulties, even with physical disease.

Sometimes in your lives as young people, you feel that no one can understand the struggles you are going through in your family relationships, with your friends and/or romantic relationships, or in your mental, emotional or spiritual health. But you must not believe that lie. Jesus knows what you are going through, He loves you, and you can trust completely that He has the power to help you change your situation and enjoy a healthy life.

3. The woman's gratitude

When Peter's mother-in-law experienced Jesus' power in her life, it's described in two brief sentences in Matthew 8:15, "...she got up and began to wait on him." These two phrases contain a verb, so they indicate an action. The conclusion we can take is that Peter's mother-in-law took action immediately after feeling al right.

First, we observe "she got up." It's important to consider what makes this response so special. It's possible to assume that many people, when healed, would decide to stay a little longer in bed "to rest and recover energy." There are two issues with that attitude. First, it would deny the healing power of God. When Peter's mother-in-law was healed, she was healed completely with all her energy and motivation. Jesus didn't do half a miracle. He took away the fever and other symptoms; she was truly healed from her disease and her health was completely restored. Second, if Peter's mother-in-law would have decided to stay in bed because she was feeling lazy, she would be denying herself the opportunity to enjoy God's blessing. In other words, to keep acting and feeling as if our problem was there when God has changed the situation stops us from receiving all the joy God has for us.

The main issue with the attitude described before is that we aren't giving glory to God for his miracles in our life We need to put aside our problems when God works in us and move forward to reach the new things He has planned for us. A good way to do this is to stop thinking about the past situation to complain and lament over it, but only to share it with others to thank God for his power and love for us. Having a thankful attitude is the best we can do, the sign of a Christian who truly experiences joy and peace from God. God is able to transform our attitudes and everything we are!

Finally, today's passage tells us that Peter's mother-in-law "began to wait on him" (Matthew 8:15). It's great to see this woman take a positive attitude, and even more, a thankful one. How sad it's to see and listen to a person who has received God's blessings and doesn't take time to say thanks! God doesn't send blessings and healing to our lives because he needs us to thank Him. He simply does it because He loves us. However, when someone thanks us for our kind actions, we feel good and it helps us to be closer to that person. A thankful attitude brings positive feelings towards another person and improves the relationship. In the same way, when we take time to serve God as a way of saying thanks, we can understand how his work in our lives is motivated by love, and how He loves communion and intimacy with us. The truth is that everything God does in our lives is to bring us closer to Him.

Review/Application

Divide the class into groups, and have each group write the definitions of the following words. Then have each group share their definitions with the whole group, and notice the different meanings that each group has given to each word. Then think what the Bible suggests to us about each word.

- Health
- Disease
- Miracle
- Faith
- Gratitude

Take some time before finishing today's class to bring to the class a list with some names of sick people (preferably that your students know). Allow each person in the class to share other names as well. Encourage them to propose personal or class activities to minister to them. End by praying for the people you have on the list.

Woman, you have an inheritance

Objective: That the students develop the awareness that God created women with rights and responsibilities, just as He did with men.

To memorize: "And the Lord said to him, 'What Zelophehad's daughters are saying is right. You must certainly give them property as an inheritance among their father's relatives and give their father's inheritance to them.' " Numbers 27:6-7

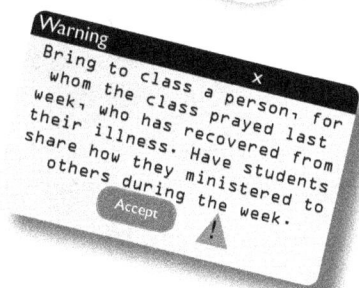

Warning
Bring to class a person, for whom the class prayed last week, who has recovered from their illness. Have students share how they ministered to others during the week.
Accept

Connect | Navigate

Introductory activity (12-17 years)
- Instructions: Ask the students to split into two groups. They must do a drama of women's role in family, and the other group will represent women's role in church. Discuss about the concept they have of women in society.

Introductory activity (18-23 years)
- Instructions: Ask your students to write a comparison between rights and responsibilities for both genres. If you want to, you can create two groups: men and women, to develop the activity.

The distorted ideas of many men about women have trampled the honor that Jesus gave to women in his ministry. Jesus was a man free of prejudices against women, He treated women in a very loving, special and compassionate way.

Mary, a sinful woman, poured perfume at Jesus' feet; a Samaritan woman met Jesus next to a well and she became "missionary"; a woman caught in adultery was brought before Him and He forgave her. Jesus challenged the law and showed a group of religious hypocrites how their oppression hurt the Father's heart.

Today we'll study a story thousands of years before Jesus. Let's meet five women who changed the ideas about women in their time. They are known as Zelophehad's daughters (Numbers 27:1-11).

Connect | Navigate

In ancient society, women barely had any rights. Jewish laws were made by and for men; i.e., created by men in important positions among the people. They dictated these laws to legitimize and protect their power structure in society.

1. Women's condition

The society in which these women were born and raised was completely patriarchal (ruled by men). This wasn't God's intention when he created Adam and Eve, but sin corrupted everything. In this world, women were considered just a little more than property. Parents had to be paid a marriage price for a daughter.

The most radicals saw women as wicked, ignorant and immoral; inferiors, mere servants. They were expected to wear a veil, not allowed to talk with men in public, nor allowed to receive an education. In this oppressive culture, five brave and purposeful women acted in a way never seen before.

The only ones allowed to receive an inheritance were men, of course. So, when Zolophehad only had five daughters, a problem arose. But the daughters were very special: (Numbers 27:1) Mahlah ("fat", "infirmity"), Noah ("movement"), Hoglah ("dancing"), Milkah ("queen") and Tirzah ("pleasing"). Incredible names!

2. Brave women

Each of these names revealed abilities, personality and adversities they faced that made them strong, persistent, courageous, wise and graceful women. When the moment to distribute the land among Israel's tribes arrived, these sisters joined together, discussed the situation, probably prayed, and decided to do something unconceivable for the times. They went before Moses, Eleazar the priest, the leaders and the whole assembly (verse 2) and asked to receive property (vv. 3-4). What would have happened? Would they be ignored? Would they be told off? Would they be considered? Would they be judged?

In Numbers 27:1-8, we read the claim of the daughters when they spoke about the margination they had endured after their father had died.

You can organize the group in teams of three or four members and ask them to read the passage and analyze it using the following questions:

1. Why did the five women have to go before Moses to ask for their inheritance?
2. What risks were they facing when they presented their plea?
3. What was Moses' answer to the women?
4. Why do you think God changed the laws to benefit these women?
5. Do you think the new law was fair for women? Why?

The central figures in the text are five women who demanded to be part of the history of Israel. As usual, Mahlah, Noah, Hoglah, Milkah and Tirzah weren't registered in their family's genealogy. The story mentions their names, but only after mentioning their father and masculine ancestors (v 1). Nevertheless, the fact that we do see their names in the Bible indicates that this is a very special story in which women are fighting for their names to be heard by everyone, even us today.

These women, facing the absence of a father figure and authority to speak for them (v 3a), decided to go themselves and present their story before the authorities (v 2). The chosen place for this is the entrance to the tent of meeting, where according to experts, only the most important issues where discussed. "Our father died in the wilderness. He was not among Korah's followers…" This opening sentence was necessary because it stated that their family was innocent and unrelated to the rebellion that happened before. Therefore, the women's plea was fair and logical, since their father didn't die for a sin that condemned the family to lose their lives and all inheritance rights.

As family, they resisted being erased from the memory of the people. That's why they claimed their right to receive property among their father's relatives (v.4). But there's something else behind this plea. The inheritance demanded by these women would allow them to support themselves. If they were left without the inheritance, how would they survive?

"…Give us property among our father's relatives." When the women saw only male individuals were registered and their family was left out, they presented their complaint before Moses and the authorities, who discussed how to make things right. This is the first pro women's rights appeal in the Bible. I'm not talking about feminism but about fair rights for women as daughters of God. These women dared to trust God as their defender, and their request was granted. These five women had a confrontational spirit about injustice, and Moses' reaction was to consider their case.

3. God acts in their favor

This had no precedent (v.5), so this case had to be brought to a higher authority, i.e., it needed to be brought before the Wise and Just. Moses didn't show any prejudice, didn't determine a decision based on the context he was living in. He didn't judge according to the traditions and what had been known. Moses placed justice before tradition. Moses took this before God, since He was the one who had the last Word, not Him. Today, many brothers, male pastors and leaders need to take the same attitude before judging if a woman can or cannot hold a leadership position in the Church. They must go before God and let Him make the decision and the call.

God's answer is surprising and marvelous (vv. 6-7). He said yes. Imagine God telling Moses, "Hear those women and their claim. They have a right to their inheritance, as I've seen their determination, braveness and will to take what belongs to them. Why should I deny that?".

Daring to tell their story provoked the creation of a new law that accepted women as inheritors (v. 8). Their claim started a story that opened doors and opportunities to the life of women among the Hebrew people.

Due to the bravery and boldness of these five women, a new law was made. We could call this the first law regarding the inheritance rights of women. We could think of a statement like this, "We solemnly declare that any heir from a deceased father without any male children will be rightfully given to the father's daughters. This will be a right from now on, as God the Judge has commanded." This is extremely shocking, as now people would know that God loves women the same way he loves men, and He would give them the same rights of inheritance.

Isn't this story amazing? The plea and claims of five women changed the rights and the law for following generations. 40 years were passed in the dessert while the women waited patiently for their land. Moses passed away and a new leader arose - Joshua. Would he forget the order that God gave to Moses? Would they need to go before the leaders to start a new claim? According to Joshua 17:1-4, they went before the leaders and reminded them of what they were granted by Moses years ago, and they received it!

When Moses heard about these sisters, he didn't know how to act. Therefore, he asked God. God saw the faith in these women and provided justice for them. God treats everyone equally.

It's important to know who you are in God. There is no reason to expect others to get what is yours. Your Heavenly Father left you an inheritance. And it's not what people say about you that makes things different. It's what God has said about you and what you say about yourself that really matters.

Faith is what matters the most to God. He says that before him there is no nationality (Galatians 3:28). There is just one Church, bought by the blood of the Lamb. We are one in Christ. Your race or the color of your skin is not what gives you advantage or value. What's in your heart is what gets God's attention. God always sees your heart.

God wants you to believe Him ... that you accept the truth that you can do all things through Him (Philippians 4:13). If you dare to believe in the inheritance you have in Jesus Christ, you'll find the strength to keep moving forward.

Review/Application

Have your students write down individually or by groups the qualities of Zelofehad's daughters that impressed them and why.

According to the biblical passage, what does God teach us about respecting women's rights and gender equality.

It's time to end with the negative past, with bad memories, with abuse, with traumas, and with the low self-esteem that have paralyzed women and made things almost impossible for them to do. It's time that they experience all that God says about them and wants them to be and have. They are heirs. They must not accept it if anyone thinks, believes and speaks less than that. They must learn from the daughters of Zelofehad and claim their inheritance today. Ask the young people to pray for the young ladies, then pray for their mothers and sisters asking God to help them to take on the role that He wants them to have in the kingdom of God.

Encourage your class to talk with people about the theme of this lesson, and come back next week ready to report on people's reactions and comments about women's rights.

She said, Yes, Lord

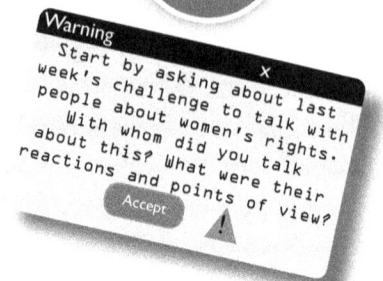

Objective: That the students understand that God wants to use women and men equally to accomplish His purpose.

To memorize: "There is neither Jew nor Gentile, neither slave nor free, nor is there male and female, for you are all one in Christ Jesus." Galatians 3:28

Warning
Start by asking about last week's challenge to talk with people about women's rights. With whom did you talk about this? What were their reactions and points of view?
Accept

Connect | Navigate

Introductory activity (12-17 years)

- Show the map for Paul's second missionary journey. (It can be found in many Bible appendices.) Divide the class into groups and give a clean map to each one of them. Write the name of the cities that Paul visited and Tiatira (even when Paul didn't visit that city in that journey).
- Instructions: Ask the students to draw a line symbolizing Paul's route, according to Acts 15:36 - 16:12. The first group to finish the whole journey will be the winner.

Introductory activity (18-23 years)

- Instructions: Write on the board the following question: "Can a woman lead a Church?" Let students dialogue or brainstorm, where everyone can express their opinion about if they agree or not with women taking leadership in a church or leading it as pastors.

Even when we enjoy more freedom of interaction between men and women, there are still people who believe women shouldn't have the same rights as men. Before God, that is simply not true. The Bible teaches that we're all equal. Before Him, we're equally responsible for our actions. And for youth, this is an important topic since they have different ideas and backgrounds. It's important for them to understand that the role of women in the Church is approved by God.

Connect | Navigate

Despite the little information we have about Lydia, we can still find very important teachings for our lives and about the care God has for His children.

When we start reading the text, we observe that Paul's plan was to keep working in Asia. He wanted to go towards Bithynia, but God told him to change course and start a new adventure in Europe. Acts 16:9-10 tells about the vision Paul had, and his understanding of people in need of the Gospel outside Asia. The first place they visited in Europe was Philippi. It's very likely that there weren't many Jews in the place, because we don't see any mention of a synagogue. Instead, people prayed next to the river. It's in this place where Paul meets Lydia. Read Acts 16:11-15.

1. Lydia, a hard working woman

Luke, Acts' author, wrote that Lydia came from Thyatira. This city was famous for the dyes made for cloth. It was also a very commercial and corrupted place. Lydia and her family moved to Philippi and Lydia worked selling purple cloth.

2. Lydia, a woman that heard God's voice

It seems that Paul and his group (Silas, Timothy, Luke and others) couldn't find a synagogue in Philippi, so they looked for a praying place. Historians tell us that at about that time, it was required to have a group of at least 10 male Jews to have a synagogue in the city. Though it appears that there was not a synagogue in the city, all the Jews respected the Sabbath and gathered together in a place to worship God. We don't know how Lydia came to be part of these reunions. But the Bible does tell us that Lydia was in a place where the true God was praised. That tells us a lot about Lydia's life, especially since she came from a pagan city.

A. She heard Paul's words. It was unusual for Jews to teach women, but Paul was sure that the Gospel was for everyone and took the opportunity to bring the message to a group of them. Lydia must have been very attentive. Putting aside personal matters, like prejudices or business, she decided to listen to this visitor.

B. She praised God. Somehow, Lydia knew God through the Jewish beliefs. But not only did she know about Him, she praised Him, which indicates she had faith in Him. It's important to comment on how many people know about God and praise Him, even without completely understanding His message for them. Lydia was one of them, praising and believing in God, but without experiencing the Gospel and a relationship with Jesus. Are you like Lydia? Do you know about God but haven't yet had a personal encounter with Him?

C. She was sensitive to God's voice. Jesus said (Juan 16:8-11) that the Holy Ghost would convince the world of sin, righteousness and judgement. This had happened in Lydia. God prepared her heart for that moment. In the same way, God is interested in all humanity, not only in Jews or those born into Christian families. God loves everyone.

D. She accepted the message of salvation. What a joy Paul and his friends must have had! God's purpose of going to Europe was becoming clearer. A European woman was surrendering her life to Christ! When she heard the message, she made the decision to accept the Good News and be baptized.

This is the reason we must pray for those who haven't heard of Christ, so that their hearts can be ready. At the same time, we must take every opportunity to share the Gospel. We don't know if there are Lydia's around us, waiting to hear about Jesus!

3. Lydia, a woman who shared her faith and served God

When Christ comes into our hearts, we can't stay quiet, we must share the Great News! Lydia did it that way. The Bible tells us about her and her family being baptized. How many there were and where they were, we may not know, but the Gospel reached her and her whole family. Faith in Christ is not to be lived in the secret. It's very interesting to note the passage where Paul and Silas tell the jailer, "Believe in the Lord Jesus, and you will be saved—you and your household." (Acts 16:31) The Gospel must influence those surrounding us. Do you want to influence others, especially your family, with the message of Jesus Christ?

Right after her life was transformed, Lydia decided to do something to help Paul and his friends. She offered her house as a place to stay. She would look after them during the time they stayed in Philippi. That way they could keep sharing the Gospel with others. Is there anything you can do to help others that are sharing the Gospel?

You can write the following guides and the texts for each section so that the students participate, reading and giving their opinions about each passage:

Lydia's life can be an example to us.

• A hard working woman.
• A woman that searches for God.
• A woman who shared her faith and served God.

Take the opportunity to ask the students if anyone would like to accept Christ as Savior. Or if you know of someone who has not made a decision for Christ, take some time to talk with him or her about making that decision.

You can also give them each a piece of paper to write the names of three people that are unaware of God's love for them, but that they would like to pray for.

Review/Application

Have your students respond to the following questions individually or as a small group, and then discuss in the large group:

1. Write two reasons why you think women should work or shouldn't work.

2. Explain how it's possible for a person to know God, but not to accept him as their Savior. Do you think there are people like that? Why?

3. Write three examples of how you can share your faith with others.

4. Write three ideas of how you can serve God, just as Lydia did.

If there is time, talk with the class about how to apply the characteristics of Lydia to each one's situation. Encourage them to put their lives in the hands of God and strive to have the characteristics of Lydia.

It can change

Objective: That the students discover Onesimus' life and the change that operated in him, to learn how our life can change radically when we accept and serve Christ.
To memorize: "I appeal to you for my son Onesimus, who became my son while I was in chains. Formerly he was useless to you, but now he has become useful both to you and to me." Philemon 10-11

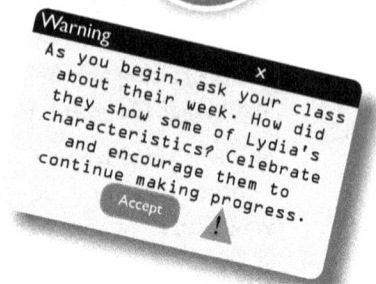

Warning
As you begin, ask your class about their week. How did they show some of Lydia's characteristics? Celebrate and encourage them to continue making progress.
Accept

Connect | Navigate

Introductory activity (12-17 years)
- Resources: Clay or molding dough
- Instructions: Give a piece of clay or molding dough to each student, and ask them to make any figure they want. Once they have finished, ask them to create another figure with the same material. Repeat this a few times. The purpose of this activity is to show to them that clay or dough can be shaped in different ways, depending on the hands that it's in. In the same way, when we let God shape us, we can be changed to serve a higher purpose.

Introductory activity (18-23 years)
- Resources: Pencils and paper.
- Instructions: Give each student a pencil and a piece of paper, and ask them to write 10 things about themselves they want to change. After this you can discuss the things that can't be changed without God's help.

Too many people have asked me this. And I'm sure that you, teacher, have heard this same question, "Does Christianity really change people?" When I talk to my friends about Christ or we share some verses, they look interested, but they aren't sure about making a decision because they don't know if it's possible to really change.

The truth is that Christ has transformed our lives. He also radically transformed Onesimus' life. We'll study now the way his character changed.

Connect | Navigate

The introductory activity has helped us to see how things in our lives can be changed, especially when we place them in God's transforming hands. But, do we truly believe in radical change? Let's talk about Onesimus' life, a clear example of the change God can do in anyone's life.

Who was Onesimus? Onesimus was Philemon's slave. In ancient cultures, slavery was an accepted social practice and practiced by many. It was not necessarily based on nationality or skin color, but on defeat in war and on debt. Philemon was a slave owner. One day, Onesimus decided to escape from Philemon's house. Many agree that the poverty and oppression these people were under were the reasons that slaves robbed their masters and escaped. The Bible doesn't mention the specific reasons for Onesimus' escape, but this might have been what happened. Onesimus traveled all the way to Rome, where he found Paul as his companion in jail. In that place he accepted Jesus! We'll study now some important things that happened in Onesimus' life when he met Christ.

1. A radical change: from slave to free man

Before starting this point, read the whole letter of Philemon.

Try to picture the anger of Philemon when he found out about his slave that escaped. A slave was very useful for the functions of a rich household, and it was bold to run away. Onesimus left to get his freedom, maybe running way from suffering and abuse. However, he was captured and was put in jail, captive of the authorities and of his own sins.

In jail, Onesimus met Paul and accepted Christ. His life changed radically; he was free from sin and his heart was filled with God's love. There he found that life had sense and purpose, and that he was valuable and loved.

In prison, Onesimus recovered his value as a person. He felt useful and his heart was moved by the needs of Paul, showing he was now a transformed individual.

A person who decides to follow Christ must show tangible evidences that he has been transformed in his way of thinking and acting. Nowadays too many people call themselves Christians, but not everyone shows in their lives that radical change. Onesimus is a great example of one whose life was transformed when he completely surrendered his life to Jesus Christ.

2. A change implies the willingness to forgive and to ask for forgiveness

Verse 12 is special. Have you ever hurt someone? Have you stolen something from anyone? How did you feel when you had to come back and ask for forgiveness? Shame is a very common answer.

In this letter, we read how Paul asked Onesimus to return to his master's house and asked forgiveness for everything he did wrong. Paul also told Philemon that Onesimus was his son (vv. 9-10) and a transformed Christian (v. 11). Paul for sure had a conversation with Onesimus about forgiving and not keeping hard feelings against his old master (slaves had a profound hatred towards their masters because they were captive and oppressed), but to see him as his brother in Christ.

Can you remember doing something that hurt other person, or are you keeping hard feelings against another? If so, you must go to that person and ask for forgiveness. I know how hard this can be, I have had to be in that situation. But when you do it, you'll feel better and your relationship with that person will be better than before. Go, ask for or give forgiveness. Confess if you did something against someone, or chose to forgive the person that hurt you. You'll realize that the community you belong to, the Church, will be better every day and love will increase.

3. Change helps us to serve others

While they were sharing a prison cell, Paul shared the Gospel with Onesimus and he met Jesus as his Savior. From that moment on, Onesimus' life changed in a radical way (v. 13). Paul considered Onesimus as a very helpful person, both to him and Philemon (v. 11). Onesimus discovered that serving others wasn't a burden anymore, but a blessing.

Ask your students to read Ephesians 6:5-7 and Colossians 3:22-24 and analyze why, when Onesimus accepted Christ, his life took on a new meaning and purpose. How was Onesimus supposed to serve after his conversion?

Has anyone called you useless? Or good for nothing? Well, it's a great time to prove that wrong. But, how can you prove that? Well, there are so many ways! The Church you go to has lots of ministries where you can serve! You know the most visible ones (like music, preaching or leading and organizing) but being in the spotlight isn't the most important thing. Remember that what is truly important is to serve the Lord in anything He calls you to do.

Try to get involved in a ministry. I'm sure you know people who need help. Onesimus served Paul when he was old, weak and incarcerated. We can act in the same way. You can organize the young people at your Church and go support people who may be in need of assistance. Little by little you'll see a gradual change taking over and everyone will be absorbed in the atmosphere of kindness.

Review/Application

Have the students answer these questions individually or in small groups about what they learned from Onesimus, explaining these three key phrases:

1. Radical change
2. Forgive and ask for forgiveness
3. Service out of love

Encourage the class to think of their friends or acquaintances who don't know Jesus. Help them think about their attitudes that can change and thus be a reflection of God. Challenge them to make radical changes in their lives with God's help.

Transformed

Objective: That the students learn about the transforming power of God in people's lives, and the grateful response of someone whose life was changed.
To memorize: "Mary Magdalene and the other Mary were sitting there opposite the tomb." Matthew 27:61

Warning
As you start, talk about the changes that were talked about last week. How has that gone? What changes have you tried to make and why?
Accept

Connect | Navigate

Introductory activity (12-17 years)
- Resources: Paper, pencils and adhesive tape.
- Instructions: Each student must write their name at the top of the piece of paper, so it can be easily spotted. Then, have them attach it to their backs so everyone can see it and be able write on the paper.

  When everyone's ready, everyone will go around writing positive things on other student's papers. Nobody can read the papers until everyone has written something.

  When finished, you can pick some students to read them or read them all if it's appropriate.

  Conclude by talking about the good things God can use in each person, and how He can even transform the negative ones into positive.

Introductory activity (18-23 years)
- Resources: Paper and pencils.
- Instructions: Fold the paper piece at ¼ of its length (see image below). Each student will use the big space to draw their portrait and write their name, and use the small space to describe themselves, writing three positive and three negative qualities.

  Help them to think of how the negative things don't have to be part of us. If we present them before God, He can help us to change.

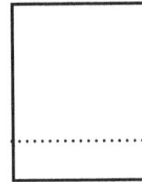

Connect | Navigate

1. The meaning behind Mary Magdalene's name

When we mention Bible characters, our mind quickly associates them with different things. Do the following experiment: Mention the names on the list below and ask the students to say out loud what comes to their minds. They may not mention exactly what's listed below, but it will still be helpful for this lesson.

- Adam = The beginning
- Joseph = Coat of many colors
- Samson = The strong man who had long hair
- David = Killed Goliath
- Jonah = A fish ate him
- Ruth = The faithful daughter in law
- Matthew = tax collector, disciple
- Judas = Traitor
- Pilate = He washed his hands of responsibility for Jesus' death

Many times our names represents who we are or something we have done or we're doing. In Bible times, names had a very important value and said a lot about how a person was or where they were from.

Mary was a very common name, the same as it's today. We can remember Mary, Jacob's mother; Mary, mother of Jesus; Mary, mother of John (Mark); Mary of Bethany, who washed Jesus' feet with a very expensive perfume.

In the New Testament we find Mary Magdalene, mentioned on many occasions. Why is she a character in the Gospels? Let's learn about her.

Mary the name means rebel, princes, beautiful, the chosen. Magdalene is a woman's name from the Hebrew

"Magdala," a town in Judea; the name Magdalene is a name that points to the place where Mary was from.

Mary Magdalene was born on the west coast of Galilee. She appears in the Gospels as part of the group of women that accompanied and served Jesus until the end (Matthew 27:57-6, 28:1-10; Mark 15:40-41; Luke 8:1-3) and she was an eye witness of his resurrection (Mark 16:9-11). The Roman Catholic Church recognizes her as a Saint and there are several churches dedicated to her.

2. What Jesus did for Mary Magdalene

In Luke 8:2, we read the miracle that Jesus did for this woman - she was set free from the control of 7 spirits. The number 7 in the Bible represents perfection or plenitude; this is the way it's used when describing Mary. She was full or saturated with evil, though the common belief of Mary being a prostitute is never specified. Serious studies point to the lack of textual and historical evidence about Mary working as a prostitute. This is a tradition that has no real support.

Jesus showed his love and compassion towards people, and Mary Magdalene was one of them. She was forgiven and blessed by her faith in Jesus. We can see how God has different ways of restoring people, depending on the situation. Mary Magdalene's name points to transformation, a change that anyone can enjoy when we decide to follow Jesus.

3. What Mary Magdalene did for Jesus

She was a woman who decided to be more than just a follower. She decided to serve Jesus. Luke 8:1-3 mentions the group of women that followed Jesus and served him, not only through economical support, but travelling along with Jesus and his disciples helping them.

In Matthew 28:1-10 and Mark 16:9-11, we read the description of a woman completely different than the woman who had first encountered Jesus.

Once Jesus restored her life, Mary was at every important event. She was committed to Jesus and his ministry. She was at her Lord's feet during crucifixion, during his death (Mark 15:40), and when he was taken to the tomb (Mark 15:47). Law forbid her and the other women from staying there, otherwise maybe they would have stayed until the third day with Jesus' body.

Her love and commitment led her and the other women to visit the tomb. Very early in the morning, they went to the tomb to find that the body of the one who had transformed her life was no longer there. How do you imagine she felt? Matthew describes an earthquake happening and an angel announcing Jesus' resurrection.

We can see in Mary Magdalene a woman who allowed God to make a radical change in her life. And she didn't let this go by unnoticed - her devotion and commitment was the best display of thankfulness.

What do people think of when they hear your name? Our name represents us too, and it's important to let Jesus work in our lives in the way that Mary Magdalene did. That way, when others hear our name, they can be thankful to God. We're called to serve, to show love, compassion and justice in this world.

I heard someone saying, "Live your life in a way that when your friends, family and colleagues think of integrity and justice, they think of you."

Are you living in that way? If not, maybe you should take time to talk to God and start working with the Holy Spirit. He can make your life be an example for your family and everyone around you, so when others see your attitude and lifestyle, they will want to know this God who can transform lives.

Review/Application

Have your students answer the following questions individually or in small groups, and then discuss as a class:

1. Why is it important to study the story of the life of Mary Magdalene?
2. What did you learn about Mary Magdalene today?
3. When studying this character, can you find an application for your life?

   Conclude the class by having your students reflect on how much God has forgiven each of them.

   Then, discuss the service opportunities that they have on a daily basis. Help them develop a plan to do a service task each day next week.

Second Chance

Objective: That the students may understand the importance of giving second chances, and God's restoring work when we make mistakes.
To memorize: "Whatever is has already been, and what will be has been before; and God will call the past to account." Ecclesiastes 3:15

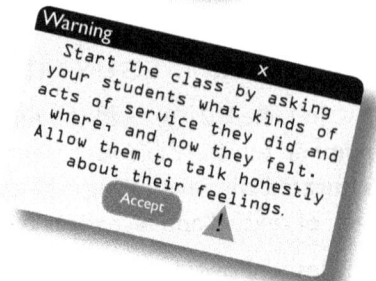

Warning
Start the class by asking your students what kinds of acts of service they did and where, and how they felt. Allow them to talk honestly about their feelings.
Accept

Connect | Navigate

Introductory activity (12-17 years)
- Resources: Paper and pencils.
- Instructions: Ask the students to make a circle and then give them a piece of paper and pencil. They must get a signature from the following people:
  1. Someone who has made a mistake.
  2. Someone who repented for a bad decision.
  3. Someone whose life was changed due to a mistake.
  4. Someone who received a second chance.
  5. Someone who has been restored and isn't judged or condemned for the past.

Give them 5 minutes to collect the signatures. You will realize it's easy to collect the signatures, since everyone or at least the majority can sign in at least one of the options. There's no need to tell why or explain their signing in each case.

This activity will work as an introduction to explain that we often make wrong decisions, but if we're willing to make changes, there can be second chances. We're going to talk about John Mark, his "bad" decision and his second chance.

Introductory activity (18-23 years)
- Resources: Paper and pencils.
- Instructions: Ask each student to write down two reasons why anyone should give / receive a second chance after a mistake. Share the answers in the group.

Connect | Navigate

All of the young people attending church have made a mistake. Some of those mistakes may not have necessarily been sins, but perhaps just poor decisions.

They need to know that they can have a second chance, that God can restore them and use them powerfully as in the life of John Mark.

1. John Mark, a young man in the early church

In the book of Acts chapter 12, we find a story about Paul being released from prison by an angel. Paul goes to the house of Mary, the mother of John, also called Mark (v. 12), where many people were meeting. According to bible experts, it's believed that John Mark's house was indeed the center of gatherings for Christians in the city of Jerusalem, during the times of the newborn church. Some even theorize that it was in this house where disciples where praying during the events of Pentecost in Acts chapter 2.

The very certain fact is that John Mark was a young son of a faithful disciple and a relative of Barnabas, a friend and partner of Paul during his first missionary journey. (Barnabas' story can be found in Acts 4:32-37.)

We could think of him in today's terms as a young member of church whose house was the meeting place for the church's activities.

2. John Mark returns home

Chapters ahead, in Acts 13 verse 5, John Mark assisted Paul and Barnabas during their journey. The plans for the journey (Acts 13:13) were to continue traveling to Pisidian Antioch, but Mark decided he wanted to go home.

In the text we can't see any explanation of the reasons behind his decision, but author William Barclay mentions a few possibilities in his Commentary for the New Testament:

- Maybe he was upset because Barnabas was replaced by Paul as the leader of the expedition. In the text, Paul is mentioned first, indicating that he was in charge.
- Another possibility is fear, since Pisidian Antioch was one of the hardest and most dangerous places at the time.
- He was from Jerusalem, so another reason could be his own doubts about preaching the Gospel to non-Jews.
- A simple reason may have been his inexperience and lack of commitment due to his young age.
- Maybe he just missed his mother.

We may never know why he returned home, a decision that the book of Acts states Paul didn't like.

3. John Mark, a reason for division

When Paul and Barnabas where ready to start their second missionary journey, they discussed and decided to continue separately. The reason behind the discussion was Barnabas' desire to bring John Mark with them as an assistant. In Acts 15:38 ,we see that Paul wasn't happy with this, and it's described that he "did not think it wise to take him, because he had deserted them in Pamphylia and had not continued with them in the work."

More than paying attention to Paul's attitude, we should focus on Barnabas', who decided to give this young man a second chance.

The Bible states nothing more than Barnabas and John Mark sailing to Cyprus.

4. Restoration

In Acts 15:39, Mark disappears from the narration. According to tradition, he went to Alexandria to start a church. Mark reappears 20 years later as a restored person. Maybe it was Barnabas' trust that gave him back his dignity and helped him to be faithful. What a blessing it's finding someone who trusts us even after we have failed! Barnabas trusted John Mark, and he didn't disappoint him.

In Colossians 4:7-11, Paul is writing from a Roman prison, and he asks the readers to receive Mark warmly once he arrived ... probably to keep people from doubting Mark after his decision. Paul writes clearly to make sure Mark's past wouldn't be an obstacle for anything, recommending him and stating his approval and trust. In the same letter, Paul declares how Mark has been very helpful for him.

Another sign of the restored relationship with Paul is in the second letter to Timothy, "Get Mark and bring him with you, because he is helpful to me in my ministry" (2 Timothy 4:11).

It's surprising how God acted through Mark. Peter himself calls him "son" in 1 Peter 5:13. It's believed that Mark wrote the very first known Gospel of the time - the Gospel according to Mark. This is a clear example of how God's grace can use a deserter to be the author of one of the 4 Gospels.

The last information we get from Mark is that he is with Paul during his last prison stay (Philemon verse 24).

Most of us, if not everyone, have made mistakes whatever the reason. Maybe by doing this we have brought wrong impressions to others or we felt "stained" by this failure. We can learn from this story that God gives us second chances and the opportunity to be fully restored, along with our relationship with others, as it happened in the relationship between Paul and Mark.

Review/Application

Have your students answer the following questions about the life of John Mark, individually or in small groups, and then discuss as a class:

1. What would have happened to young John Mark if Barnabas and Peter had not supported him in continuing his ministry?

2. What things did John Mark accomplish in his service to God after being restored?

3. What is your attitude when you or someone fails in the church?

4. What do young people in your church do to support a young person when he or she fails?

5. What do you think about giving a second chance to those who have failed in their service to God?

In conclusion, have them think about the times God has given them a second chance. We also need to give others a second chance.

What a sister!

Objective: That the students learn God's plan to use us in His Kingdom if we're willing to, despite our mistakes and weaknesses.

To memorize: "I brought you up out of Egypt and redeemed you from the land of slavery. I sent Moses to lead you, also Aaron and Miriam." Micah 6:4

Warning
Let the class share their feelings about last week's subject: A second chance. Encourage them to share some testimony of how this affected them this week.
Accept

Connect | Navigate

Introductory activity (12-17 years)
- Resources: Paper and pencil.
- Instructions: Ask every student to think of a Bible character and write next to the name what that person had to offer to God. Example: David – his songs and prayers (even today we sing his compositions).

  Help them think about these characters and what they achieved when they surrendered to God.

Introductory activity (18-23 years)
- Resources: Paper and pencil.
- Instructions: Ask each person to write down something they can do well (drawing, singing, technology related skills, decorating, talking, etc.). After that, ask them to share with the group what they wrote and how they think that God could use that talent or skill to bless others.

We find many examples of people in the Bible who gave their lives, gifts and talents with the desire of being used by God for the well-being of others. We may not be in a situation where we would be asked to do something that endangers our lives, but if we're asked to, we must think if we're willing to do it, letting God using us according to His plans.

After everything, we must remember that we're His creation, and everything we have is His. But He respects our decision and waits for us to be willing to surrender everything we have and do for his glory.

Connect | Navigate

The book of Genesis finished with the Israelites enjoying the life in Egypt, but that situation quickly changes when we move to the first chapter of Exodus. Joseph and that generation had passed away, but their descendants multiplied (Exodus 1:7). Then, a new pharaoh that didn't know Joseph rose to power (Exodus 1:8). So Joseph's descendants went from being favored to being enslaved by the Egyptians.

In this situation, the Egyptians didn't like how much the Israelites were growing in number and strength, so they started planning on how to control them to avoid an uprising. So they gave them hard tasks under strict surveillance (Exodus 1:10-14). They even ordered the midwives to kill the newborn male children (Exodus 1:15-16). All of this failed, so Pharaoh ordered them to throw all the male babies into the Nile river (Exodus 1:22). Even in these horrible circumstances, God had a plan.

You can organize the students into three teams and let every team read and analyze a part of Miriam's life (Exodus 2:2-10; 15:19-21; Numbers 12:1-16) and share with the group the traits of her personality. Discuss what you can learn from her example, and apply it to your daily lives.

1. Miriam, the clever girl

Miriam and her family, all from the Levite tribe, were living in Egypt during this chaotic time. To add to the problems, her mother Jochebed gave birth to a baby boy! They kept him hidden for three months, but when they couldn't do that anymore, "She got a papyrus basket for him and coated it with tar and pitch. Then she placed the child in it and put it among the reeds along the bank of the Nile" (Exodus 2:2-3). They made this plan hoping God would perform a miracle.

Here is where Miriam started her task, she "stood at a distance to see what would happen to him" (Exodus 2:4). Surely Jochebed trusted her daughter to do this task - look after her baby brother and make sure he was safe.

Miriam observed how the basket reached the Egyptian princess. Imagine the fear Miriam felt when she saw this! But her heart was filled with hope when she saw the princess having compassion on the baby. What Miriam did next was very clever. She offered to help the princess raise the baby. She was clever enough to bring her own mother to do the job! What a miracle! Jochebed had the permission of the Egyptian princess to raise her own child!

2. Miriam, worship leader and prophetess

After that episode, we don't hear from Miriam until Israel was set free and crossed the Red Sea. This miracle was so wonderful that a celebration was needed! Moses led the people in a victory song and Miriam directed women, starting a song and a dance, "Sing to the Lord, for He is highly exalted. Both horse and driver He has hurled into the sea" (Exodus 15:21).

The same Miriam that looked after his brother in the river is now worshipping and dancing before God. That young girl, scared but filled with hope, was now a prophetess! (Exodus 15:20). She didn't hesitate to use her gifts to rejoice in the Lord as gratitude for what he had done.

3. Miriam, the not-so-wise woman

Miriam was now an older lady, and she had witnessed God's miracles during all this time. But that wasn't enough to stop her from acting and murmuring against Moses. The specific criticism was about Moses marrying a woman who was not from the Hebrew people, but an Ethiopian or Midianite (maybe Zipporah). They challenged Moses' authority as a prophet (Numbers 12:1-2). They were correct in their claim since Aaron and Miriam both acted as prophets. So yes, God did speak through them too. But what was incorrect was their attitude, so He told them, "With him I speak face to face, clearly and not in riddles" (Numbers 12:8).

When they finished their conversation, God's presence left the tabernacle and Miriam found she had leprosy. This punishment was a representation of her impure heart. God considered Miriam's attitude as a very severe fault, and so was the punishment. Miriam was excluded from the camp until she was clean. And we can assume she returned not only cured, but also repentant.

Miriam had to be clean in her heart so God could use her!

God wants us to be willing to surrender our gifts and talents for his glory. God is, in fact, recruiting brave men and women willing to follow his lead and guide his people. People like this are remembered as part of history! (Micah 6:4)

Review/Application

Have your students answer the following questions, individually or in small groups, and then discuss as a class:

1. In what political situation did Miriam grow up? (When Pharaoh ordered the baby boys to be killed.)

2. What motivated Miriam to speak directly with Pharaoh's daughter? (The desire to save his brother.)

3. What does "prophetess" mean? (Someone who spoke in the name of God.)

4. What did Miriam celebrate with her songs? (The crossing of the Red Sea.)

5. Why did Miriam and Aaron murmur against Moses? (Moses chose a Cushite woman.)

6. Why was God so upset? (Because they were comparing themselves to Moses.)

Based on what was learned in the lesson, discuss the topic. Encourage your students to accept God's call to serve Him from their young age.

I'm a temple

Objective: That the students develop awareness that they must take care of themselves as the temple of the Holy Spirit.
To memorize: "You were bought at a price. Therefore honor God with your bodies." I Corinthians 6:20

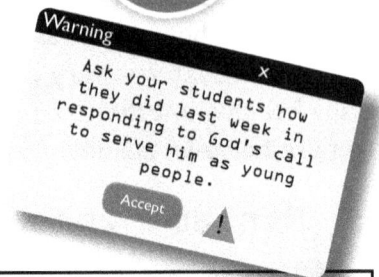

Warning x
Ask your students how they did last week in responding to God's call to serve him as young people.
Accept

Connect / Navigate

Introductory activity (12-17 years)
- Resources: Paper and markers.
- Instructions: Create signs with positive attitudes (honesty, service, compassion, patience, etc.) and others with negative ones (dishonesty, cheating, violence, etc.). Chose a group of students and use adhesive tape or a piece of string to attach the signs to their chests. The rest of the students will find a partner to hold hands creating a "house." The objective is to let in only a person with a positive attitude (each "house" can only hold one person at a time). If a student with a negative attitude occupies a "house," the students will lose. After a few rounds, the "house" that remains will be the winner.

This activity is designed to explain that it's us who decide which attitudes we have in different circumstances in life. It's also a lesson on how there are negative attitudes that will want to take over but we have to resist them.

Introductory activity (18-23 years)
- Instructions: Ask the students to write down activities they do or they would like to do to take care of their bodies. They must describe them in detail. Example: if they write "healthy eating," they must write an example of a nutritious menu for a meal. Other examples are: exercise, sleeping enough, sports, have skin treatments, etc.

A temple is a building sanctified by God's presence, dedicated to worship Him. In Hebrew, it was called "God's palace." A temple was different than other buildings because of the fact of God's presence dwelling in the building.

Connect / Navigate

Many times young people say, "I can do whatever I want with my body, because it's mine," but as we can see in I Corinthians 6:19-20, our body isn't ours. The text states, "You are not your own; you were bought at a price." If God gives us this value, why shouldn't we be careful with what the Bible calls "Temple of the Holy Spirit"?

In the Bible we can find many texts where we see the care God expected when people built the Tabernacle and later, the Temple. Exodus 35:4-29 narrates how Moses, after receiving God's instructions, explains to the people about the resources and materials to be used: gold, silver, purple yarn and olive oil for the light. It's also detailed in how only the most skilled people would work on the construction. Everyone gave their best in both resources and skills to make the Tabernacle as good as possible.

Can you imagine what the temple was like that was built by Solomon? I Kings 5 and 6 details the process of the construction. We can see that similarly, only the best materials were used: the finest woods and statues overlaid in gold were used in the 27 meters x 9 meters building.

The New Testament draws an analogy between our bodies and the temple where God dwells. If He was so careful about the construction and decoration of His temple, can you imagine the care he took as the "builder" of our bodies?

We can learn:

1. God made our bodies perfect

I'm not talking exclusively about our physical appearance, but also about the way we function. We can get everything we need from the food we eat, and we dispose of the things we don't need; even during sleep, our body can perform lots of tasks like breathing.

Genesis 1:26 explains that we were created in God's image and likeness. He created humans with lots of care, and made them very different from other species. Genesis 2:7 says that God himself gave us the breath of life to become living beings!

Since God took so much care in creating us, why wouldn't we do our part by taking care of ourselves? We must look after our physical appearance (the front of the temple) but also the inside: our soul and heart, even more if we have invited God to dwell in us.

Our bodies are the temple of the Holy Spirit (1 Corinthians 6:19). When the Holy Spirit dwells in a body, it's because it belongs to God. That's why Paul says, "You are not your own." When someone surrenders their life to Christ, they have decided to surrender their body too.

When Jesus was on Earth, he also talked about his body as a temple, and he said, " 'Destroy this temple, and I will raise it again in three days.' But the temple he had spoken of was his body." (John 2:19, 21)

2. Our body was purchased at a very high price

Again, 1 Corinthians 6:20 tells us that we have been bought at a price. We must value our bodies, not only because God created us, but also because He paid such a high price for it. This action implies an acquisition, a change of ownership. We aren't owners of our lives anymore, but God is.

The question that emerges is, what was the price He paid for our lives? Yes! Jesus' life! That's the value that God gives to your being. Can you imagine that? You are so important to God that He thinks his only Son's life is a fair price for you. That price not only gives us value, but makes us clean from all sin, to make us ready for his Spirit to dwell within us and make us pure and holy.

We have been bought at a very high price. If God is giving us this enormous value, we must appreciate it and be careful too. If we want to keep intimacy with the Holy Spirit, we must also do our bests to guard our "temple" from the threat of sin. No one can come and tell you that you aren't worthy. Remember ... you are worth Jesus' life!

3. We must honor God with our bodies

Honor means respect and worship. This text (1 Corinthians 6:12-20) talks about sexual immorality, but it can be expanded to any other kind of immorality: selfishness, pornography, lust, bad intentions, hate, vanity, pride, etc. We must understand that we must not participate in anything sinful, not only with our physical body, but also with our thoughts and motivations.

Our bodies become a resource to honor God, so everything we do with it must be wise. Have you ever considered that everything you do with your body or to your body says a lot about the God you claim to serve and love? This is the image of Christ we're showing to others. If you are asked to help, do you do it with a bad attitude or to be in the spotlight, or because you don't have any choice or because you truly want to honor God? Next time, before doing anything with your body, consider carefully if it will honor God.

4. God considers us a worthy dwelling place

When Jesus was dying on the cross, the veil inside the temple tore, as a sign that God wouldn't dwell in a house made by human hands. He would now be with us through His Holy Spirit.

If a very important ambassador came to our country and they commissioned you to find a house for him to live in, what would you do? I'm sure you are thinking about a house in a very exclusive place, or at least an apartment in a luxury building - a place where he or she could feel content, safe and respected.

Now picture God saying, "I need a dwelling place, and the best place is in my children's hearts." Isn't it a privilege to be his temple?

Exodus 40:34 tells us how God's presence filled the Tabernacle. In the same way, we can ask Him to be within us and let his presence dwell upon and within us. But we must be ready to live in a way that the Holy Spirit is honored.

Review/Application

Write the memory verse on the board or on a card, "You were bought at a price. Therefore honor God with your bodies" (1 Corinthians 6:20). Ask your students to read the passage and share how they can glorify God in their body and spirit, and what situations of daily life are preventing them from glorifying God and being temples of the Holy Spirit.

Challenge your students to start a special daily time with God. Challenge them to grow spiritually in the same way that they are growing physically.

How do I eat?

Objective: That the students learn the way we eat is an important part of the care we have to our physical body, as Holy Spirit's temple.
To memorize: "But Daniel resolved not to defile himself with the royal food and wine." Daniel 1:8

Warning
Generate a discussion with the theme of physical and spiritual growth. Ask how they did in their daily time with God last week.
Accept

Connect | Navigate

Introductory activity (12-17 years)

- Instructions: Bring to class cutouts from magazines about different types of food: fruits, vegetables, meat, cereals, sweets, etc. Every student will pick three things and will share with the group the reason why they don't like those foods.

  The teacher will ask which group of the food pyramid the chosen elements belong to. Conclude by talking about which group they like the most and if they are good for a healthy lifestyle.

Introductory activity (18-23 years)

- Instructions: Put together a menu. Write a list of food on the whiteboard. They must create a menu with the options.

  After they do that, you will present the caloric content of each element presented and they will do the math. Let them know that the recommended number of daily calories for a young woman is about 2,200, while a young man needs about 2,800. Many young people consume more calories than they burn, therefore accumulating fat. Others won't eat enough and will suffer from malnutrition.

A portion of grilled beef	401
Broccoli	32
White rice	343
Banana	85
Fatless pork chop	276
Potato	76
Pasta	369
Mandarin orange	43
Ham	296
Carrot	42
Bread	269
Melon	44
Chicken	170
Tomato	22
Corn tortilla	50
Peach	52

The digestion process consumes and absorbs most of the nutrients in food. When these functions act properly, the result is health, strength and energy for daily life.

To obtain any food's nutrients, the first necessity is a proper eating schedule. If a person eats properly, his immune system will improve. A balanced diet is key to good health.

The same happens in God's kingdom. A good relationship with God depends upon spiritual health, which depends upon a balanced spiritual diet. Food for the soul comes from studying God's Word and worshipping Him.

Connect | Navigate

Start reading Daniel chapter 1, emphasizing the verses that talk about food. This story narrates a particular event in the life of a group of young Jews who were taken in captivity. The Hebrew word used to describe this group of guys is "Yeled," which indicates an age between childhood and the time a person was ready to marry. This term was applied to people from 12 years old.

Let's see the close relationship between these men's diet and their relationship with God.

1. Chosen to be strong

According to Daniel 1:3-4, these young men were chosen because they came from important families and because of their good physical shape. A beautiful, healthy body, in eastern culture, was associated with wisdom. It was true in the case of the young men. They fulfilled the requirements that the king had set, which made them eligible to be chosen to serve him. Daniel and his friends already knew God, and they surely had a good relationship with him. This is something they couldn't learn in captivity; this was something they learned at their home.

These young men decided not to eat from the king's food, not only as a way to care for their bodies, but mainly as a measure of care for their spiritual lives; as Hebrews, they had a diet based on God's commandments (Leviticus

11:1-47 and 17:10-16). They decided to obey God before men, risking their lives by disobeying the king. Today, we must do good when managing our physical and spiritual life. Our convictions must stay strong in any circumstance.

Somehow, the king understood the relationship between diet and intelligence, because in verse 5 we read that the king ordered them to be fed the best food for three years. Only after that time would they be ready to serve him.

In ancient Babylon, physical appearance was very important, similar to the way in our day that looks are made a priority. This has brought a way of thinking and acting where health and beauty can be swapped, going to the extreme of thinking that being pretty means to be extremely thin. Eating disorders, such as bulimia and anorexia, are emerging because of this. As Christians we must be aware of this and don't let fashion, gluttony or trends dictate our diets, but follow what's better to keep our bodies healthy and honor God in the process.

2. The royal food

Bible doesn't narrate specifically what the diet was in Babylon (Daniel 1:5), but the Hebrew word used here is "patbág," defined as candies and delicacies. We can say for sure they were offered something appealing, only the best of Babylon's kitchen.

The king also offered them wine, but this word is used to describe any kind of alcoholic beverage. Babylon was famous for producing a drink similar to beer, and it was very common to drink a lot during the meals.

Nowadays, we're also under a bombardment of publicity and invitations to the world of alcohol.

Not all food from the king of this world is nutritious. They may be very appealing, but their end will be malnutrition and death.

We can find a variety of fast food and sweets that can bring pleasure but won't be good for us. You can ask students to list some foods that aren't nutritious or are harmful for health: alcoholic beverages, fast food, sodas, etc.

3. Daniel didn't defile himself

In verse 8-16 of the chapter we're studying, we can see Daniel's conviction. He set his mind on a goal and had a strong resolution to stay away from the king's food. This is an indicator of a mature personality and character. Also, Daniel's friends Hananiah (Shadrach), Mishael (Meshach) and Azariah (Abednego) had the same background and they were together in this goal.

For the ancient world, food and idols were closely connected. Many cultures had rites of sacrificing and dedicating food to their deities before consumption. When Daniel and his friends chose not to defile themselves with the food, they were also taking a stand against participating in those rituals, and staying loyal to the beliefs they had. Daniel decided to abstain from that food not because he was picky but to honor God. His example was followed and supported by his friends.

Today we don't have rigorous diet restriction because we aren't ruled by Jewish laws (Acts 10:9-15), but we're called to make a difference in the world, and that includes a healthy lifestyle.

God commands us to care for our temples, and that includes a balanced diet, according to our different needs. Vegetables and water might look like something unappealing, but it had good results. Maybe it was hard for them to get used to this diet because their Hebrew diet did included meat which they weren't getting in Babylon. The point here is to emphasize their commitment to making a difference. Whenever you agree to not defile yourself, you aren't only looking after your physical being, but also after the temple of the Spirit and you are honoring God. If you do your part, God promises wisdom and health (v.17), so the challenge is on the table. What would you do if you were in Daniel's shoes?

Review/Application

Divide the class into three teams and assign three principles for good nutrition to each group, who will then analyze the biblical passages, and make 3 posters to explain each principle to the class. (Use card stock, markers, colored pencils, old magazines, white glue and scissors.)

Nine important principles for good health.
1. Eat at regular intervals and avoid eating between meals. (Ecclesiastes 3:1)
2. Eat to live and not live to eat. (Proverbs 23:1-2)
3. Rest in accordance with God's plan. (Exodus 20:9-11, Psalm 127:2)
4. Keep your body clean. (2 Corinthians 7:1)
5. Have control over yourself. (Philippians 4:5; 2 Timothy 1:7)
6. Keep joy in your life. (Proverbs 17:22, Philippians 4:4)
7. Avoid fats. (Leviticus 3:17; 1 Corinthians 6:12)
8. Trust in God and obey Him. (Proverbs 4:20-22)
9. Give glory to God in everything you do. (1 Corinthians 10:31)

Ask your students to suggest a healthy substitute for junk food. Daniel replaced the contaminated food with healthy food. How will they do it?

Freedom to say no

Objective: That the students may be aware of the danger that addictions represent and the physical, mental and spiritual damage they can cause to our bodies.
To memorize: "'I have the right to do anything,' you say—but not everything is beneficial. 'I have the right to do anything—but I won't be mastered by anything.'"
(1 Corinthians 6:12)

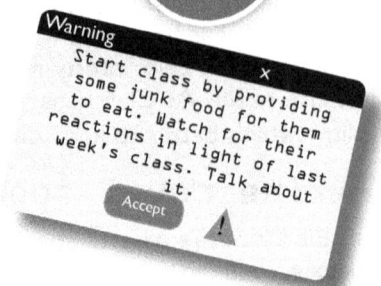

Warning
Start class by providing some junk food for them to eat. Watch for their reactions in light of last week's class. Talk about it.
Accept

Connect | Navigate

Introductory activity (12-17 years)
- Resources: Three small balls of one color and three of another (6 total). The balls can be made of colored paper.
- Instructions: You will need two couples of volunteers: one of two boys and one of two girls.

  Each team will choose a person to be the guide and the other to be the follower. The follower is responsible to take the balls to the goal, but they can't do anything if it's not indicated by the guide.

  The team that takes the three balls to the goal first, will win. After the activity, ask the guides and followers what were their experiences. The purpose of the activity is to represent how a person controlled by harmful habits isn't free to make his own decisions and how this will stop them from having a full life.

Introductory activity (18-23 years)
- Resources: A whiteboard and a chair in the middle

of the classroom. A hammer and a table (optional, for the "judge").
- Instructions: Pick a student to be the judge and another to be the secretary. Split the group into two teams. The first team will present to the judge reasons why drugs should be legal. The second one will defend the opposite statement. The secretary will write down the arguments against and for legalization of drugs in two columns. Set a time for them to prepare their arguments and ideas and then start the debate giving time to each team to present an argument, and to the opposite to refute.

  After a few rounds, the judge will make a decision. Try not to intervene in the debate, but encourage dialogue until all the ideas have been properly argument.

  The purpose is to introduce the topic, allowing the students to reflect on it.

Connect | Navigate

Addictions aren't something new. It's not a trend started by the newest drug mafia. Although the word "addiction" isn't mentioned in the Bible, it always speaks about the results that many addictions have on the human being. An example is Noah's story in Genesis 9:20-23. A person that becomes an addict has lost control over his thoughts and decisions, letting the addiction control him and put him in risky situations. Addictions affect all areas of human beings: physical, emotional, interpersonal and spiritual.

1. Our body, temple of the Spirit of God

"Do you not know that your bodies are temples of the Holy Spirit, who is in you, whom you have received from God? You are not your own" (1 Corinthians 6:19).

The Bible portion we'll study today talks about physical stewardship, this is, the responsibility we have to look after the body God has given to us. We as Christians belong to God for two reasons. First, because He created us and He is our maker. Second, because we were purchased at a high price to become children of God.

Belonging to God may sound to some as a very authoritarian statement. But in this case, it means that God's love is acting in the lives of those who surrender to Christ. It's precisely that surrender that gives us the balance necessary to enjoy an abundant life.

2. Say no to addiction

"Do not get drunk on wine, which leads to debauchery. Instead, be filled with the Spirit" (Ephesians 5:18).

Though this is a text that talks only about wine, we can extend its meaning to any substance that alters our state of consciousness and leads us to addiction. The definition of addiction is, "the impulse that leads a person to use any substance or stimulus on a regular basis to obtain pleasure or gratification."

When we talk about addictions, the first thing that jumps to our minds is all the illegal drugs. But addiction can come from things legal drugs too. A good example of this is alcohol and cigarettes, which cause chemical dependence and are legal for people over 18 in most countries. Addictions can come from unhealthy habits and actions, like gambling, social media, masturbation, etc. Though these practices don't lead to physical dependence, they do cause a psychological or emotional dependence and are harmful to us. Whatever it is, we know as a fact that addiction has very damaging consequences. The Bible lists some: Problems among family (Genesis 9:18-29); lack of wisdom (Proverbs 20:1); poverty (Proverbs 21:17); harming our relationship with God (Isaiah 5:11-12); lack of understanding (Hosea 4:11); slavery (Titus 2:3).

A. Physical consequences

The consequences depend a lot on the habit or substance that the person is addicted to. Some of the consequences of substance abuse are: deterioration of brain cells - these are responsible for our reasoning and mental processes. Degeneration of organs and tissues due to the overload of uncommon substances that may turn into cancer, cirrhosis and others. Adding to that, the risks of diseases like AIDS which come from the way the drugs are administrated, like syringes. Finally, the abuse of drugs can end with overdose or death by the evolution of the problems mentioned.

B. Emotional consequences

It's proven that the use of narcotics can induce psychological disturbances due to the disequilibrium these substances cause to the organism. Bipolarity and schizophrenia are some of them, happening even with "not so hard" drugs. Some drugs can bring a sensation of happiness and freedom from reality, but after the effects comes the depression, irritability, panic attacks, etc. It's not uncommon that these consequences lead an addicted person to commit suicide.

C. Spiritual consequences

Addictions sidetrack us from God's plan for our life. The most harmful consequence is that they take us away from God. This separation is visible through the sad, hard life addicted people have. We lose the peace and love of someone who is in communion with God, and we get into a depressed life, filled with guilt, shame and a feeling of inferiority. The worst consequence of being a slave of addiction is the loss of the gift of eternal life, "Do not be deceived ... no drunkards ... will inherit the kingdom of God" (1 Corinthians 6:9-10).

3. So, why do some people say "yes"?

When it comes to addiction, there are many reasons that can lead a person to addiction. The same way that adult drinkers have difficulties admitting that alcohol can turn into a problem and into an addiction, young people who experiment with drugs or other habits won't accept those realities. Knowing who we are in Christ, the value we have through Him, and knowing we have a purpose can help us avoid the trap of addiction. Buying and drinking alcohol at 18 may be legal, but that doesn't mean we're free. Freedom is making choices that honor our convictions (Daniel 1:8).

The Bible gives us good advice in how to stay out of addictions, "Instead, be filled with the Spirit" (Ephesians 5:18b). Habits can only be substituted for by other habits. We'll have bad habits if we don't fill our lives with good ones. We'll stay away from alcohol addiction if we stay close to God and are filled with the Spirit. Many believe that young people are addicted because they are the most vulnerable to social pressure, curiosity and a rebel attitude. But 1 John 2:14b tells, "I write to you, young men, because you are strong, and the Word of God lives in you, and you have overcome the evil one." In other words, youth is not synonymous to weakness; it's the opposite! We'll be strong if we let the Word of God live in us.

Form groups of 2-4 students, and give them the following questions. They will discuss them and then share their answers with the group. (You can prepare the questions on paper so they just write the answers.)
- What is impeding you from being filled with the Holy Spirit?
- Where are the places where it's easier to have access to drugs?
- Have you been in one of those places?
- Which are the most common invitations that young people receive to take drugs?
- If a friend in school asked you why you don't drink, smoke or do drugs, what would be your answer? Before the situations arise regarding any addictive actions, what's your personal conviction?

Review/Application

Allow time for your class to answer the following questions individually or in small groups, reflecting on the subject of addictions, and discover what the Bible tells us about it.
1. What is the Biblical perspective of addictions? Read 1 Corinthians 6:12. (We must not let something dominate us.
2. 1 Cor. 6:19 tells us about who we belong to and what we serve. Could you write the verse in your own words?
3. Read the following Biblical passages and discover the consequences of the use of wine.
   a. Family problems (Genesis 9:20-23)
   b. Lack of wisdom (Proverbs 20:1)
   c. Poverty (Proverbs 21:17)
   d. Not considering the works of Jehovah (Isaiah 5:11-13)
   e. Lack of judgment (Hosea 4:11)
   f. Bondage (Titus 2:3)
4. According to 1 Corinthians 6:9-10, what would be the worst consequence of addiction?
5. The Bible gives us very interesting advice on how to live free of addictions. Read Ephesians 5:15-18 and say what that advice would be.
6. Regarding addictions, how does the example of Daniel apply to your life? Read Daniel 1:8.

Help them understand that they must take a strong stand against addictions. Motivate them to write their personal commitment statement. If you wish, beforehand you can prepare sheets for them to write their personal commitment.

The good kind of sex!

Objective: That the students understand clearly the biblical concept of sexual relationships and how it's meant to be exclusively for marriage.
To memorize: "That is why a man leaves his father and mother and is united to his wife, and they become one flesh." Genesis 2:24

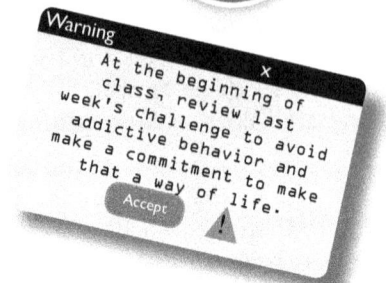

> **Warning** x
> At the beginning of class, review last week's challenge to avoid addictive behavior and make a commitment to make that a way of life.
> Accept ⚠

Connect / Navigate

Introductory activity (12-17 years)

- Instructions: Have the student form a circle or a line.

  Take one of the students away from the others and give him a message using gestures, not words or sounds (you will have one minute to do this). Bring the student back to the group and he will have to whisper what the message was in the next student's ear. Each participant will transmit the message to the next person until the message reaches the last student. The last student will say out loud what message he received, and everyone can compare it to the one they heard, and finally with the original.

  Explain to them that sexuality works similarly to this activity. We hear lots of opinions, but very often the message that reaches us is very distorted.

Introductory activity (18-23 years)

- Resources: Paper and pencil.
- Instructions: Split the group into two teams. Ask both teams to write a list of things that one can't share with others because they are meant to be exclusively personal. Give them 3 minutes, and then compare the lists, giving 10 points for each valid item. If both groups have the same one, they'll receive 5 points each. The team with more points at the end will win.

  Explain to them that sexuality is meant to be shared between a husband and a wife, in a relationship that is exclusive and faithful.

Connect / Navigate

Every day we receive messages about sex and sexual relationships. We hear a wide range of depictions, such as: they are exciting, everyone does it, they may be boring, they are enjoyable, my parents say they are forbidden, they are gratifying, they are mysterious, they are wonderful, they are painful, they are disappointing, it's a routine, Pastor says they are sin, they are fun, etc.

When we hear so many different opinions, it's easy to see why sex is a favorite topic among youth. With so much information, yet so much confusion, everyone wants to discover or define what exactly sex and sexual relationships mean.

1. Sex is something really good!

In the first two chapters of Genesis, we see how God created humans intentionally and with a clear purpose. The Bible specifies that when God created mankind, he said it was very good. God didn't say only a few parts were good. He saw that everything in his creation was good.

Sexuality is a gift from God to both men and women. It's important to say that, even though we're born with sexual characteristics, it's when we reach adolescence that we start being aware of it in a clearer way. It's during that stage of life that the traits of personality and physical characteristics are defined clearly and there is a bigger differentiation between genders.

It's precisely during this time that our body develops and starts preparations to enjoy and participate in sexual relationships with others. However, we must consider Genesis 2:24, "That is why a man leaves his father and mother and is united to his wife, and they become one flesh." This means that the plan is to reserve the gift of sexual relationships for the time when we're not only physically, but emotionally mature enough to share it with the person we love and we're committed to, within the context of marriage, for the rest of our life.

The first two chapters of Genesis explain why God created man and woman. First, having two different genders would allow a relationship where sex could be enjoyed (2:24). Second, sex is a way for couples to express physical affection and to please each other (2:24). Finally, God created sex for humans to reproduce (Genesis 1:28).

2. Is sex always good?

Yes and no. Confusing? Well, let me explain it this way: Eating meat or solid food is not bad in and of itself, but for a newborn baby, it's very bad. It's not the proper time yet. There's nothing wrong with being a dad or a mom, nor enjoying our sexuality, but if it's done out of the proper time and context, it will become a nightmare.

Speaking of nightmares, we live in a world that looks just like a nightmare. A world that because of sin, saw the distortion of the image of God imprinted on humans, affecting the whole creation. This means that even God's plan for sexuality was distorted. The original desire of love and the search for mutual satisfaction turned into selfish lust. The plan of faithfulness, commitment and exclusivity was changed into temporary satisfaction that disregards who the other person is. The natural order was changed into acts of rebellion (homosexuality, lesbianism, etc.). And this has brought consequences: damaged relationships, broken homes, physical and emotional illness, frustration, hate in families and individuals, unplanned pregnancies and forced marriages, single mothers, abortions and separation from God.

But even when we live in a world with darkness, God's plan is still at work. So all the good of sexuality is still a reality for everyone who has accepted Jesus as savior and lives by his standards.

The Bible invites us to not follow the customs of this world (Romans 12:2); it encourages us to act with more than just instincts. It calls us to act using our reasoning and will, obeying God.

It's clear and easy to agree with everything we have said, but we cannot deny the pressure we undergo and the exposure that we have to television, advertisements, magazines, internet, music, films, friends, coworkers and so on. This is surrounding us and bombarding our senses with more and more sensual and erotic content that pushes us to act with lust and based on instincts.

Pressure to use our sexuality selfishly is powerful, but the Bible promises that if we remain in Christ, the sin will have no power over us. God will help us live accordingly to his will. In Him, we are more than conquerors! (Romans 6:6; 8:37; 11-14; 2 Timothy 1:7; 1 John 5:4-5).

God created sexuality to be enjoyed as an important part of marriage ... marriage that honors God through sexual purity ... marriage committed to care for each other and satisfy each other. Fast forwarding our sexuality is not right, and the Bible speaks against it (1 Corinthians 6:18-19; Galatians 5:19; Colossians 3:5; 1 Thessalonians 4:3).

But honoring God with our sexuality is not only for married people. As a single person, it's possible to honor Him by avoiding situations, places, and people that can push our sexual limits, surrendering all our thoughts to Christ, being responsible with our actions and desires, and staying pure for the person that we'll chose as husband or wife. This will show our commitment to God, the giver of the wonderful gift of sexuality.

Review/Application

Ask the students to answer the following as individuals or small groups, and then discuss as a class:

1. Define the word "sexuality."

2. Would you classify sexual relationships as sin? Why yes or why no?

3. What were sexual relationships created for?

4. Is sex always good?

   a. Mention some of the ways in which we're pressured to give in to the idea of having sex before marriage.

   b. What would be the two main reasons why you would be willing to abstain from having sex until marriage?

   Reflect: Will there be some specific actions that you should put into practice now?

Are there some practices that you should stop doing now because they can become a serious threat to keep you pure sexually?

Discuss the biblical challenge of sexual purity. Help them understand what this looks like in today's world. Encourage them to write a creative phrase about God's call for them to live sexually pure lives.

Warning! Danger!

Objective: That the student develops awareness about sexually transmitted diseases and about the responsibility we have over our bodies as temples of the Holy Spirit.
To memorize: "For the Spirit God gave us doesn't make us timid, but gives us power, love and self-discipline." 2 Timothy 1:7

> Warning
> Remember to start the class by reviewing last week's challenge of committing to sexual purity.
> Accept

Connect | Navigate

Introductory Activity (12-17 years)
- Resources: One or two apples (depending on the size of the group. You can use any other fruit that is available or any other treat, like chocolate), a knife.
- Instructions: Use the knife to share the apple (or what you chose to bring to class). Make sure you share until there's nothing left.

  Ask them: How was the apple? Did you like it? Could you eat the same apple again? Could it again be a delicious fruit? Of course not.

  May times in life we do things that harm our bodies. When we don't look after ourselves and we act irresponsibly, we'll never be the same. We'll face situations in life that will look appealing and tempting, like an apple, but that aren't good. If we forget that our body is the temple of the Holy Spirit, we'll suffer the consequences of our wrong decisions.

Introductory activity (18-23 years)
- Resources: Whiteboard and markers.
- Instructions: Ask the students to list all the sexually transmitted diseases (STD's) that they know. Ask them to explain what they know about them.

When we're talking about sexual relationships outside of marriage, we must also be made aware of sexually transmitted diseases (STD's) and unplanned pregnancy. Today the topic is STD's and their consequences, and what God says about it.

It's very important for young people to know the consequences we have when we don't say no to situations that endanger us.

Connect | Navigate

Sexually transmitted diseases are infections that are spread through sexual relationships, by genital contact and fluid exchange. Many of these diseases have no cure; others have a cure but they leave consequences. We'll study them and also learn what God's will for our lives is.

1. Our world

In recent years, the World Health Organization has been expressing concern due to the growing number of STD's cases, about 15 million per year in people between 13 and 19 years old.

In a world where we're under constant pressure about everything related to sex through all the media, we have become familiar with the expression "safe sex." This is a phrase used to justify having sexual relationships outside marriage, and to describe the use of condoms to avoid the spread of STD's. But, is "safe sex" really safe? Ask the students for their thoughts on the use of this phrase.

Today, there are about 65 million people suffering from an incurable STD, all because they bought the "safe sex" propaganda and acted irresponsibly. God established parameters and limits to help us avoid getting these diseases. He created sexual relationships as a gift to be enjoyed inside the boundary of marriage, and disobedience to those boundaries has brought suffering and increasing numbers of people having STD's.

2. A big problem

(NOTE: This section is to be used considering the group you are talking to. If you think your group is mature enough, use this information. Otherwise, you can share a simple overview using the basic information in the table below.)

You can complement this information with pictures to create a clearer idea and impact about the risks of STD's. Sunday School is an appropriate time to talk about these topics and discuss them in an ideal environment.)

What do we know of STD's? Today we'll study the most common ones.

Name	Transmission	Symptoms	Treatment	Yearly cases
Chlamydia	A bacteria, spread through sexual relationships and fluid exchange	Pain in the pelvic region, sterility, secretions from penis or vagina, pain, irritation.	Antibiotics, effective when detected early. If detected later, antibiotics will work but there's a chance of becoming sterile.	3 million
Gonorrhea	Bacteria, spread through sexual relationships and fluid exchange, infected underwear	Infertility, bad smelling secretions, irritation, ulcers in genitals, pain. Advanced cases can affect other organs.	Antibiotics, Penicillin	650 million
Syphilis	Bacteria, through sexual relationships and fluid exchange	Ulcers in genitals, irritation, pain, bad smelling	Antibiotics	70 million
Herpes	Bacteria, through sexual relationships and fluid exchange	Irritation, pain and burning. A rash with a dark liquid.	No treatment	1 million
Human Papilloma virus	Bacteria, through sexual relationships and fluid exchange	Warts on the genitals, increases the chances of developing cancer.	Chemotherapy and radiotherapy, many cases have no cure	5,5 million
Hepatitis B	Virus, through sexual relationships and fluid exchange, syringes, blood transfusions.	Fever, pain in articulations, nausea, vomit and diarrhea.	No effective treatment	120 thousand
Trichomoniasis	Through sexual relationships and fluid exchange	Foamy secretions, intense irritation.	Antibiotics	5 million
HIV AIDS	Virus, through sexual relationships and fluid exchange, blood transfusions, syringes, from mother to baby	Virus attacks immune system leaving the body vulnerable to all other diseases.	No cure	There are more than 41 million cases in the world.

3. A biblical insight into STD's

God established sexual relationships to exist in marriage, but we have seen the consequences to that disobedience.

It's believed that HIV was transmitted to humans when someone decided to have sexual relationships with a monkey, which is clearly against God's plan (Leviticus 18:23). Humans have perverted their acts, leading them to dishonor their bodies (Romans 1:21-32). God created sex (Genesis 1:27) and sexual relationships (Genesis 1:28) but within clear boundaries that must be respected.

Our world offers attractive, tempting things (Genesis 3:3-4), and creates a society where this looks like something normal and necessary. Everywhere we hear about safe sex, creating a false idea that condoms and other methods are completely safe, which is a myth. We must have self-discipline and look after our bodies because they are temples of the Holy Spirit, and we aren't our own. It's sad to see how the numbers of people suffering STD's is rising. This point to the lack of self-discipline, and it's a warning for us to trust that God gave us a Spirit of love, power and self-discipline (2 Timothy 1:7). So when temptation comes to you, use that power to bring unclean thoughts captive to Christ (2 Corinthians 10:5). God gives you his Spirit to dwell in you, but also to give you prayer and the Bible as tools to resist the enemy. Be responsible, take care of your body and don't forget our actions have consequences. Stay close to God, He will take you by the hand and won't leave you alone.

Review/Application

Form teams and answer the questions:

1. If God created sex as something beautiful for the couple, why has man distorted that gift and turned it into something harmful and sinful?
2. Why do you think God said that sexual relationships were only for marriage?
3. What are the consequences of having sex outside of marriage?

Ask them to write or answer false or true for each sentence, and then discuss as a class. Be sure to correct any wrong ideas or answers.

1. Sexually Transmitted Diseases are transmitted through sexual intercourse, fluids and sexual contact.
2. All sexually transmitted diseases are curable.
3. AIDS is transmitted through a hug, a kiss, or by shaking hands.
4. AIDS only affects homosexuals.
5. I can have sex as long as I protect myself.
6. The condom is a safe method for not contracting this type of disease.
7. Our body is the Temple of the Holy Spirit.

Discuss the consequences of doing the wrong thing. Make them aware of how important it's to properly use of the body that the Lord gave us.

Good habits, bad habits

Objective: That the students learn that there are habits, like pornography and masturbation, which destroy a person's life and draw them away from God.
To memorize: "Flee the evil desires of youth and pursue righteousness, faith, love and peace, along with those who call on the Lord out of a pure heart." 2 Tim. 2:22

> **Warning** x
> Talk about how they used their bodies to glorify God during the last week.
> **Accept** ⚠

Connect / Navigate

Introductory Activity (12-17 years)
- Resources: Two paper sheets (big size) and markers
- Instructions: One paper will have the title "good habits" and the other "bad habits." Ask the students to write on the paper a short sentence about what they think of each title and some examples from their daily life.

Introductory Activity (18-23 years)
- Resources: Paper and pencil.
- Instructions: Make teams with 2-3 students each and ask the teams to think and write down their thoughts on masturbation and pornography. After that, each team will share their answers and discuss about it.

Start with the next question: How flexible can the world be with sin? We hear about lifestyles that are well known, accepted, and even admired. There's a supposed freedom where it's possible to try and experiment, because as long as we aren't affecting others, we can do whatever we please.

In this flexibility, we see trends and experiences that are carried out with excess and perversion, harmful habits that are dangerous and hurtful to people. God tells us in 1 Corinthians 6:12, " 'I have the right to do anything,' you say—but not everything is beneficial. 'I have the right to do anything—but I won't be mastered by anything.' " Young people must be alert to everything the world offers through practices and experiences that are done in secret, but with a popularity, like masturbation and pornography.

Connect / Navigate

Teenagers and young people must understand that their bodies are in development, and it's normal to feel impulses and sexual desires. God created men and women, and one of their purposes was to enjoy sexuality in an appropriate way.

A man and a woman are called to "become one flesh" (Genesis 2:24) in spirit, soul and body. Physical unions (sexual relationships) are one of the ways God gave humans to express love.

Through the appropriate use of our sexuality, we can reproduce and be part of the experience and gift given by God of contributing to giving life to another being. It's correct that human sexuality (impulses, desires and sexual relationships) have that purpose of reproduction, "be fruitful and increase in number" (Genesis 1:27-28), and pleasure (Genesis 2:24) within marriage.

Human sexuality is given to the people along with the freedom of choice. Sadly, usually people make wrong decisions and use things for a different purpose. Sexuality isn't an exception.

The lives of people are shaped by values, ideologies and habits. Habits are practices, customs and uses that become a routine. We can, of course, find that there are good and bad habits.

Good habits are those that are formed in us through discipline, and help us to live a healthy life. For example, the habit of eating on a regular schedule, the habit of exercising, the habit of sleeping enough, etc. Bad habits are those which harm us and affect other areas of our lives. Among those are the ones we're discussing today: pornography and masturbation.

1. Masturbation: a sinful activity done secretly

Some mental health professionals (psychiatrists and psychologists) recommend that people explore their bodies and discover their sexuality, because in that way they will get to know themselves and what brings them pleasure.

The dictionary defines masturbation as, "the stimulation of the genitals of oneself (or others), usually until reaching an orgasm, through hand stimulation or means that don't include sexual penetration."

It's clear that in masturbation, there is a search for sexual pleasure. During the transition from childhood to adolescence, it first occurs naturally (almost accidentally) and without inappropriate intentions, as part of our physical development and self-knowledge. However, as we read in the dictionary, we can also see that masturbation can occur purposefully and with clear intention, and this can be harmful for three reasons:

A. It challenges God's purpose of creating sexuality to be a means of reproduction and pleasure within the marriage.

B. It's often accompanied by an external stimulus that can be a fantasy or thought that can be sinful. This creates and feeds sexual desire for someone who is not one's spouse (very often the person practicing masturbation isn't married). These are incorrect thoughts that can be classified as sexual immorality, which the Bible tells us is wrong (1 Corinthians 6:8-10).

C. It affects other areas of life because there is a lack of sexual self-control. The actions will be repeated with more and more frequency. Therefore, masturbation is a practice that can take control over the person. As young people, it's important to look for the presence of the Spirit in our lives, so we can have strength and self-discipline to have control over any situation, no matter how innocent or simple it may look (2 Timothy 1:7).

2. Pornography: a distorted vision

Pornography is the exhibition of sexual content in an obscene way with the intentions of awakening lust. There's something wrong in someone when he or she creates a product with these intentions, and in doing so, uses perverse, awful means.

Many people from all ages believe that pornography won't affect anyone because it takes place in private. However, research indicates that this will develop a heavy addiction. Generally the people who started watching pornography won't be satisfied by a glance. It will become a curiosity that grows and will lead the person to an addiction.

This harmful habit will produce insensitivity where the addict becomes tolerant to images that are explicit and every time more grotesque or impersonal about the sexual act. And it won't stop there. To keep satisfying the sexual desire, the habit will become stronger and stronger, and will search for more perverted and degrading images, until only seeing won't be enough. This will lead to a search for actions that can end in rape, violent sexual acts, etc.

Dr. Victor Cline, clinical psychologist and human behavior expert from Utah University reports, "When someone is exposed repeatedly to pornographic material, he or she will start creating a mental 'library' full of images that won't disappear. It will be there, ready to be remembered, even when the individual won't want it".

When this moment arrives, it's a clear sign that the person (man or woman) has lost control over their mind and won't be able to fulfill the purpose of living in harmony with God and others (1 Peter 1:16).

As a preventive action, Paul writes, "Let the message of Christ dwell among you richly as you teach and admonish one another with all wisdom" (Colossians 3:16). We can create a "spiritual library" so we can act accordingly in every situation.

Let's also mention that behind the pornography industry exists a network of sexual crimes: human trafficking, children and women abused and exploited, etc. ...

3. What to do as young Christians?

Have the students form teams and find practical ways to flee from these two harmful habits, using the memory verse (2 Timothy 2:22). If you think it's appropriate, separate the groups by gender. Let them share their answer and discuss their ideas.

One would think that these situations are far away from the life of Christians, and some will deny that these desires have been in their hearts and minds. But if anyone has experienced these two situations, we can reassure you that there's no reason to be alarmed - you aren't alone. We know that today's world keeps trying to convince us that certain things are no longer wrong, trying to change our understanding of what is good and bad, as we read in Romans 1:18-32. But we have to be aware too that God wants us to be free from sin. We can read an exhortation for this in Colossians 3:5. When God asks us to do something, it's because He knows it's possible. It may be time to surrender everything you are - mind, body and spirit - repent, and let God help you be free and flee from any habit that draws you away from Him and threatens to sink you in sin.

As a Christian, you must flee from all evil. That's the commandment in Hebrews 12:14, and when we do it, there are blessings (Psalm 1:1-3). We must understand there's forgiveness in Christ (1 Corinthians 6:10).

Review/Application

Read the following case study to the class and have them carefully answer the questions as small groups or as a class:

I'm 17 years old and a few months ago I started to masturbate. I have tried to leave this vice. I'm a Christian and all I want is to please God completely. I recognize that the vice of masturbation prevents me from doing so every day. I started about 6 months ago. Compared to other cases, that is not a long time, so I may have time to stop and get rid of the great consequences that may affect me.

1. What faults or sinful acts do you identify in the case?

2. In the light of the Word and what was seen in the lesson, how could you help the young person?

3. If you know of someone who is about to fall into these habits or has experienced some problem with masturbation or pornography, what advice from the Word would help him or her stop from continuing.

Help the students to not feel guilty about asking for forgiveness for bad thoughts. Lead them to find the solution that God gives them. Take time and pray for one another, asking for divine help in the face of temptation.

Set Limits!

Objective: That the students can identify sexual harassment; know the risk of being a victim, respect their own limits and learn to respect the limits of others.
To memorize: "The Lord was with him; he showed him kindness and granted him favor in the eyes of the prison warden." Genesis 39:21

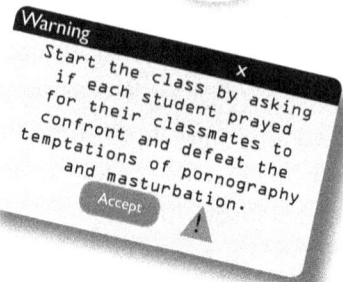

Warning
Start the class by asking if each student prayed for their classmates to confront and defeat the temptations of pornography and masturbation.
Accept

Connect | Navigate

Introductory activity (12-17 years)
• Directions: Divide the class into two groups, one group of girls and another of boys.

Have the boys go to the center of the room. Then ask them to intertwine their arms and legs as strong as they can. The girls will try to separate them one by one and take them out of the center of the room until only one of them remains.

Then if you want to and there is enough time, do it with the girls in the center and the boys trying to separate them.

At the end of the activity, you should explain to them that in the same way that they held on to their companions in order not to let them go, they must have firm convictions, based on the Word of God. They need to be firm in what they believe and fight to the end, with all their strength and with passion for what they want to take care of.

Introductory Activity (18-23 years)
▪ Instructions: Form two groups, mixed males and females. One group will be the victims and the other the stalkers. The bullying group should ask the victims questions and they should answer 'No!' They should answer seriously without even smiling.

Then explain to them that if they want to be taken seriously, they should respond seriously without doubting about the things they don't like.

Sexual harassment is a problem that occurs in any social environment, at home, at work, at school, university, on the street and even in some religious centers. In the latter case, there are those who go so far as to use one's faith to take advantage of the naivety or the fear of the parishioners and thus obtain sexual favors.

Connect | Navigate

First explain the concept of sexual harassment so that everyone understands what you are referring to:

• Sexual harassment includes a range of assaults from discomfort to serious abuse that may involve sexual activity. Sexual harassment is considered a form of unlawful discrimination and is a form of sexual and psychological abuse.

• Sexual harassment typically is unwelcome touching among peers or non-peers, but it also includes lascivious comments, arguments about superiority of sex, sexual jokes, sexual favors to get status, etc.

1. Two cases of sexual harassment in the Bible

One was carried out on a woman and another on a young man. The two had different endings, according to their context.

Since these two passages are known by the majority of young people, the class can be organized in two teams: the girls to look at the case of Tamar and the men at the case of Joseph. They should analyze each case and find out how each one solved their problem of sexual harassment.

A. Sexual harassment begins in the mind: the case of Amnon and Tamar [2 Samuel 13:1-16]

The Bible shows us in a realistic way the presence and results of sexual harassment within the people of God. Amnon is a clear example of someone who didn't respect the boundaries, harassing and causing great harm in Tamar's life and finally in his own life as well.

2 Samuel 13:1-16 says that Amnon fell in love with his sister Tamar to the point of becoming ill. But since she was a virgin, it seemed to him that it would be difficult to do anything to her. Together with Jonadab, he planned what he would do. The plan was that Amnon would pretend to be ill. "Jonadab said, 'When your father comes to see you, say to him, 'I would like my sister Tamar to come and give me something to eat. Let her prepare the food in my sight so I may watch her and then eat it from her hand.' " (v.5).

The plan worked. The king sent Tamar to attend to Amnon. Once there, she approached his bed to feed him, and while she was there Amnon took advantage of the occasion (v.11). Being stronger, he forced her and raped her. He used deception, seduction and persuasion to get away with it, ignoring her protests. Amnon manipulated the circumstances to get away with it. He didn't want to hear Tamar's objections (vv 13). "He refused to listen to her, and since he was stronger than she, he raped her" (v.14). Having harmed his sister Amnon "hated her with intense hatred. In fact, he hated her more than he had loved her" (v.15).

Amnon connived with Jonadab to make a strategic plan to fulfill his wish. This plan was not the right one, neither for him nor for his sister. Later, we see that Amnon paid for his rape of Tamar with his own life (vv. 28-29).

B. You must be astute as Joseph [Genesis 39:6-20]

Often, we can see sexual harassment coming and we should run or escape. Let's look at the biblical example of Joseph. He was taken as a slave to Egypt to work at Potiphar's house. He did his work well and found favor with his master, "For the Lord was with Joseph" (v.2). Verse 6 tells us that Joseph was "well-built and handsome." This fact led to an incident with Potiphar's wife.

It seems that his master's wife was not a good person. Taking advantage of her husband's absence, she looked at Joseph, wanting to go beyond the limits that are allowed between a woman and a man who are not married. She said to him "Come to bed with me!" (v. 7).

In verses 8 and 9, we find that Joseph refused. " 'With me in charge,' he told her, 'my master doesn't concern himself with anything in the house; everything he owns he has entrusted to my care. No one is greater in this house than I am. My master has withheld nothing from me except you, because you are his wife. How then could I do such a wicked thing and sin against God?' "

The woman didn't understand this so she continued to harass him, with daily invitations to lie with her (v.10). On one occasion she became insistent and took him by the clothes, drawing him towards her (v.12). In this case, unlike Tamar, Joseph was able to resist the invitation and flee from Potiphar's wife, but in flight he left his clothing behind (v.12-13). She used this to accuse Joseph, and he was sent to prison (v.20), despite being innocent.

Joseph was in the palace working as a slave. He knew perfectly well that if he didn't run and escape from that situation, it would get worse. He knew God. Although he was harassed on several occasions to do something that he knew was wrong, he feared God and fled from that situation, even though Potiphar's wife lied about him and he ended up in prison.

2. God is with us

No one should mock us in any way. Of course, we must take care not to provoke risky situations. "Be alert and of sober mind. Your enemy the devil prowls around like a roaring lion looking for someone to devour" (1 Peter 5:8). We must always be in a constant and good relationship with God. We must be careful to have our eyes open to see all that happens around us, and above all, we must try to keep ourselves at the center of God's will.

On the other hand we shouldn't mock others or push people beyond their limits, respecting them when they express that they don't like or feel comfortable with the situation, whatever it is. We have to keep the golden rule, "So in everything, do to others what you would have them do to you" (Matthew 7:12).

3. Some tips to keep in mind

- We must be careful how we dress, since we may confuse other people or we may be misunderstood.

- When speaking, we shouldn't use double meaning in conversations, because if we do, we can open doors for others to misunderstand us.

- We have to be careful with the phrases used in the form of hints.

- We need to put limits on how we express ourselves physically with friends, girlfriends or boyfriends. We need to respect other people's limits too.

- If a person makes us feel uncomfortable with their looks, what they say or by their attitude, we should avoid being alone with them.

- We shouldn't let anyone intimidate or threaten us by saying that we shouldn't tell anyone what he or she says or does. Even if it's a member of our family, girlfriend or boyfriend, friend, teacher, school friend or a brother or sister in Christ, we need to share this with our parents or the people who love us the most, or even the authorities. No one can force us to do something that we don't want to do, or that denigrates or displeases us.

Ask your students if they have some other practical suggestions about how to be careful to prevent being harassed or abused by others, as well as not abusing others.

The greater or lesser psychological impact of sexual harassment on the victim depends on the greater or lesser intensity of the aggression and the psychological and social support found in the victim's environment. The concealment of the harassment is frequent because of fear of receiving accusations of lack of credibility or defamation, or of having provoked the harassment, etc. This cover-up tends to increase the psychological impact on the victim.

The fall of the human race into sin and depravity has warped what God had designed and wanted from the beginning for this world, especially for our interpersonal relationships. While it's true that sin drastically affects human life, few sins tear the fabric of our relationships as painfully and miserably as the sin of sexual harassment / abuse. It disfigures the image of God in people, devalues the created human beings made in His image and devastates its victims. The church must be committed to preventing and helping people who are harassed or sexually abused.

Review/Application

Ask your students to respond:

Sexual harassment is considered a form of illegal discrimination and is a form of sexual and psychological abuse ... it encompasses lascivious comments, discussions about superiority of sex, sexual jokes, sexual favors to achieve other status, etc.

1. How can you detect a stalker?
2. What should you do to avoid getting the attention of a stalker?
3. What can we do about a stalker?

Take a few minutes and do something to memorize the biblical text. Help them understand that in addition to knowing the biblical text, they need to allow the text to impact them and give them assurance that God is with them and helping them, regardless of the situation.

Finally, ask them to memorize I Peter 5:8 this week - "Be alert and of sober mind. Your enemy the devil prowls around like a roaring lion looking for someone to devour."

Pure Youth

Objective: That the students clearly understand what sexual purity is and how it's possible to live a pure Christian life.
To memorize: "But just as he who called you is holy, so be holy in all you do." 1 Peter 1:15

Warning
Ask your class if they gave any more thought about sexual harassment. Did anyone experience it last week, and if so, how did they respond? Have them quote 1 Peter 5:8.

Accept

Connect | Navigate

Introductory activity (12-17 years)
- Materials: Two roses or flowers that have petals.
- Directions: Divide the class into two groups. Give each group a rose, and ask each member to take off a petal until they have finished. When the petals are all off, then you as the teacher will pick up the stem that has no petals and explain that it represents a person who uses sex for fun. Explain that the body has to be cared for gently. The body is not to be played with because it was designed for a divine purpose. When

we have sex without giving it the importance and the place for which God designed it, we're playing with our body and our whole life will be affected.

Introductory activity (18-23 years)
- Materials: Paper and pencil.
- Instructions: Ask each student to mention some of the circumstances in which they may be tempted to lose sexual purity and how they can look for ways out.

When we speak of sexual purity, several aspects of a person's life can be affected. We saw in previous classes that we were designed as sexual beings, male and female. God made us so, yet he also clearly stated that we should use our sexuality responsibly.

God reveals in his Word the importance of sex in marriage. Sexual intercourse outside of marriage can cause diseases, sadness, suicide, family problems, divorce, etc.

Connect | Navigate

In our society, young people are being bombarded with ads and media where explicitly naked and semi-naked bodies are displayed, creating all kinds of thoughts or arousing their sexual curiosity. One of the biggest problems is that at this age, boys and girls are in a stage of exploration of new experiences, amongst them, the sexual ones.

We must teach our youth that God created intimate caresses and sex specifically for marriage. We must also show them that it's normal to feel attraction for someone, but also we must teach them how to control their emotions. When hormones are activated, they cancel out neurons. That is, when people face sexual temptation, they often think only of the momentary satisfaction, not of the consequences.

1. God and sexual relations

God established sexual intercourse as a means of having children and enjoying marriage. He knew it was good. In the divine plan, the union of two people who love each other was a perfect union of two bodies, but also the union of the spirit and soul (Genesis 2:24). God blesses that union. The Bible teaches that sexual relationships outside of marriage is considered a sin, which the Bible calls fornication It goes against God's mandate of sexual purity before marriage. But today, this divine principle has been attacked by modern ideas, where we're told that marriage is out of fashion, that young people can have sex at any time they want and with whomever they want as long as they "protect" themselves. They say that the idea of staying pure until marriage is an old-fashioned ideal.

Divide the class into groups of 3-4 students and have them analyze the following passages so that they can discover God's advice about how to keep sexually pure.

In the Bible we find the following tips for dealing with sexual temptation:

- Isaiah 26:3 - When we're tempted, we're not at peace. Yet if we keep in our minds what we have read in the Scriptures and always trust in it, we'll receive peace.

- I Corinthians 10:13 - God always gives us a way out. It's very common for us to use phrases such as "I couldn't stop," or "the temptation was too strong," but God in His Word says He gives us all sorts of ways to overcome temptations.

- 2 Timothy 2:22, I Corinthians 6:18 - God tells us that when we're about to fall into temptation "we must run away," "escape the snares of the devil." That doesn't mean that as young Christians, we're fearful, but in critical moments in which passion is greater than reason, it's better to flee, not to fall into temptation.

- 2 Timothy 1:7 - God doesn't control our body. He is very respectful and doesn't deal with you if you don't want him to. But if you give Him complete control, including your sexual needs, He will give you the self-control you need.

2. Young people and holiness

The biblical passage to memorize today tells us that with God's help, it's possible to live a life of holiness in all areas of our lives, even in the area of our sexuality. "But just as he who called you is holy, so be holy in all you do" (I Peter 1:15). To be holy means to live apart from evil, to be clean and pure before God.

Sometimes we believe that temptations come to us because we're Christians. However, sexual needs come to us because we're human. We must understand fully that just being children of God, going to church and Sunday school, etc., doesn't makes us live in a bubble where no one can touch or influence us. It just isn't true. The devil wanted to tempt Jesus, so how much more will he seek to tempt us? Paul tells the young men of Corinth that if they cannot wait to have sex, it's better that they marry soon, lest they fall into the sin of fornication (I Corinthians 7:2). There are many young Christians who, in courtship, have so much physical contact and intense caresses, that they take the risk every day of falling to the temptation of having sex before marriage.

Therefore, it's very important that you take care of this vulnerable area of our lives as young Christians, so that you can live a life of holiness: praying, reading and learning from the Bible, choosing your friends well, remembering your commitment to sexual purity that you made a few Sundays ago, fleeing temptations, setting goals for yourselves to achieve the most important things in your lives.

Review/Application

Discuss with the class:

Maybe you have not experienced what a sexual relationship is. There are many pressures from media and friends to give in to this kind of temptation. Ask the class to respond:

1. What would be your answer if a young man or woman of your age asks for your opinion regarding sexual purity?
2. When you are alone, what do you do to avoid thoughts that don't please God?

Considering that on television, in movies, on the Internet, and at school, the majority of young people today have sex during their courtship, justifying themselves with these phrases: "Virginity has gone out of style," "Everyone does it," "Have safe sex and enjoy your sexuality," etc.

Ask them to respond:

1. What do you think about those statements and justifications?
2. What does the Word of God say about relationships before marriage?
3. What practical strategies would you use to avoid falling into sexual impurity or fornication when maintaining a relationship of courtship?

Talk about how important it's to set aside some time daily to read the Bible and pray to learn and be strengthened. Guide them to make a commitment in this regard.

Silent Death

Lesson 28

Wendy Ayala • Guatemala

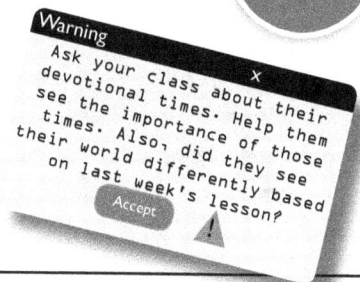

Objective: That the students may recognize God as the author of life from conception onwards, and the only one with the authority to end life.
To memorize: "For you created my inmost being; you knit me together in my mother's womb" Psalm 139:13.

Warning
Ask your class about their devotional times. Help them see the importance of those times. Also, did they see their world differently based on last week's lesson?
Accept

Connect | Navigate

Introductory activity (12-17 years)

- Instructions: Begin by explaining that they are in a difficult situation. They all went to a distant place, but when they returned home, they realized that everyone was acting weird. They don't know what to do because the price of everything had increased a lot. Gasoline went up three times, people were being dismissed, there was no work and there was no money. The situation was so extreme that in every home, parents had to sacrifice someone, so everyone must defend themselves and say why he or she shouldn't die.

After each of the students have explained why they shouldn't die, ask them how they felt when thinking about that possibility.

Then reflect with them as you tell them that there is a large group of small people, who die daily and cannot say anything, cannot defend themselves, and the saddest thing is that they didn't ask to be in this world.

Introductory activity (18-23 years)

- Instructions: Form two groups. Explain that today they will be part of the Congress of their country and they will discuss a very important issue for the nation - abortion. They need to make a law which, if accepted, will make abortion legal.

One group will be in favor of abortion and will defend it so that its legality will be approved, while the other group won't agree and will fight for abortion to be condemned. Each group must defend their position and explain why they hold to it.

After a while of listening to them, start with the points of the lesson.

In this verse, the psalmist is affirming that God who has formed us knows us perfectly. We are a miracle or a wonder that came from the hand of God, showing too the omnipotence of our Creator.

Connect | Navigate

When we talk about abortion, it's important to know the definitions. For example, etymologically, abortion means "deprivation of birth." Abortion is the death of the product of conception (union of the ovum and the sperm) and its expulsion from the maternal organs at any stage of its pre-natal development.

1. We are made in the image of God

Genesis 1:27 says, "So God created mankind in his own image, in the image of God he created them; male and female he created them." This verse makes two affirmations clear: first, that we are God's creation and second, that we are made in his image. After these affirmations, can we take someone's life? God created life, and that is why life belongs to Him. Psalm 24:1 states, "The earth is the LORD's, and everything in it, the world, and all who live in it." It's clear that we come from Him, life is sacred, it's a gift and therefore we must respect it.

2. Why say 'no' to abortion?

The world wants us to believe that abortion is permitted and is an ethical solution for human beings. They want to deceive us by making us think that there is no life in embryos, but this is a big lie.

We know that every action has its consequences, and when we disobey God's commands, problems come. With this we don't mean that pregnancy is a problem, but it must occur within a home, where the new being is loved and wanted and not just the product of passion. When an ovum is linked to a sperm in a sexual relationship, it's called conception or fertilization. Medically, from this moment on, there is already life in that embryo. The Word of God clearly says, "Your eyes saw my unformed body" (Psalm 139:16). So, from the moment of fertilization, there is already life and nobody can disprove this. So if someone decides to have an abortion, she is definitely committing murder. The commandment in Exodus 20:13 says, "You shall not kill." Many studies have been done where the pain suffered by the fetuses during an abortion has been proven. Their gestures of pain, their silent screams, their writhing. Although we may not believe it, they suffer not only during the abortion but even before when they that feel rejection. Children are our inheritance given to us by God.

We're all children here, therefore we are a blessing for our parents, we are their inheritance. Psalm 127:3 says that, "Children are a heritage from the Lord, offspring a reward from him." God says that children are special for parents, so we must take responsibility for our actions. It's true that many times children are conceived with no love. For example, there are cases of sexual abuse or rape, but God gives the necessary strength to manage these situations, without taking the lives of his little creations.

Ask your students the following reflection questions:

- What are the biblical bases for saying "no" to abortion?

- How would you advise if someone you love a lot asked for advice, because her boyfriend wants her to get an abortion?

3. Types of abortions

It's sad to talk about this, but we must know the terrible methods that are used for an abortion. This information can help us at some point when someone asks us our opinion. As for the methods used, it will depend on the trimester of pregnancy in which the person who wants to have an abortion is. For example:

If it's in the first trimester, from one to three months, the following methods are used:

- Suction: Here they use a tube that sucks the fetus out. It's 29 times more powerful than a normal vacuum, pulling apart the fetus in a brutal and ugly way. This is the most used method in abortion clinics.

- Dilation and Scraping: Another method is also frightful, where a device such as a sharp spoon is introduced into the dilated womb of the woman and the fetus is scraped out.

- The Pill (RU486): This is a medicine that is taken to interrupt pregnancy. It's combined with other medicines causing contractions which cause the expulsion of the fetus.

If the pregnancy is between three and nine months they will do the following:

- Dilation and evacuation: In this method, the cervix is dilated and a pair of pliers are introduced that destroy the fetus, since at this age they already have bones and it's more difficult not to leave bits behind.

Sometimes, women have miscarriages. These occur in people who don't want to have an abortion, however the womb or something else doesn't allow the pregnancy to continue. This is not condemned by God, because the person didn't want that to happen and did all they could to prevent it.

In many towns, villages or very distant places, abortion is practiced through village wives, (non-professional women), but they do it in an insecure and unhygienic way, causing the death of many people. They do it by means of knitting needles, bicycle cables, wires, etc., in a brutal and unhygienic way.

4. Consequences after abortions

In sexually active couples, there is no 100% safe method to avoid pregnancy. But many people think that they can take risks and that if they get pregnant, an abortion will solve their problem. Maybe nobody will notice, or nobody will find out, but what they don't know is that this will leave indelible marks on their mind and heart. Studies have shown that abortion brings, especially for women, serious consequences such as:

a. Problem of low self-esteem: She feels very ashamed, sad, and despises herself and feels that she no longer has value as a woman. She believes that no one is going to accept her as a woman, and sometimes this can lead her to prostitute herself or commit suicide.

b. Having a guilt complex: The woman who has had an abortion feels very guilty, has sleep disorders, anxiety and suffers a great weight of guilt, which only Christ can take away from her.

c. She can become infertile: Many times, a young woman who has an abortion, is attended to by incompetent and unscrupulous people who damage her womb or ovaries. It's sad that often when this lady later marries and wants to start a family, she cannot because the abortion harmed her reproductive system.

Review/Application

Ask your students to fill in the underlined blank space according to the biblical passages:

1. Children are the _____ of Jehovah. Psalm 127:3 (Inheritance)
2. We were created by God, in his _____. Genesis 1:27 (Image)
3. We are the _____ of God. Mark 10:6 (creation)
4. In the beginning _____ created the heavens and the earth. Genesis 1:1 (God)
5. The gender opposite to Male. Genesis 1:24. (Female)
6. The union of a sperm with an ovum. Psalm 139:16. (Embryo)
7. Product of love between a father and a mother, and the inheritance of Jehovah. Psalm 127:3 (children)
8. Name given to the male. Genesis 1:24. (man)

Ask them to answer false or true:

1. Abortion is allowed by God when it's a couple of teenagers. F
2. Abortion doesn't affect the embryo because it doesn't feel anything. F
3. God is the giver of life, and therefore he alone can take it away. T
4. I own my life and can do with it what I want. F
5. All contraceptive methods are safe. F
6. God formed me in the womb of my mother. T
7. Life begins from the union of a sperm with an ovum. T

After what you have learned in the lesson, talk about the fatal consequences of abortion. Guide them to commit themselves to God and reject the practice of abortion even when society agrees and passes laws that favor it.

Hmm, what a temptation!

Objective: That the students will understand what temptation is and that it's not a sin until we give in to it.

To memorize: "No temptation has overtaken you except what is common to mankind. And God is faithful; he won't let you be tempted beyond what you can bear." (I Corinthians 10:13a)

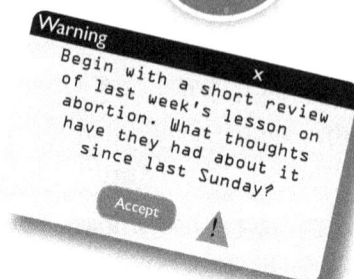

Warning
Begin with a short review of last week's lesson on abortion. What thoughts have they had about it since last Sunday?

Accept

Connect | Navigate

Introductory activity (12-17 years)

- Instructions: Divide the class into two teams. On a piece of paper, have each team write down five decision options that a teenager might face in their daily life. For example, "Copy a friend's answer to an unexpected test, or leave the question blank." Once each team has its five situations, they will present them to the other team, and the students of the other team must decide which is the correct option. The students of each team can decide how easy or how difficult to make the decisions. The teacher should be prepared to guide the debate and offer some verses that enlighten the students.

Introductory activity (18-23 years)

- Materials: Paper strips and pencils or pens.

- Instructions: Ask your students to write individually on their paper strips a temptation that they have had during the last week. (They shouldn't put their names on their strips.) Then they will give the teacher their strips and the teacher will pass out the strips to the students. Each student will read the temptation and say in a few words how he/she would escape from that temptation. The activity ends when everyone has read and responded to the strip that they received.

As humans, we experience difficult situations in our lives that cause us pain and anguish. During these situations, we wonder why this situation came into our lives, and when we don't find a clear answer, we experience even greater discontent and uncertainty. We tend to want to know the cause of situations, and what benefit or consequence they will have on our lives.

Connect | Navigate

Begin by defining temptation as one of the ways that proves our faithfulness to God. According to the Beacon Theological Dictionary, "The intention is to prove the character of the person. The purpose can be to strengthen the life of a person by exposing the latent defects of his character."

Temptations are difficult situations that we all face in our lives. Many times, we don't have people around us in whom we trust enough to share what we're going through, and receive encouragement and consolation. It's important to remember that Jesus himself went through temptations while living here on earth, and that He understands perfectly when we're passing through them. Likewise, Jesus can help us have victory over situations and emerge stronger from the tests. Truly, Jesus has the power to help us, and studying his example in the Bible can encourage us to trust Him.

1. What is temptation?

The word temptation can be defined as an opportunity to make a decision. In every temptation that presents itself to us, we have the opportunity to make the right decision or the wrong one. It's important to recognize that in a situation of temptation, making the right decision is often difficult. The wrong decision is often the most attractive one, and often the one the tempted person likes best.

When talking about temptation, we often experience feelings of shame, and to recognize that we're tempted by different situations is usually a very difficult thing that requires honesty and courage. When we turn to the Scriptures, we read that Jesus himself, when he lived here on earth, went through temptations, and that with the power of the Holy Spirit, he was able to endure them. Hebrews 4:15 tells us, "For we don't have a high priest who is unable to empathize with our weaknesses, but we have one who has been tempted in every way, just as we are—yet he didn't sin."

It's important to recognize that temptation is not a sin. That is, when tempted we're not sinning. The situation becomes a sin and takes us away from God when, instead of saying 'no' to an incorrect option, we accept the negative or sinful opportunity that temptation offers us. When a girl's mother forbids her to eat the cookies that are on the kitchen table, the mother won't punish the girl for wanting to eat them. The mother understands that obviously the girl might want to eat the cookies. However, her mother will punish the girl if she eats the cookies, since she had asked her not to. Although this example is not the ideal, it can help us understand that God considers it sin when we turn away from Him and disobey His perfect will for our life. But God wants to help us defeat temptation. In 2 Peter 2:9, we're reminded that the "Lord knows how to rescue the godly from trials." That is to say, good people suffer temptations, but God helps them so that they don't sin.

We must remember that temptation is not a "game" God is playing with our lives. When we face trials as human beings, we tend to begin to ask ourselves, "When will God do something about this? Why doesn't this situation disappear from my life?" The Bible itself reminds us about the natural love of God, and tells us that "When tempted, no one should say, 'God is tempting me' for God cannot be tempted by evil, nor does he tempt anyone" (James 1:13). Remember that God allows situations in our lives for a purpose, and that the love of God is eternal and we can rely completely on Him.

2. What is the purpose of temptations?

The purpose of facing temptation in our life is for us to grow. In His Word, God reminds us of the following, " Consider it a sheer gift, friends, when tests and challenges come at you from all sides. You know that under pressure, your faith-life is forced into the open and shows its true colors" (James 1:2-3 MSG).

It's important to recognize that temptation is a test, that is, a way to help us see how strong our faith and commitment to God is. It's similar to the experience of a five-year-old boy who wants to learn to ride a bicycle. His dad will explain how to climb up, how to sit on the seat, where to put his feet and hands, how to pedal and how to steer the bike with the handlebars. However, the little one won't know if he can ride a bicycle until he starts pedaling himself, and finally rides the bike by himself. In the same way, God instructs us and teaches us, but with time there come tests or temptations into our life, which although difficult, just like when the child begins to walk alone, allow us to strengthen ourselves and put into practice what God has taught us.

God has a wonderful plan for our lives, and even though various trials or temptations come into our lives, God is overseeing everything (Jeremiah 29:11). The greatest purpose of a temptation must be to bring us closer to Him and help us to experience His love and care for us in a fresh way (Romans 8:28).

3. How to overcome temptation?

One of the most important things we must remember is that temptation can be overcome. For us as people, many of the temptations we confront may seem impossible to bear; However, God never leaves us alone, and offers us all his help, especially in difficult situations. We must know how to approach God. Reading the Bible and prayer are practices that can strengthen us and fill us with God's presence, enabling us to overcome temptation. Jesus reminds us that God won't leave us alone, but will give us the comforter, the Holy Spirit, to help us and remind us of the things that we have learned.

In Luke 4:1-13, we read that Jesus himself is our best example of how to overcome the temptations that come into our lives. When Satan tempted him 3 times, Jesus Christ answered, "It's written ..." since He knew and had memorized the Scriptures from childhood. Just as it happened with Jesus, memorizing verses from the Bible is a discipline that can help us overcome temptation as we recall verses when we face a situation in which it can be difficult to make a godly decision. Hebrews 2:18 tells us that "Because he himself suffered when he was tempted, he is able to help those who are being tempted."

It's also important to remember that Jesus Christ was an obedient son to his Father, and tried to please him in everything he did. Everything he did in his life was to honor Him. So, when temptation arises in which we're invited to do wrong, if we say that we are his children, we must make the decision to please and obey God in everything.

Finally, it's important to recognize that the only sure way to overcome temptation is by having confidence and depending on God. God loves us with an infinite love. He is interested in everything that happens in our lives, and he promises us his help and presence. This week, try to believe, trust and memorize the word that God gives us in 1 Corinthians 10:13, "All you need to remember is that God will never let you down; he'll never let you be pushed past your limit; he'll always be there to help you come through it" (MSG).

Review/Application

Teamwork: Read the following story to the students and ask them to reflect and answer the following questions.

"The story is told of a lady who was interested in the gold purification process. She visited a jewelry manufacturing center in her city. Approaching the smelter, she asked him some questions about the process. "Tell me," she said, "Is it true that you use fire to purify the gold you use to make the jewelry, and that you always keeps your eyes on the process?" The smelter replied, "The gold arrives here full of impurities, and the only way to separate the precious metal from the impurities is through the use of fire. At high temperatures, the fire burns off all the impurities, and only the pure gold remains at the end. During the process, it's very important that I don't turn my eyes away from the gold for a moment, for if I'm not careful, the gold itself can melt along with the impurities. I pay close attention during the whole process." The astonished woman asked, "How do you know when gold is completely purified?" The smelter replied, "Ah, that's easy. The gold is completely purified when I can see my image reflected in it."

1. How does this story resemble the temptations we face in our lives?

2. What are some of the questions that you have asked while you were experiencing temptations in your life?

3. How do you feel knowing that God, as the smelter, is attentive during the entire formation process of our life?

4. What are some of the things you have done when temptations have come to your life?

5. How do you think temptations can actually help us become better Christians?

6. What new ideas or encouragement have you found through studying the biblical passages of the lesson that can help you in your life from now on?

Talk about the temptations they commonly face as teenagers and young people. Encourage them to always trust God and His Word.

Why am I a Christian?

Objective: That the students might know how to explain and defend their faith.

To memorize: "But in your hearts revere Christ as Lord. Always be prepared to give an answer to everyone who asks you to give the reason for the hope that you have. But do this with gentleness and respect" (1 Peter 3:15).

Warning

Don't forget to ask about last week's challenge. Ask them if they felt strengthened knowing that the Lord was with them in the midst of their temptations.

Accept

Connect   Navigate

Introductory activity (12-17 years)
- Materials: Paper and pencil
- Instructions: Ask each student to draw a characteristic of a Christian. For example, you can draw a young man reading the Bible. Then they share their drawing with others.

Introductory activity (18-23 years)
- Instructions: Form two groups and place them one in front of the other, in debate position. Then tell them that one group will be in favor and the other against the following sentence: "Christians are ashamed of the gospel."

  Allow each group to present their opinions and reasons for a few minutes. Check that they don't go on for too long.

Apologetics is the defense of biblical and Christian faith. Essentially, Christian apologetics is speaking for God according to what God has revealed of himself. The apology is the rational defense of the Christian faith, which seeks to establish the truth of Christianity.

Biblically speaking, apologetics is "Always be prepared to give an answer to everyone who asks you to give the reason for the hope that you have." (1 Peter 3:15)

Connect   Navigate

Most Christians today prefer to experience Christianity rather than to think about it or explain it. But considered these verses:

1. "But the seed falling on good soil refers to someone who hears the word and understands it. This is the one who produces a crop, yielding a hundred, sixty or thirty times what was sown" (Matthew 13:23). Everyone heard it, but only the "good earth" understood it.

2. "The Spirit told Philip, 'Go to that chariot and stay near it.' Then Philip ran up to the chariot and heard the man reading Isaiah the prophet. 'Do you understand what you are reading?' Philip asked. 'How can I,' he said, 'unless someone explains it to me?' So, he invited Philip to come up and sit with him" (Acts 8:29-31).

3. Paul in Corinth, "Every Sabbath he reasoned in the synagogue, trying to persuade Jews and Greeks" (Acts 18:4).

4. Paul in Ephesus, "Paul entered the synagogue and spoke boldly there for three months, arguing persuasively about the kingdom of God" (Acts 19:8).

5. "Consequently, faith comes from hearing the message, and the message is heard through the word about Christ" (Romans 10:17). Again, the emphasis is on hearing with perception.

6. "We try to persuade others," says Paul (2 Corinthians 5:11). The Greek word used for each of those terms (persuasion, dialogue, discourse, arguing, discussing, presenting evidence, reasoning with) are used to give the idea of communication, and are at the heart of Paul's classic evangelistic model.

Can there be saving faith without understanding? Can there be understanding without reasoning? The Bible seems to say 'no'. Paul encourages believers in 2 Timothy 2:15, "Do your best to present yourself to God as one approved, a worker who doesn't need to be ashamed and who correctly handles the word of truth."

Many ask if any participation of the mind in the exchange of ideas seems too much like human effort, and in reality only dilutes the work of the Spirit. But Christianity thrives on intelligence, not on ignorance. We must love God with the mind as well as with the heart and the soul.

1. What we believe

In this lesson, we'll define and illustrate the parameters of why we need to use reason to understand why we are Christians. In other words, we'll talk about what we believe. You can divide the class into groups and distribute the biblical passages among the students. Ask them to tell the class what the verse tells them about their beliefs. For example: Genesis 1:1; Isaiah 45:22; Colossians 1:16 tells us to believe "in one God Creator of all things."

a. We believe in one God, Creator of all things (Genesis 1:1, Isaiah 45:22, Colossians 1:16).

b. We believe that God is Triune: Father, Son and Holy Spirit; three different people and only one God (Isaiah 9:6-7, John 1:1, Romans 9:5, Ephesians 4:6).

c. We believe the Mystery of the Incarnation; that is, that Mary conceived by the work and grace of the Holy Spirit (Luke 1:29-30-35; Matthew 1:18).

d. We believe that the second person of the Trinity already existed in eternity, but that through the mystery of the incarnation, he participated in human nature, thus being the "EMMANUEL" (God with us) (Matthew 1:23) "God manifested in the flesh "(1 Timothy 3:16).

e. We believe that because Jesus Christ was fully God and fully Man (without sin), his sacrifice on the Cross was of infinite value to redeem us from our sins (John 1:18, Romans 9:5, Titus 2:14, Hebrews 4:15; Revelation 5:9).

f. We believe that the Bible is the Word of God, written by men but under the direction and inspiration of the Holy Spirit, and we believe everything that is spoken in it (2 Peter 1:20-21).

g. We believe that Jesus died for our sins and that He was resurrected for our justification (Romans 4:25).

h. We believe that the risen Jesus ascended to heaven, where he is at the right hand of the Father and where he also intercedes for us (Romans 8:34).

i. We believe that Jesus Christ is the only mediator between God and men. "For there is one God and one mediator between God and mankind, the man Christ Jesus (1 Timothy 2:5).

j. We believe that every man is a sinner, not only because he is a descendant of Adam, but because he himself has sinned voluntarily and, as the Bible says, "There is no one righteous, not even one" (Romans 3:10).

k. We believe that man is justified only by faith. "What then shall we say that Abraham, our forefather according to the flesh, discovered in this matter? If, in fact, Abraham was justified by works, he had something to boast about—but not before God. What does Scripture say? 'Abraham believed God, and it was credited to him as righteousness.' Now to the one who works, wages are not credited as a gift but as an obligation. However, to the one who doesn't work but trusts God who justifies the ungodly, their faith is credited as righteousness" (Romans 4:1-5).

l. We believe that Jesus Christ was sent so that men could be saved, "For God so loved the world that he gave his one and only Son, that whoever believes in him shall not perish but have eternal life" (John 3:16). And St. Peter says; "Salvation is found in no one else, for there is no other name under heaven given to mankind by which we must be saved" (Acts 4:12).

m. We believe that the believer in Christ, that is, the one who with a living faith believes that Jesus Christ died for his sins and accepts him as his only and sufficient Savior, already in this time has the assurance of eternal life. Jesus said, "Very truly I tell you, whoever hears my word and believes him who sent me has eternal life and won't be judged but has crossed over from death to life" (John 5:24). "Very truly I tell you, the one who believes has eternal life" (John 6:47).

n. We believe in the Holy Spirit, the Third Person of the Divine Trinity, that He is always present and effectively active in the Church of Christ and together with the church, convincing the world of sin, regenerating those who repent and believe, sanctifying believers and leading to all truth which is in Jesus Christ. (John 7:39; 14:15-18, 26; 16:7-15; Acts 2:33; 15:8-9; Romans 8:1-27; Galatians 3:1-14; 4:6; Ephesians 3:14-21, 1 Thessalonians 4:7-8, 2 Thessalonians 2:13, 1 Peter 1:2, 1 John 3:24, 4:13).

2. I believe in Jesus

There can be no Christianity without Jesus Christ. In Matthew 16:13-17, men gave several answers to the question, "Who do men say the Son of Man is?" Peter said, "You are the Christ, the Son of the living God." Why do I believe that Jesus is the Son of God?

a. Because even history recognizes that Jesus lived on earth - The history of humanity is divided by the fact of the life of Jesus. The years are counted before Christ and after Christ. Famous men of antiquity and ancient writings such as Barnabas, Clement, Ignatius, Polycarp, filled their documents with facts of the life and teachings of Christ, and didn't retract their testimony.

b. Because the Bible declares the existence of Jesus - John recounts the power of Jesus in seven major miracles and declares their purpose. See John 20:30,31. The disciples knew Jesus better. They believed in Him in such a great way that all but John and Judas gave their lives as martyrs. Many of them left written in the Bible those experiences they had lived alongside Jesus Christ.

c. Because Jesus transforms our lives - No human being is the same after having met Christ. Because if we let him take control of our lives, we'll never be the same. Paul in 2 Corinthians 5:17 confirms that everything is new in Him.

d. Because Jesus is still working - Because Jesus can take the sinful and petty life of the sinner and transform it into a useful and clean vessel for His work.

God is not ashamed to be our God; nor Jesus to be our savior, but what makes Jesus ashamed of us is that we're ashamed of his words. Are we ashamed of the words of Jesus? Are we ashamed of the Scriptures? Are we going to be embarrassed or are we going to feel proud?

Review/Application

Ask them to write in their own words what the following beliefs mean to them.

- Christ
- Christians
- Holy Spirit
- Bible

Encourage the students to think of two non-Christians to whom they could share their faith. Encourage them to finish the class by praying for each other, and in the week ahead, to tell someone what they learned in class.

Why am I a Nazarene?

Warning
Start by asking them how they did during the week and if they were able to share their testimony with the people they have been praying for. If so, how did it go?
Accept

Objective: That the students will be sure why they are Nazarenes.
To memorize: Make every effort to live in peace with everyone and to be holy; without holiness, no one will see the Lord (Hebrews 12:14).

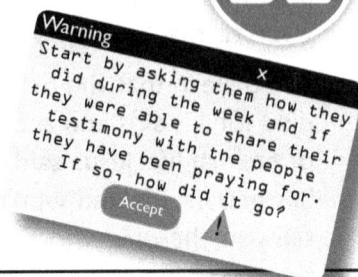

Connect / Navigate

Introductory activity (12-17 years)

- Instructions: Ask the students to tell you how they recognize that a person is a fireman, a soldier, a policeman, a doctor, a pastor, etc., without talking to them.

  Ask the students if someone asked them, 'Why are you Nazarene?' What would you respond? Let them give some answers.

Introductory activity (18-23 years)

- Instructions: Form two groups. Each group must present a drama of a known comedian, but without identifying who the comedian they are talking of is.

  The teacher will ask the groups to guess the identity of the comedian the other group is representing.

  After they have made some guesses, the teacher can ask them how they identified the comedian in question or why they think he is a comedian?

  Ask the students: "If people ask you: 'Why are you Nazarene?' what would you answer?" Let them give some answers.

Today we'll see some important points to help us answer this question clearly, of course based on the Sacred Scriptures.

Connect / Navigate

Before answering the question "Why am I a Nazarene?" we need to know that the Church of Nazarene is a Christian organization and consists of those people who joined voluntarily in accordance with the doctrines and government of that church; people who seek holy Christian fellowship, the conversion of sinners, the entire sanctification of believers, and their edification in holiness. This means that the church proposes to serve God so that His Kingdom will grow through the preaching and teaching of the gospel throughout the world. And not only this, but it has a well-defined mission, which consists of preserving and propagating Christian holiness as established in the Sacred Scriptures, through the conversion of sinners, the restoration of persons and the entire sanctification of believers.

In the lesson we'll answer the question, "Why am I a Nazarene?"

1. Because I identify with what the church of the Nazarene believes about Christ

We are a Christian church. What does that mean? Allow the students to respond.

We believe in Jesus Christ, the son of God (John 1:18). He is God, but he became a man and he lived among us. Through his redemptive work, he brought us salvation, "But when the kindness and love of God our Savior appeared, he saved us, not because of righteous things we had done, but because of his mercy. He saved us through the washing of rebirth and renewal by the Holy Spirit" (Titus 3:4-5). He is our savior and the only mediator between God and men, "For there is one God and one mediator between God and mankind, the man Christ Jesus (1 Timothy 2:5).

2. Because I identify with the doctrine of the Church of the Nazarene

You have probably heard the word "doctrine" many times, but you have asked yourself, what does it mean? Doctrine is a coherent set of teaching or instructions based on a system of beliefs.

The doctrine of the Church of the Nazarene is based on the Bible, which is the Word of God and leads us to live lifestyles different from the model that the world presents to us. The Bible says, "But just as he who called you is holy, so be holy in all you do (1 Peter 1:15).

God who is Holy, calls us to a life of holiness (Hebrews 12:14, Leviticus 20:26). We believe that the Holy Spirit wishes to effect in us a second work of grace, known in various terms including 'entire sanctification' and 'baptism with the Holy Spirit,' cleansing us from all sin; renewing ourselves in the image of God; giving us the power to love God with all our heart, soul, mind and strength, and our neighbor as ourselves (Acts 2:42); and producing in us the character of Christ. Holiness in the lives of believers is more clearly understood as a resemblance or likeness to Christ.

3. Because I identify with its mission

The Church of the Nazarene is a missional people. This means that we are a sent people that respond to the call of Christ and are enabled by the Holy Spirit to go to the world to testify of the lordship of Christ and to participate with God in the building of the church and the extension of His kingdom (Mark 16:15, Matthew 28:16-20).

As Nazarenes, our mission begins in:

a. Worship: As we gather together before God in worship by singing, listening to the public reading of the Bible, giving our tithes and offerings, praying, listening to the Word, practicing baptism and participating in the Lord's Supper, we know more clearly what it means to be God's people. Our conviction that the work of God in the world is achieved mainly through congregations that worship, leads us to understand that our mission includes receiving new members in the fellowship of the church, and organizing new congregations for worship. Since worship is the highest expression of our love for God, it's worship centered on God, honoring Him who has redeemed us in His grace and mercy. So, the primary context of worship is the local church where the people of God meet, not in a self-centered or self-glorifying experience, but as a self-surrender and an offering. Church worship is carried out as a service of love and in obedience to God.

b. To minister to the world in evangelism and compassion: Through this mission in the world, the church demonstrates the love of God. The history of the Bible is the story of God reconciling the world to himself completely through Jesus Christ according to 2 Corinthians 5:16-21. The church is sent to the world to participate with God in this ministry of love and reconciliation through evangelism, compassion and justice.

c. To encourage believers to Christian maturity through discipleship: We affirm that Christian discipleship is a way of life. It's the process of learning how God really wants us to live in this world. As we learn to live in obedience to the Word of God and in mutual responsibility towards one another, we begin to understand the true joy of a disciplined life and the Christian meaning of freedom. The ultimate goal of discipleship is to be transformed into the likeness of Jesus Christ as mentioned in 2 Corinthians 3:18.

d. To prepare men and women for Christian service through higher Christian education: Higher Christian education is essential for the development of our understanding of what we believe. In education, faith is not divided into parts, but is beautifully integrated with knowledge as faith and learning develop together. The whole person is cultivated, and each area of thought and life is understood in relation to the desire and design of God. Higher Christian education contributes, significantly to being a missionary people offering the broad panorama of knowledge and that is necessary for effective service to God in our different vocations. The Lord's desire is for men and women to develop who can take their place as Christian leaders who can serve in the church and in the world.

Any organization that remains through time is based on a deep combination of shared purposes, beliefs and values. The same thing happens to us. Our church was founded to transform the world by projecting biblical holiness. We are a church. Our mission is to make disciples in all nations, in the likeness of Christ.

The present and future life of the Church of the Nazarene is defined by its participation in the mission of God. That is why today we can say that it's an organization that is distinguished not only by its beliefs, but also by the particular way in which it contributes to the Kingdom of God.

Review/Application

Ask them to respond with their words:
1. Why do you call yourself Christian?
2. Why are you a Nazarene?
3. What do you understand by the affirmation "we identify with missions?"

Encourage students to ask other brothers/sisters of the church during the week or family members why they are Nazarenes and share their experiences and what they learned next Sunday in class.

Cults

Objective: That the students might know how to identify the characteristics of a cult.

To memorize: "For false messiahs and false prophets will appear and perform signs and wonders to deceive, if possible, even the elect" (Mark 13:22).

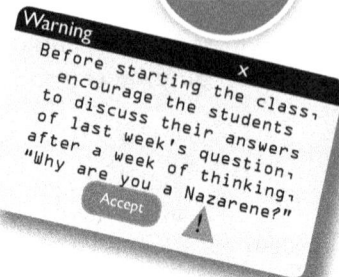

Warning

Before starting the class, encourage the students to discuss their answers of last week's question, after a week of thinking, "Why are you a Nazarene?"

Accept

Connect | Navigate

Introductory activity (12-17 years)

- Instructions: Ask the students to form pairs and blindfold everyone. Then ask everyone to spin around in circles 20 times. One person of each pair will try to lead the other to an established goal. The pair who reaches the goal first wins.

  Explain that the blindness produced by cults and false philosophies can make people dizzy, preventing them from reaching the correct goal. They are like the blind leading the blind.

Introductory activity (18-23 years)

- Instructions: Ask that each of the students, or in groups if you prefer, look for ads in the newspaper that have to do with cults and comment how they have proliferated within societies.

This activity will allow the feelings and concerns of young people to flourish on the subject. Irvine Robertson, in his book What Cults Believe (1991) says that today cults can be classified into four groups:

1. Pseudo-Christian cults: Those that pretend to be Christian and are not. Although they use the Bible, they have very particular ways of interpreting it and even use other writings to which they put the same value as the Bible, and even consider them to be superior. They also claim to have the only source of salvation and that their leader has a new revelation.

2. Eastern cults: They are part of the movement that promotes "oriental mysticism," which is very fashionable, to be sure. The strongest roots are found in Buddhism and Hinduism. They try to make people look for "the truth" in themselves. The Bible is just one more sacred book and they believe in reincarnation, monism and that God is in everything and is everything.

3. Hindu Christian cults: These make a mixture between Christian doctrine and the teachings of Hinduism. Among them are Christian Science, Theosophy, Unitarians, among others.

4. Personality cults: They revolve around a leader or its founder. Many of these cults disappear with the death of their leader.

Connect | Navigate

One of the characteristics of the last times will be the emergence of false doctrines and false prophets or teachers who try to deceive people, both believers and non-believers. Another feature is that crowds will gather around these kinds of erroneous doctrines.

This has caused a great revival and appearance of false cults and doctrines in our times. Hence our responsibility as Christians to rise up as Defenders of the Faith, responsible for making known to a thirsty and lost world the true gospel of Jesus Christ, based on the teachings of the Bible (the only true and reliable word of God).

For this reason, we'll study what the Bible tells us about these erroneous doctrines and their false teachers. We'll see what the warnings are that God gives us, what is the mode of operation of these movements and what we should do as sons and daughters of God.

1. Deception

A basic characteristic of a cult is the lack of truth or the misrepresentation of the truth. The Bible tells us clearly that Jesus is the way of truth and life and that no one comes to the Father except through Him (John 14:6). This is interesting because the characteristic of a cult is precisely to distort the concept of who Christ is. Jesus Christ is God, Lord of all there is, the only source of salvation. Colossians 2:8 tells us, "See to it that no one takes you captive through hollow and deceptive philosophy, which depends on human tradition and the elemental spiritual forces of this world rather than on Christ."

A religious cult will always accompany this truth with something else that, according to them, is as necessary to achieve salvation. In other words, they will have some rite, doctrine or custom that is equal to Christ; or a group will have a religious leader who is equal or similar to Christ. That is, even when some cults know Jesus, they will always claim that something else is necessary to reach heaven.

Examples of some prerequisites to reach heaven established by these groups are: Hare Krishna - the Sabbath, doing good works, Mary, only Jehovah, Buddha, you yourself are your god, etc. Religious cults teach that salvation is obtained through Christ, plus their little variation or doctrine. Some cults don't recognize Christ at all! They may equal Christ with their teachers or with some "great man in history." The most efficient way to recognize a cult or religious cult is by identifying the way in which they consider Jesus Christ.

2. They don't believe in the Bible as a divine revelation

I Timothy 6:20 says, "Timothy, guard what has been entrusted to your care. Turn away from godless chatter and the opposing ideas of what is falsely called knowledge." This verse warns about deceivers who use vain philosophies, deceitful arguments and even false prophets. We currently see a number of books of false philosophies that are promoted much more than reading the Bible.

There are many cults and erroneous doctrines that don't claim to have a new truth, but have as their source the Bible. However, they make interpretations that go against the true meaning of the Scriptures; they usually take passages out of their context and arrange them according to their own opinions. According to them, they possess the only true way of interpreting the teachings of the Word of God. The Bible is not their only source of authority. In other words, they have other sources of authority that they consider on the same or even higher level than the Bible.

Many cults attack the teachings of biblical Christianity, arguing that the Christian church has moved away from true faith. Their doctrines constantly suffer variations, because their foundation is not solid. On many occasions, the leaders of the cults "inspired" by God dare to make predictions of the future, which are never fulfilled. Keep in mind that by their changing theology, they accommodate the meaning of their false prophecy by convenience.

3. Exalted concept of leadership

Colossians warns us of human traditions within these groups, and this is precisely because man is exalted in an exaggerated way. There are cults that have leaders who are the center of authority and believe themselves to be the messengers of God, so they are the only ones responsible for establishing "doctrine" and defining the behavior and course of the cult. This makes them people of great influence on the members of the cult.

Jeremiah 29:8 says, "Yes, this is what the LORD Almighty, the God of Israel, says, 'Do not let the prophets and diviners among you deceive you. Don't listen to the dreams you encourage them to have.' " Jeremiah 29:9 says, " 'They are prophesying lies to you in my name. I have not sent them,' declares the LORD."

Cults often center around a man or woman who try to gain power, money or influence by manipulating group members. They often try to instill fear in their followers. The 'believers' are constantly taught that their salvation is only obtained by remaining in that cult.

How to avoid falling into deception?

a. Join a strong Biblical church: A church where there is constant fellowship and Bible study; a biblical church and Christ-centered church that teaches that the Bible is the word of God for his people (Titus 2:1) and that Jesus Christ is the cornerstone of Christian and spiritual experience.

b. Examine and study seriously any offered teaching: In this sense, it's important that people take notes and then at home, take time to openly scrutinize, with seriousness and responsibility, the claims/teachings that have been made (1 Thessalonians 5:21).

c. Put aside feelings and try to be rational: In Romans 12:1-2 we find that our faith must be a rational faith; that is, a belief that can be articulated and presented in a reasoned and understandable way. As human beings, we have an emotional part. However, we shouldn't pretend to nourish our faith solely with emotional elements or with rare experiences; we must demystify the Christian experience and understand it with a balanced approach.

d. Help those who have fallen into the networks of religious deception: In Jude, verses 22 and 23 he speaks of the need to take action against deception and error, seeking to rescue those who have been prey to the teachings of cults and false religions.

True Christianity is the one that points out that the Bible is where we'll find God's truth for his people, and that the person of Jesus Christ is the center of our Christian and spiritual experience.

Characteristics of people prone to religious deception:

- They go in search of religious novelties: They are always looking for people coming from outside that bring new spiritual things or experiences to be "in tune with fashion."

- Their faith is too impressionable: They are highly emotional people, whose faith is based on things they see and that appeal to their emotions. Every miraculous or marvelous event must have a biblical basis; if it doesn't it shouldn't be accepted as a Christian.

- Tendency to look for hidden and dark things.

- Read books or writings of doubtful origin that open the door to spiritual confusion, or that question the truth of the Word of God.

- They constantly go from church to church and from group to group: they are constant pilgrims, instead of looking for and joining a bible-based Christ-centered church.

Review/Application

Divide your students into groups, assign them a cult that exists in your country and provide basic information about it. Let them discover the three characteristics mentioned in the development of the lesson about the cult:

- Deception
- The Bible
- The Leader

Ask them to make a chart that shows the difference between what they believe is the Church of Jesus Christ and what the cult that they were assigned believes.

This cult believes in ...	But as a Christian, I believe in ...

Encourage students to look up the Church of the Nazarene's Articles of Faith and memorize them. When they know what we believe, it's easier to distinguish what is not true. Ask them to memorize them to be able to share during the next class session.

New Age

Objective: That the students might get to know how to distinguish the characteristics of the New Age movement.

To memorize: "See to it that no one takes you captive through hollow and deceptive philosophy, which depends on human tradition and the elemental spiritual forces of this world rather than on Christ" (Colossians 2:8).

Warning
Start the class by citing the articles of faith of the church of the Nazarene and get the students to repeat them after you.

Accept

Connect | Navigate

Introductory activity (12-17 years)

- Instructions: Distribute a piece of paper for each student. The young people should write on one side of the paper a characteristic of themselves that is true and on the other side something that is false. When everyone finishes, they should read them aloud and the other students should discover which of the characteristics are true and which of the characteristics are false.

Comment that there is a movement that wants to present lies, trying to mix them with truths, and we must be careful not to be taken in by them.

Introductory activity (18-23 years)

- Instructions: Previously ask your students to bring a newspaper. Ask them to look in the newspaper for elements that speak about esotericism, yoga and oriental elements. Discuss how these practices have been incorporated into society.

Connect | Navigate

The New Age movement is not a cult, or a church, nor even a religion. It's a way of looking at life, a philosophy, a way of thinking and acting that many people and organizations have adopted to change the world according to certain beliefs they have in common. But it has no leader, nor rules, nor fixed doctrines, nor do they have a common discipline.

The New Age movement speaks of many things that touch our faith: God, creation, life, death, meditation, the sense of our existence, etc., but it's not a religion. It takes various aspects of many religions and also of science and literature and mixes them with a certain originality to give far fetched answers to the most important questions of human life. Sometimes it even uses Christian language to express ideas that are very contrary to Christianity.

In this lesson, we'll see what these people believe to avoid falling into deception.

1. What is the New Age Movement?

The New Age Movement has taken a variety of names including the Human Potential Movement, Third Force, Aquarian Conspiracy, Cosmic Consciousness and Cosmic Humanism. While most refer to it as the New Age Movement, many in the movement don't like that title, and many others wouldn't even consider themselves part of the movement, although they may practice many of the core beliefs of the New Age Movement.

Defining the New Age accurately is a difficult task for several reasons. First, the New Age Movement is a mix of many things and tries to unify them. The unifying factors are a shared ideology rather than an organizational structure.

Secondly, the New Age Movement is difficult to define because it emphasizes and encourages change. The New Age Movement is syncretistic, and therefore evolutionary in nature. Many proponents change their perspectives, so it's often difficult to define their main beliefs. We could say that New Age is a mixture of oriental philosophies, Hindu and even science. Beliefs have permeated even the medical and educational spheres.

2. Main beliefs of the New Age

Their basic belief is monism. Those of the New Age believe that "everything is one." Ultimately, there is no real difference between humans, animals, rocks, or even God. Any difference between these entities is only appearance, not real. A Christian vision of reality rejects the concept of monism (everything is God and God is in everything). The Bible teaches that God's creation is not an indivisible unit but a diversity of created things and beings. Creation is not unified in itself, but sustained by Christ, in whom "all things subsist" (Colossians 1:17).

- The belief in pantheism: Everything is god. All creation participates in the divine essence. All life (and even that which is not alive) has a spark of divinity inside. Christianity is theist, not pan-theist. Those of the New Age teach that God is an impersonal force, while the Bible teaches that God is an imminent, personal, triune and sovereign God. God is apart from His creation, instead of simply being a part of creation, as pantheism teaches.

- The belief that we are gods: The logical conclusion of the other two. If "everything is one" and "everything is god," then we should come to the conclusion that "we are gods." We, according to the New Age, are ignorant of our divinity. We are "gods in disguise." In fact, this was the deception that caused the fall of man (Genesis 3:4-5). Yes, we're created in the image of God (Genesis 1:26), and therefore we have dignity and power (Psalm 8), but at no time does this make us gods. Those of the New Age teach that we are gods, and therefore we have divinity within our humanity.
- The belief of reincarnation: Most New Age believe in some form of reincarnation. The Bible tells us clearly that this cannot be possible:, "Just as people are destined to die once, and after that to face judgment" (Hebrews 9:27). The Bible teaches the resurrection of the body (1 Corinthians 15), not the reincarnation of the soul. Likewise, the doctrine of karma is foreign to the gospel. Salvation comes from grace, not through works in this life (Ephesians 2:8-9) or in any supposed past life. We won't be reborn after death. Hebrews 9:27 clearly teaches that we'll only die once.
- The belief in moral relativism: Those of the New Age Movement think in terms of grays, instead of black and white. By denying the law of non-contradiction, those of the New Age will often believe that two opposing statements can be both true. Therefore, they will teach that "all religions are true" and that "there are many paths to God." We as Christians must be clear that only Jesus is the way to God (John 14:6). On the other hand, the Bible tells us to be "cold or hot," "light or darkness," "salty or tasteless."

When the doctrines of the New Age are examined, they are not really new at all. Many of these concepts can be found in a basic form in Genesis 3. Note these statements made to Eve in the Garden: "You will be like God" (pantheism), "You won't die" (reincarnation), "Your eyes will be opened" (change of conscience), and "Did God really say?" (moral relativism).

3.   Where do we see the influence of New Age?

- Literary infiltration: Nowadays New Age literature is excessive; by 1991, only in the US, there were 2,500 specialized bookstores, not counting the New Age sections in all bookstores, with 25,000 titles in circulation and growing rapidly, making this line a source of "big profits", according to the newspaper "Journal do Brazil."
- Audiovisual infiltration: The following influences are evident in movies, videos, video games, music and also in books and magazines: taste for terror, for the imaginary and fantasy, for the cosmic-magic, the ugly and monstrous, extra-sensorial experiences, para-psychological powers such as telepathy, communication with spirits through games such as the Ouija Board, trips to the afterlife, talismans, witches, witchcraft, etc. and some are even expressly satanic. Satanic films abound and are frequently broadcast on television.
- Infiltration by symbols: The satanic symbols can be seen abundantly in newspapers, magazines, art, advertising, television, movies, clothing, etc.
- Infiltration into music: The so-called "New Age Music," with the repetition of sounds in alternating sequences, is made to create atmospheres that lead the listener to a state of relaxation that favors the alteration of states of consciousness.
- Drugs: In the New Age Movement, drugs are used above all as a means to achieve, through the alteration of states of consciousness and the manipulation of the nervous system, alleged divining experiences.
- Progressive disregard to morality and the law of God: This is a form of infiltration evident in all sectors of society, through the media, both in fictional programs (novels, films) and in non-fiction (opinion programs, scientists, etc.).
- Faces of the New Age: Apparent acceptance of all religions; it doesn't go against any, but neither accepts any that is not pagan: Hinduism, Buddhism, Zen, Taoism. It introduces pagan beliefs (for example, reincarnation). In this way, if Christians "annex" these false doctrines and beliefs to our faith, we end up losing the true Faith. Thus, the Christian Faith is weakened and destroyed, which is one of the purposes the New Age wants to achieve: to integrate all religions in one.
- Search for health: A typical case is that of "universal energy" cures; also, "Transcendental Meditation" to achieve emotional and psychic balance. Practices such as yoga and acupuncture are classic examples of this.
- Search for ecology: True environmentalism seeks to conserve the planet and respects all forms of life, especially human life that has a value far superior to all others since man was made 'in the image and likeness of God'. The exaggerated environmentalism of the New Age says that man has the same worth as a whale or a forest or a tree. They come to regard mankind as the planet's worst enemy instead of seeing us as its guardian and administrator.

Review/Application

Individually or in small groups, have the students read the provided scriptures verses, and see which New Age belief it contradicts:

Scriptures	New Age Beliefs
Colossians 1:17	Reincarnation
1 Corinthians 15	Everyone is a god.
John 14:6	Monism
Genesis 3	All religions lead to God

Challenge your students to look around (at T.V., radio, businesses, in your own home, online, etc.) and spot the influences of the New Age Movement and share these with the class next week.

The Occult

Objective: That the students may be able to distinguish the characteristics of the occult to not get caught or deceived.

To memorize: "For our struggle is not against flesh and blood, but against the rulers, against the authorities, against the powers of this dark world and against the spiritual forces of evil in the heavenly realms" (Ephesians 6:12).

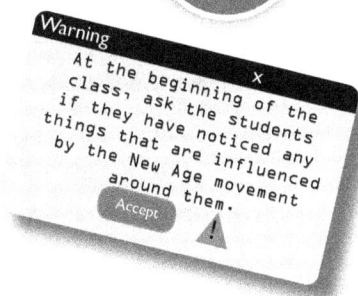

> **Warning** x
> At the beginning of the class, ask the students if they have noticed any things that are influenced by the New Age movement around them.
> Accept ⚠

Connect | Navigate

Introductory Activity (12-17 years)

- Instructions: Choose five young people who can tell a scary story or legend about their city. Take a story with you in case the young people don't know any. Get someone to surprise them by making a loud noise behind them at the back of the class to try to frighten them. You will notice that the majority will be frightened since they were paying attention to the dark story the others were sharing. Ask them why they think that people are fascinated with the occult.

Introductory Activity (18-23 years)

- Instructions: Present the following statistics to the young people: A research team carried out a study among 115 middle and high school students where they had to respond to this question. Do you want to know about occultism? The survey provided the following revealing statistics: more than half of the respondents (54%) said they have an interest in the occult and the supernatural world, and a quarter (26%) indicated that they are 'very interested.'

Discuss with the students why they believe that this phenomenon is occurring among young people. Does the supernatural exist? We live in an era in which people seek answers to the basic questions of life: What is the purpose of life? Is there life after death? Are there proofs of the existence of a supernatural God?

According to the Bible, there is a continual supernatural conflict (Ephesians 6:12). This present spiritual battle is between the kingdom of God and the kingdom of Satan.

Although the Scriptures make it clear that the supernatural is real, and that the spiritual struggle is still in place, there are some who would like to demystify what is said about the devil, demons, and demonic possession. But it's evident that the supernatural exists, because if we take the supernatural out of the Bible, we would have an empty gospel that lacks power and transforming life. Something that we should be very clear about is that it's a supernatural reality and it's very dangerous to try to infiltrate this totally spiritual world. That we have knowledge of their existence shouldn't create in us a desire to experience occult powers.

Connect | Navigate

The word "occultism" comes from the Latin word "occultus" and contains the idea of things that are hidden, and that are secret and mysterious.

1. What is meant by occultism?

We can mention three different characteristics of the occult:

a. To try out secret or hidden things.

b. It has to do with actions or events that seem to depend on human powers beyond the five senses.

c. It has to do with the supernatural, with the presence of spiritual forces.

Within the occult we can mention the following: sorcery, magic, palmistry, fortune-telling, divination, tarot cards, Satanism, Spiritism, demonism and the use of crystal balls. Undoubtedly, many more can be added to this list, but we'll look at these and others in this study.

The Bible condemns categorically, without exception, all occult practices. Deuteronomy 18:9-15 shows us very clearly how God commands all the people of Israel to not practice the occult, by passing their children through fire, divination or witchcraft etc., for these things are clearly an abomination to God.

Both the Old Testament and the New Testament condemn meddling in the occult (Galatians 5:20). At Ephesus, many of those who practiced occultism became believers in Jesus Christ and renounced their occult practices. "Likewise, many of those who had practiced magic brought their books and burned them before all ..." (Acts 19:19).

2. What does the occult apparently offer?

The occult offers several attractive things that anyone would want to possess. For this reason, because they are very attractive, many people are involved in this terrifying world of the occult. But what is occultism trying to offer?

Apparently, it offers:

a. Power: Logically this refers to a totally supernatural power because it crosses the boundaries of natural laws, this apparent power given by satanic forces is able to affect other people, physical elements and so on.

b. Knowledge of the unknown: Primarily of the supernatural and of future events. They (demons) are allowed to communicate with the dead and sometimes exercise authority over the dead who are really demons acting as people who have died.

c. Cure for diseases: They manage to bring about truly amazing cures, especially for psychic illnesses. Regularly these cures are carried out by witch doctors and shamans, as well as many others.

The supernatural can only come from two sources of power: the triune God or Satan. God uses his power to bless and to build up Christian people and for the salvation of the lost. In contrast, Satan creates confusion and ignorance to destroy us. Satan is deceitful, dresses up as an angel of light (2 Corinthians 11:14), and tries to involve in his evil occult network all sorts of people, even Christians.

3. What are some occult practices?

a. Divination

Divination seeks to know the past and future by hidden methods. As well as the past, Satan knows the present, he is spirit along with his angels and he is in different places even though he is not omnipresent. His demons help him to find out what is happening in the world, and he uses the fortune-tellers to create confusion.

No doubt divination is inspired by Satan. The devil tries to amaze people through fortune-tellers. For a child of God, future divination doesn't make sense because, besides being forbidden by God, our life is in His hands, the future for the children of God is safe. Divination makes use of several methods to deceive:

- Astrology: Alleged influence of the stars on the human destination.

- Cartomancy: Guessing the past, present and future through cards. The tarot is a set of special cards for divination.

- Palmistry: Guessing the future by reading the hands, palmistry is similar to the cartomancy because the goal is to guess the future but in a different way.

- Guessing something about the person when smelling objects belonging to him.

- Clairaudience: Listen to voices that appear inexplicably informed of what is happening or will happen to a person.

- Clairvoyance: Having visions related to knowing the past, present and future of a person. Most of the time they use a crystal ball.

- Necromancy: Guessing with the help of the spirits of the dead.

- Oneiromancy: Guessing through dreams. God gave the gift of interpreting dreams to Joseph and Daniel as special and particular cases to show the power of God. Satan uses this to deceive us. The fortune tellers have created a dictionary where each type of dream has its meaning. (Dreaming of: flood = bad luck, owls = deadly accident, rain = good luck).

- Oracles: Those fortune tellers who interpret flights and songs of birds or astronomical signs.

- Ouija: The Ouija board is sold in toy stores as a simple 'toy,' but it's so dangerous that the same occultists don't recommend using it for danger to be possessed by the spirits invoked.

- Psychometry: Guessing through personal objects of the person concerned.

- Dowsing rods: a type of divination employed in attempts to locate ground water, buried metals, may have some scientific support.

In 1 Chronicles 10:13-14, we can see the decision that God made regarding Saul for consulting a fortune-teller. This shows that God doesn't like divination, and consulting the fortune-tellers brings terrible consequences. He forbids going to the fortune tellers (Leviticus 19:31) and listening to them (Deuteronomy 13:1-5 and 10-11) God "sets his face" against "those who turn to mediums and spiritists" (Leviticus 20:6).

b. Spiritism

Spiritism has to do with the invocation of spirits of the dead. This practice is very dangerous because you can have a direct talk with some real demons. Satan is very cunning and does anything to deceive people into thinking they are talking to a deceased relative.

c. Spiritual Manifestations

These can be visions of apparitions, souls, spirits or ghosts of humans or animals in homes, factories, streets, cemeteries, hospitals, roads, etc. Many times, this may be due to a mere suggestion, or a hallucination, or mental disturbances, but we cannot omit the truth that often these are not mere suggestions but really manifestations of satanic spirits disguised as human kindness, or something terrible.

The Bible is very clear about this practice. Spiritism claims to invoke and speak directly with a spirit of a known dead person, be it a relative or not, and people who consult spiritists are deceived into thinking that they actually receive the message from their ancestor. But the truth is that according to the Bible, this is impossible. Hebrews says that "Just as people are destined to die once, and after that to face judgment" (9:27).

In the Bible, we find that all practices of Spiritism are an abomination to God (Deuteronomy 18:11), and according to Leviticus 20:27, those who invoke spirits of the dead deserve to be stoned.

d. Magic

The purpose of magic is to cause health or illness, love or rejection, good or bad luck, protection or damage, wealth, death, etc., by means of hidden methods. Some believe that magic can be white or black, "white is good and black is bad." The truth is that it's not possible to separate the one from the other, because both are influenced by Satan, since there are only two sources of power, from God or from Satan. The power of God is not manifested through magic but through the Holy Spirit. Satan uses black and white magic to divert men from the truth of God.

There is no doubt God doesn't like magic since it's one of the favorite weapons of Satan to deceive people so that they don't put their faith in God. The Bible is clear as to what God says about magic:

- Exodus 22:18 - God hates sorcerers.
- Deuteronomy 18:10 - God doesn't want sorcerers.
- Revelation 21:8 - Sorcerers will be thrown into the lake of fire.
- Leviticus 19:31 - God forbids going to enchantments.
- Leviticus 20:6 - God hates those who meet with occult practitioners.

Review/Application

Instruct your students to read the following biblical verses, and based on them, establish a biblical argument against the practices that are indicated.

Passages:

- Leviticus 20:6; Leviticus 20:27; Leviticus 19-31; Deuteronomy:18:10-11; Isaiah 47:9-10; 2 Kings 21:2,6, Acts 8:9-24; 13:4-12.

Practices:

- Witchcraft/Magic (Leviticus 19:31; 20:6; Deuteronomy 18:10-11)
- Spiritism (Leviticus 20:27; Deuteronomy 18:10-11)
- Divination (Leviticus 19:31; Deuteronomy 18:10-15; 2 Kings 21:2,6; Isaiah 47:9-10 and Acts 13:4-12)

Now motivate them to see how occultist beliefs have filtered in different ways throughout modern society, and this week, they should look around for occult influence and bring the information to the next class.

Satanism

Objective: That the students can identify the characteristics of Satanism so as not to fall into it.

To memorize: "And having disarmed the powers and authorities, he made a public spectacle of them, triumphing over them by the cross (Colossians 2:15).

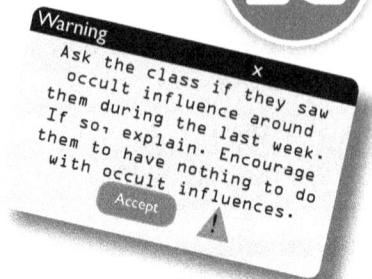

Warning
Ask the class if they saw occult influence around them during the last week. If so, explain. Encourage them to have nothing to do with occult influences.
Accept

Connect | Navigate

Introductory activity (12-17 years)
- Instructions: Form a circle with your students, having previously chosen three to five people. These three (or 5) must not reveal their identity or that they have been chosen as attackers. Tell everyone that within the group there are three or five enemies that will be killing with a wink. The attackers will be shooting at others with the wink of their eye. When they wink at someone and they realize that they "shot him," he must say "dead" and he must leave the game, but if any of the others discover the attackers they must say "I found the spy" and identify who the murderer is.

Introductory activity (18-23 years)
- Instructions: Discuss with the young people about the existence of satan, what they think about him and what they know about his work etc.

This study will serve to identify some of the enemy's tricks today. The Christians' enemy is Satan and his army of fallen angels. We have to oppose and struggle against spiritual forces, which are invisible.

What is an enemy? "A person or a force who is actively opposed or hostile to someone or something." The Hebrew word in the Old Testament means, "observer, or someone who is watching or observing with an attitude of criticism." The name of Satan means, "adversary or the one who accuses."

Very few people, both Christians and non-Christians, have a clear concept of who Satan is and his place in the world. Satan unleashes his destruction and ruin on marriages and relationships, families in churches, communities and nations. However, the Christian in his full armor can face it.

Connect | Navigate

Satan was a good being until the moment he wanted to exalt himself above God. His beauty filled him with pride, which led him to lose his sanctity. He wanted to receive the praise that only belonged to God. When Satan didn't recognize the authority of God, who had created him, he was thrown out of heaven (Isaiah 14:12-14 and Ezekiel 28:14-16).

The other time we see Satan, after having lost his place in heaven, is in the Garden of Eden, where he deceived Adam and Eve (Genesis 3:1-13), causing them to rebel against their Creator, marking the line of battle between the two kingdoms, the kingdom of light and the kingdom of darkness.

1. The names and strategies of the enemy

Let's examine some of Satan's names that we find in the Holy Scriptures, so we can understand better the character of this enemy. Many of these names not only reveal the nature and how our enemy is, but also shed light on the tactics of warfare used against the body of Christ.

Divide the students into groups and give each group a name with the passages. Ask them to explain how they would describe the enemy according to those passages.

- Devil: Matthew 4:5,8,11; Revelation 12:9, 12; 20:2. (Answer: They describe him as deceitful, cunning, knowledgeable and ancient.)

- Father of lies: John 8:44. (Answer: Murderer and liar.)

- The god of this age: 2 Corinthians 4:4. (Answer: blinds people to way of salvation.)

- Unfaithful or unbeliever: 2 Corinthians 6:15. (Answer: He has no relation with the Christian.)

- Angel of light: 2 Corinthians 11:14. (Answer: Deceiver)

- Enemy or avenger: Psalm 8:2. (Answer: Enemy and vengeful.)

- Adversary: 1 Peter 5:8. (Answer: Adversary who prowls around like a "roaring lion looking for someone to devour.")

His strategy

First, we must recognize that to fight against Satan must be done in the spiritual world. Spiritual things are discerned spiritually. We shouldn't try to understand them with human reasoning. You are not fighting against flesh and blood, but with the powers of darkness.

2. Satanism and various beliefs

Satanism

The worship of Satan has deep historical roots. Worshipping him, known as Satanism, is expressed in different ways. Black magic, black mass, certain aspects of the world of drugs, and blood sacrifices all have to do with Satanism. In Roberta Blankeship's book "Escape from Witchcraft", she recounts that in 1973 a corpse was found in the outskirts of Daytona Beach, Florida. It was the severed and mutilated body of a seventeen-year-old boy named Ross "Mike" Cochran. Information from the Associated Press news agency read: "The police verdict is that Cochran was a victim of Satan worshipers, and was killed in the midst of a frenetic sacrificial rite."

Satanism exerts other chilling and bloody rites, consisting mainly of sex clubs that are embellished with orgies with satanic rituals. Although the church of Satan sounds like a conceptual contradiction, this church was founded in San Francisco in the year of 1966 by Anton Szandor Lavey.

The black mass

It's perhaps one of the most chilling practices that Satanism has. A black mass is a gathering of Satan-worshipers who, led by one or more of their priests, commit acts outside of morality by turning their gatherings into orgies and lewdness while making sacrifices to Satan. A young Mexican acquaintance that in this study we'll call "Rigo" to keep his anonymity, recounts his personal experience of attending black masses and says, "Out of ignorance I was involved in a satanic sect in the city of Guadalajara, and I had many problems, including being possessed by more or less seven demons. In the mass, several people met together to worship Satan and we offered sacrifices to him. The most chilling thing I remember is having sacrificed a girl and an adult, offering them to Satan. Once we had made our offerings, we drank their blood and we ate their flesh. Now thanks to the help of many Christians, I was able to get away from that sect, and thanks to God I was able to receive the gift of eternal life. Now I know that I'm saved and that I will be with Jesus in heaven for eternity." 'Rigo' like many other young people, are involved in these satanic practices in ignorance. In the United States alone there are approximately 60,000 human sacrifices every year in black Masses.

3. The defeat of Satan at Calvary

What do the following passages tell us?

- "Just as Moses lifted up the snake in the wilderness, so the Son of Man must be lifted up" (John 3:14).

- "And having disarmed the powers and authorities, he made a public spectacle of them, triumphing over them by the cross" (Colossians 2:15).

- "Then I heard a loud voice in heaven say, 'Now have come the salvation and the power and the kingdom of our God and the authority of his Messiah. For the accuser of our brothers and sisters, who accuses them before our God day and night has been hurled down. They triumphed over him by the blood of the Lamb and by the word of their testimony; they didn't love their lives so much as to shrink from death' " (Rev. 12:10,11).

They show us that the cross was the means that God used to overcome the enemy of humanity. The only way we can be saved is through the suffering sacrifice of the death of Jesus on the cross, where his blood was shed for us.

There cannot be a permanent victory in the lives of the children of God until we can see and appreciate the fact that Satan was defeated on the cross of Calvary. The church of God, as a unit, cannot face satanic attacks if it doesn't first learn to submit to the power and victory that Calvary gives us as the clear testimony of the defeat of the devil.

The church of God is in its last battle and this means a last conflict with Satan. Facing this conflict from another point of view other than Calvary is impossible. Hence the need for the clearest possible understanding of how the Christian can exercise authority to obtain victory over satanic invasion. Around us we see the satanic powers growing, threatening to destroy everything in their path, and it's only through Christ that we can overcome them.

In Hebrews 2:14,15, we can see that the Cross has destroyed the power of Satan over man. Jesus by his death broke the "power of him who holds the power of death—that is, the devil."

Destroy him. Could we say anything stronger than that? In the Greek, destroy means "to leave without power or to put out of action."

Review/Application

Ask the students to look up the passages and discover the advantages that the children of God have over the enemy.

An enemy with no advantage:

1. 2 Thessalonians 3:3 (Christians are protected from Satan.)
2. 1 John 2:13 (Christians have defeated him.)
3. Luke 10:19 (Christians have power and are not harmed.)
4. 1 John 5:18 (Satan can't harm the righteous.)
5. James 4:7 (The Christian submitted to God has the power to resist Satan and make him flee.)
6. 1 Peter 5:8-9 (The devil is our adversary and wants to devour us, which we can resist through faith.)

Ask the students to look up the biblical passages and discover some recommendations that the Scriptures give us in order to not give a place in our lives to the devil.

Some recommendations:

1. Ephesians 4:26-27 (Don't give the Devil a foothold in your life.)
2. 2 Corinthians 2:10-11 (Forgiveness keeps us from falling under the power of Satan.)
3. Ephesians 6:11 (With all the armor on, we can stand firm against the traps of Satan.)
4. Romans 16:20 (God's grace and power is with us to defeat Satan.)
5. John 12:30-31 (Don't be afraid of Satan, because Jesus is more powerful than he is and will throw him out of your life and out of this world.)
6. 2 Thessalonians 2:8 (Satan's past, present and future is defeat.)

What a joy to be a child of God! Help students appreciate the gift of salvation that God has given them. Tell your students that this is a gift that we should share with those who are still trapped in devil's bonds. Share your testimony with someone who doesn't know Him.

Differences

Objective: That the students might know that our personality and character are a part of being created in the image of God as human beings.
To memorize: "Then God said, 'Let's make mankind in our image, in our likeness'" Genesis 1:26a.

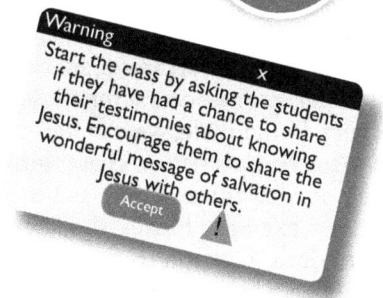

Warning
Start the class by asking the students if they have had a chance to share their testimonies about knowing Jesus. Encourage them to share the wonderful message of salvation in Jesus with others.
Accept

Connect Navigate

Introductory activity (12-17 years)
- Materials: Clippings from newspaper or magazines of the game "find the differences."
- Instructions: Divide the students into groups. Give each group a clipping and ask them to solve the puzzle. When they have finished, ask them what they would think if there were two places or two people in the world as similar as in the activity they just did?

   During the discussion, the issue of twins may arise or there may be twins in your class. You can take advantage of this situation to have them think about how they would feel knowing that there is another person so similar to them in the world.

   Then have them think about the biblical text that expresses that we have been made in the image of God.

Introductory activity (18-23 years)
- Materials: Cards and pencil.
- Instructions: Divide the class into two groups, and ask one group to make a list with characteristics of human beings and the other to make a list with characteristics of God. At the end, make a comparison of both lists, highlighting those that are repeated in the two lists. Then ask: What do you think the similarities are due to? And the differences?

   Did you know that people can be blinded by money? It's true! For money, people can stop seeing their relatives, stop seeing the people around them, stop seeing the world in need, a need that gets bigger every day and is all around us. But above all they cannot see the Word of God, and as a consequence, are a long way off from God's kingdom.

Considering how limited the human mind is, the memory verse can be surprising. As humans, we tend to see God as a supreme and distant being, and even though we establish a relationship with Him, it's difficult for us to think that He and us are not really very different, at least according to our original human nature. We have the same image ... we're similar. This means that we resemble God. Maybe up to now we have not taken much time to consider this truth and understand what it means for us today.

Connect Navigate

1. God's Creation

   All of God's creation is good (Genesis 1:31) and has a purpose. Human beings are not the exception. God planned us to be in His image and likeness. This means that God expected us to be like Him, "Then God said, 'Let's make mankind in our image, in our likeness' " (Genesis 1:26a).

   Unfortunately because of sin, some things changed in our human nature. Despite that, many years after the creation of man and woman, Paul claims God's purpose for us, "For we are God's handiwork, created in Christ Jesus to do good works, which God prepared in advance for us to do" (Ephesians 2:10).

   We're the most complex creation of God. Unlike the other creatures, God decided to give us qualities similar to those He has, which make it possible for us to have a will to decide and accomplish what we were created for.

2. Humans: personality and character

   When we see people, we notice that we're not the same. No person resembles another and therefore the idea that God designed us in his image can be confusing. We know that God is a Spirit and therefore the affirmation that man was made in the image and likeness of God goes far beyond a physical appearance. Our likeness to God refers rather to that which is immaterial (Genesis 1:26). From a biological point of view, it's easy to understand that all human beings are equal and function in a similar way, but when we explore further we realize that there can be a great number of differences between one person and another.

a. Personality

What makes a person different from others is their personality, which can be understood as the characteristics of each individual that define their behavior, their way of thinking and feeling, (introverted, extroverted, pessimistic, calm, controlled, passive, careful, sensitive, fickle, restless, sociable, etc.). Although there are specific personality classifications, each person has characteristics that are so unique to themselves that they are able to distinguish themselves from others. In the Bible, we can find characters with different personality types. We can even see how each of the disciples of Jesus had particular characteristics in their behavior, ways of feeling and thinking. We also note that regardless of their particularities, God used them to fulfill His purpose.

For example, Moses, the liberator of the people of Israel, and Peter, one of Jesus' disciples, were both men with a lot of determination to act. We could even point them out as impulsive or voluble, but God had a plan for them. Their personality helped them achieve God's purpose; their determination gave them the impetus to do great things for God.

Because of the size of the task that Noah received, we can see him as a very patient and dedicated man. Not everyone would be suitable for this task; the particular characteristics of Noah's personality allowed God to use him.

Jesus considered John, the beloved disciple, as the one who could take care of his mother. He had shown himself to be a careful, dedicated person who showed his love; these characteristics allowed Jesus to ask him to perform this specific task.

We have seen how different people are able to do something for God; up to this point it might seem difficult to understand how it's possible, since we're all so different, to be similar to God. But we must not forget that God is creative. Just as the body has many parts, each with a different function, each of the characteristics of the human personality can be used by God in different ways if we allow Him.

b. Character

One of the elements of personality is our character, which is specifically linked to the moral nature of a person and related to ethics and social context. Character represents the way a person reacts or their habits of behavior in the face of the circumstances they face. It's precisely through our character that we allow our personality to be used by God. It's then in this aspect as humans that it's important to reflect on our resemblance to God. Unfortunately, sin damaged aspects of God's original design in us, but we have the ability to change our character, and the work that God does in us allows this restoration.

Although our personalities can be diverse, that is, our way of thinking, feeling or the way we do things, our reactions are defined by our character. God needs people with different characteristics but all capable of self-control. He can use different people, regardless of their personality, as long as they allow their reactions to be controlled by God's will (Colossians 3:10).

A person can have an aggressive personality, but if he is able to show it in the right way and at the right time, God can use that characteristic to fulfill his purpose (Peter, Moses). In the same way, someone can be very serene and their way of reacting can also be timely (John). As long as our personality is subject to our own impulses, it will be difficult for others to see the likeness of God in us. Our task as Christians should be to imitate the character of God (Ephesians 4:13, 24).

In the case of Moses and Peter, we can clearly see how their lack of self-controll led them to commit actions that were not part of God's plan (for example, when Moses killed the Egyptian or when Peter cut off the Roman soldier's ear). Once they surrendered their will to God and acted with justice and holiness, knowing the truth, God used them to impact the history of His people.

Review/Application

Ask your students to discuss these questions in small groups or as a class:

1. How would you describe Peter after reading John 18:10-11? (As someone impulsive, who acts without much consideration for their actions, someone daring, perhaps courageous and challenging authority.)

2. What would be your description based on what Acts 2:13-15 says? (As someone determined, who defends and responds to others with actions and is not intimidated.)

3. There was not much time between one event and the other. What differences and similarities do you find between Peter's first reaction and the second? (Peter is still the same impulsive man, who responds to others according to what he thinks, without fear of what others say, although between the first event and the second his response is more accurate, presents a defense with more control, not aggressive but better.)

As you wrap up, motivate your students to make the necessary changes so that their reactions are more reflective of the righteous, holy and loving character of God.

Mirror, Mirror on the Wall

Warning

Before starting the class, ask the students if they have been thinking about areas of their character that might need changes.

Accept

Objective: That the students may learn the Christian concept of self-esteem.
To memorize: "The LORD doesn't look at the things people look at. People look at the outward appearance, but the LORD looks at the heart" (1 Samuel 16:7).

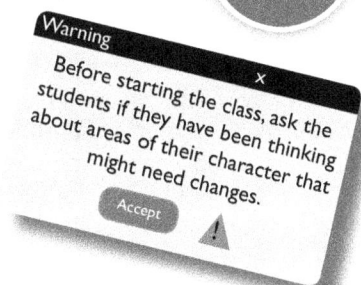

Connect | Navigate

Introductory activity (12-17 years)
- Materials: Magazines and newspapers.
- Instructions: Divide the class into two or three groups, and ask them to look for articles/photos of people they think might represent: an intelligent person, a builder, the next Miss Universe, the next president of their country, a doctor, a secretary and an athlete.

  At the end, ask them to present the chosen selections and discuss the reasons why they chose them. It's possible that some will make comments about what the news reports or articles said about these people. In other cases they will find that they chose what they did because the people had the appearance that they considered appropriate.

  Explain that in this activity, they judged people by appearance (unless the news explains who they are), and labelled them by appearance as well, but God doesn't do that with us.

Introductory activity (18-23 years)
- Materials: Paper and pencil.
- Instructions: Ask each of your students to write a description of the person on their right. Tell them that they won't have to reveal what they wrote.

  When they finish, ask them to think about what they wrote and discuss what they needed to know in order to write about that person. You will notice that those who know each other better will make a more complete description of the partner, and that those who don't know much will make a description only of the person's appearance.

  Explain that to correctly describe someone, you have to know more about them (tastes, desires, wants, etc), and not just about their appearance.

Connect | Navigate

The human tendency to concentrate on appearances has not changed much over the years. It's natural to look, and then from what we see, we make a judgment about something or someone. This situation places the image as the main evidence of quality; we see this with products and unfortunately, it happens when we deal with people. It's rewarding for all, regardless of appearance, to understand the way in which God sees us; perhaps until now your students have been considering values to determine who they are, which are not necessarily appropriate for developing correct Christian self-esteem.

1. What is self-esteem?

Self-esteem is the consideration, appreciation or value of one has of their self; the way in which people appreciate themselves determines their behavior. Therefore self-esteem is a very important aspect to take into account.

In Romans, the apostle Paul asks Christians to pay attention to the concept they have of themselves. His particular invitation is not to have a higher self-concept than one ought, "For by the grace given me I say to every one of you: Don't think of yourself more highly than you ought, but rather think of yourself with sober judgment, in accordance with the faith God has distributed to each of you. For just as each of us has one body with many members, and these members don't all have the same function, in Christ we, though many, form one body, and each member belongs to all the others" (Romans 12:3-5).

Since people act on the basis of what they think. Paul wanted to make sure that Christians were sure of the potential they possess so that they could develop their specific role within the body of Christ. The passage also mentions that it's God who gives each one gifts that enable them to fulfill their purpose.

The self-concept that a person has of themselves is determined by different factors. As Christians, God must be the most important factor to consider when defining our self-esteem.

2. How is self-esteem built?

During adolescence, people suffer from many changes, and this situation can cause anxiety because they are constantly comparing themselves with others to see if they 'measure up', which in their opinion, is the ideal. The comparisons they make will be mostly related to physical aspects which can directly affect their self-esteem. That is why it's important that the students know all the factors that determine who they are so that they can make an informed judgment.

a. Family

Our parents greatly influence the way we think about ourselves. Mainly during childhood, the value and view that parents have of their children is crucial, since children usually want to impress their parents and do the things they are expected to do. Parents can strengthen their children's self-esteem or weaken it.

You may notice among your students some who have received encouragement in their homes, and others who, on the other hand, have not been valued enough. If you know your students' parents, you may have a good idea of the type of adolescent you have in front of you. Let your students know that although their family has helped determine their concept of themselves, there are other things that they should consider.

b. Society

Another factor that influences our self-esteem is the environment in which we live. During adolescence, the opinion of peers (people of the same age) exerts more influence than that of adults. It's very likely that your students are now redefining their self-value based on peer pressure; not considering what their parents think of them as very important. It's very important that you emphasize the care that should be taken when choosing friends, as Paul recommends to Timothy in his letter (2 Tim. 3:2-5).

The values that society exalts define the standards that people aspire to; the students are exposed to all of this and for them it represents something which is very important. Exalting a certain style, fashion or appearance as necessary to stand out in the world is a situation that teenagers have to deal with. Paul writes in 2 Timothy 3:3,5 that loving yourself to the extreme and boasting are foolish attitudes that shouldn't be imitated. Your students should know that what society shouts at them shouldn't be what determines the value that they have of themselves.

C. God

By this point in the lesson your students have already considered many opinions that they have received, and have an idea about themselves; who they are and how much they value themselves. It's probable that until now, they have not thought much about God's opinion of them when determining their self-esteem. It's important that you remind them of the special care that he took in forming them (Genesis 1:27), and what is important to God (1 Samuel 16:7).

Some of your students will be facing difficult situations, and the image they have of themselves may not be correct; others may have paid too much attention to their appearance and at the moment it seems to be the only thing that counts. Remind them that the works of God are wonderful and formidable (Psalm 139:13-17), and that each one of them was planned by God for a special purpose (Ephesians 2:10). Let them see that what really matters is God's opinion of them; that is where they will find the right value and self-esteem.

3. A correct self-esteem

Problems of self-esteem are not only due to having a poor concept of themselves, but also to having a higher concept than what is real. Not having an adequate self-esteem causes difficulties in interpersonal relationships, in addition to diminishing the joy or ability to enjoy daily life. So, it's possible to feel superior or inferior to others. But an even greater problem occurs when the potential to serve God is affected by an incorrect self-concept.

A weak self-esteem is a source of insecurity. People who feel inferior to others are constantly comparing themselves with others. On the other hand, people with arrogant ideas about themselves don't develop all their potential because they don't consider it necessary. In the end, both situations are the result of focusing too much on ourselves and not considering what is really important: How God values us.

God designed us in a perfect plan and decided to give each of us a function, as long as we don't accept God's plan for our lives, we cannot fully enjoy everything for which we were created. Under this perspective, no one can say that he/she is less or more important than others since we all play a vital role in the building of God's kingdom (1 Corinthians 12:14-18).

Review/Application

1. How would you define self-esteem in your own words.
2. What do you think of yourself?
3. What do others (family, friends) think of you?
4. What does God think of you?
5. Are there any differences between what you, others, and God think of you? If so, why do those differences exist?
6. How does the opinion of others and of God affect the opinion that you have of yourself?

After your students have answered the questions, invite them to meditate on the concept they have of themselves and the ideas that they have allowed to define and value them. Remind them that only by looking in God's mirror can they have a correct idea about themselves.

Being Alone

Objective: That the students understand the meaning of being alone and loneliness.

To memorize: "Turn to me and be gracious to me, for I'm lonely and afflicted. The anguishes from my heart have increased; lift me out of my sorrows" (Psalm 25:16-17).

Warning
Ask the students if they have thought this week about how much God values them.

Accept   x

Connect | Navigate

Introductory activity (12-17 years)
- Materials: Sheets of paper on which are written the words "alone'" and "loneliness."
- Instructions: Glue or tape the sheets of paper with the word "alone" and others with the word "loneliness" in different parts of the classroom as decoration and to draw the students' attention. Form groups to reflect on the following questions: When do you feel alone? How do you feel when you are alone? Do you want to be alone? What do you understand by solitude?

  Once they have finished, ask each group to explain what they have said and then summarize.

Introductory activity (18-23 years)
- Materials: a large piece of paper and markers or a whiteboard. Sheets of paper for students to write on and pens.
- Instructions: Ask them to write on their paper two fears regarding the topic of loneliness. Then ask each person to read what they wrote without explaining it. Write up on a large paper or on the whiteboard your summary of their comments so that everyone can see what they are saying. Speed up this step and encourage students to make the effort to listen to each other. List the data, then ask the students to choose, from the list they gave, what got their attention or the impressed them most. Take a few minutes to analyze the fears.

  This activity will allow the feelings and concerns of the young people to surface on the topic of loneliness.

Connect | Navigate

Psychologists consider that someone is alone when they don't maintain communication with other people or when they perceive that their social relationships are not satisfactory.

The dictionary gives at least three definitions of what solitude is:
- Being lone in order to meditate and have an encounter with ourselves.
- We can be in a solitary place such as in a deserted place or uninhabited land.
- Sorrow and melancholy that is felt by the absence, death or loss of some person or thing: feeling helpless without the loved one or the thing we esteemed.

This last definition of loneliness is deep within those who suffer in this way. It cannot be seen, and is so profoundly imbedded in the affected person and it's difficult to get rid of this inner pain. Although this idea is very paradoxical among Christians, because at all times we know that God is with each one of us, there are times when we have felt that we're the most alone helpless beings. We see it in the cry of King David in Psalm 102, which is called 'an afflicted man's prayer.'

1. Alone and lonely

Actually, there are two types of loneliness: on a personal level (absence of an intimate relationship with someone) and on the social level (lack of friendships). Loneliness is an unpleasant experience for those who live it. Sometimes it can be accompanied by depressive elements, and in many occasions, it's confused with social isolation. Sometime they say that shy people are loners, but this is not true - they just have a reduced social group.

When our ability to relate is deficient, it increases the likelihood that we'll remain alone since the relationships we maintain are less enthusiastic, and others don't identify either mentally or emotionally with us.

However, there are certain people who are inclined to convince themselves that they are not worthy of being appreciated. They reject any kind of potential friends in order to protect themselves from possible rejection and distance themselves from others, although other people don't necessarily put a barrier between them. The most common definition of loneliness is lack of company, and that tends to be linked with states of sadness, lack of love and negativity and not seeing the benefits that occasionally come with solitude.

2. We are not alone

Young Christians cannot say that they are exempt from feeling lonely sometimes. We're imperfect human beings and we all fall prey to falling into weaknesses. We don't always have to carry our pain and suffering, because hope in Christ is greater than all adversity.

We have also seen in different passages several men of God walk through painful loneliness. The best example is David, crying out in different psalms, "Turn to me and be gracious to me, for I'm lonely and afflicted" (Psalm 25:16). "I'm like a desert owl, like an owl among the ruins. I lie awake; I have become like a bird alone on a roof" (Psalm 102:6-7). We see an afflicted David, perhaps sunk in a terrible sadness at being persecuted, without friends, without family close to him, and maybe even feeling helplessly separated from God himself.

We still see the pain of loneliness vividly embodied in Jesus Christ when he utters, " 'Eloi, Eloi, lema sabachthani?'" (which means 'My God, my God, why have you forsaken me?')" Mark 15:34. Clearly, we're not exempt from feeling lonely, helpless, afflicted, anguished and sad. But in those moments, the cry must be addressed to God.

In addition, a child of God - whether young or older - will rarely fall into chronic and depressive loneliness because they have brothers and sisters by their side, through whom God shows them His love and companionship.

When Jesus Christ rose from the dead and ascended to the right hand of God the Father, his disciples felt helpless and went to hide. Some returned to their work. But God sent the Holy Spirit to be with them and accompany them always.

Through his Word, God shows us that apart from sending us the Holy Spirit as our comforter, He left us in community within the church (Romans 12:15-16 and Philippians 2:2-4); we're a family. Through the church, we're called, among many other things, to be together, not only physically, but united in fraternal love, crying with those who mourn, laughing with those who laugh, watching over our brothers and sisters, accompanying them at all times. So, we're not alone; we are a body in Christ and as such, we must be intertwined in a bond of peace, love and companionship.

3. Personal encounter with God

Together with the church, there is someone more important who never leaves us nor forsakes us: Our God. It's true, many people endure pain and suffer from this chronic and painful loneliness. Many in their solitude have seen their lives sink to the point where they have even been admitted to psychiatric units, or have committed suicide.

However, many also in their solitude, have sought God and found him. Loneliness is also a moment of reflection, of knowing ourselves thoroughly and of being sincere with ourselves.

There is a time to communicate with others and a time to establish contact with the deepest part of ourselves ... in solitude. Today's culture doesn't put much value on being alone. Neither does it appreciate the benefits of separating some time to be alone with God. When we're alone with God, we can take an honest look inside ourselves to see faults that we must correct. It's in the sincere analysis of our actions that we find the weak points of our obedience to the Word of God. That's why someone said, "solitude is like going to the desert." There the naked motives of our soul are undressed, and the will of God becomes clear. The expression, 'desert' is used many times in Scriptures, not as a physical place, but as a life situation in which there is loneliness, sadness and pain. There are no vanities that trap the heart there. There, a person is alone with God and with himself.

Therefore, loneliness - as sadness - is an opportunity to grow in God, to hope in Him, so that the sweet and precious character of our beloved Lord Jesus Christ may be built up in us. Furthermore, we must know that in many difficult situations, God has brought us victories, and loneliness won't be the end when loneliness refers to moments of sadness and pain. Even in unwanted moments of loneliness, God will strengthen us, because his Word says that His power is perfected in our weakness. There is value in crying, going through sadness, desolation, feeling helplessness, and loneliness. But it's not okay to stay in our suffering, because we know who to turn to, to cry out to, and to hold on to - God.

Throughout our lives with God, sometimes we'll be standing, sometimes walking, but on other occasions we'll be down, or weak; but we're sure that we'll rise again and again, not because of our own strength or because we're very strong, but because our Heavenly Father has promised to help us.

Review/Application

Have the students complete the following statements (with their own words), and then discuss as a class if the want to.
1. There are three definitions of loneliness: the first is the lack of companionship, the second is about an isolated place and finally it's feeling of sorrow and _____. (melancholy)
2. In psychology, there are at least two types of solitude, the personal and the social. What does each of them consist of? (Personal: absence of an intimate relationship, Social: lack of friendships.)
3. When one wants and looks for ways to be alone, what is being done and what is being sought after as a Christian? (An honest look inside.)
4. How should young Christians face the feeling of loneliness, based on the example of David? (We must cry out to God.)

Talk to your students about the blessing of spending time alone with God. Help them to value solitude. Encourage them to separate a time alone with God next week.

Count to 10

Warning
Don't forget last week's challenge - ask the class to share about times spent alone with God during the last week.
Accept ⚠

Objective: That the students understand that anger is not a sin, but must be controlled.
To memorize: "Do not be quickly provoked in your spirit, for anger resides in the lap of fools" (Ecclesiastes 7:9).

Connect | Navigate

Introductory activity (12-17 years)
- Materials: A piece of paper for each student that has written on it an emotion: joy, sadness, anger, frustration, surprise, distrust, horror, etc. (considering the number of students, make sure that the same emotion is not repeated more than twice, except for the word "anger" that may appear more times to emphasize the lesson).
- Instructions: Give each student a piece of paper and ask them to not show it to others. Then one by one they will have to act out the emotion assigned to them; the rest have to discover what it is.

At the end, ask some of them how they felt. Let the students who acted out 'anger' speak at the end so everyone can discuss what anger makes them feel like. It's possible that some of your students who acted out anger expressed some violent actions such as hitting a chair or showing fists. Note this feature and comment on it.

Introductory Activity (18-23 years)
- Instructions: Read to your students the following excerpt from the story "Let the anger dry up" and then ask them to comment on it.
Let go of anger
Mariana was very happy to have been given a blue tea set as a gift. Julia, her little friend, came early to invite her to play. Mariana couldn't go, since she had to go out with her mother. Julia then asked Mariana to lend her the tea set.

Upon returning from the walk, Mariana was amazed to see her tea set lying on the floor. Some cups were missing and the tray was broken. Crying and very upset, Mariana rushed to her mom. "Do you see what Julia did to me? I lent her my tea set and she didn't take care of it."

Mariana wanted to go to Julia's house to ask for an explanation, but her mother said to her, "Do you remember that day when you went out with your new dress and a passing car splashed your clothes with mud? When you got home, you wanted to wash the dress immediately, but your grandma didn't let you. She said that you had to let the mud dry, because later it would be easier to remove the stain. Anger is the same - let anger dry up first, then it's much easier to deal with the problem."

Ask your students what they think about Mariana's mother's advice, and what results they have had when they let themselves be carried away by anger, and or when they decided to wait a little. Have you ever heard the phrase "when something angers you, count to ten before you answer"? This is a method that can help you avoid doing something that you will regret afterwards.

Connect | Navigate

Anger is a normal human emotion; it helps us recognize the effect that certain circumstances have on us and allows us to be alert to any threat to defend ourselves. The drawback with this emotion is not being able to control it, since out-of-control anger can be destructive and cause problems for ourselves and our relationships with others.

Although anger is an emotional state that varies in intensity, sometimes it can dominate us so much that we feel that it controls us and unleashes anger in us, causing us to react aggressively.

While anger is a natural human reaction, this doesn't imply that we can let it run loose and uncontrolled. The Bible urges us to not let anger dominate our actions and not give in to anger precipitously; before reacting, we must consider if the reason that provokes it's a correct one.

1. 'In your anger don't sin'
Anger is an emotion that can appear at any time. Paul's exhortation in Ephesians 4:26a, "In your anger don't sin," is at the same time a warning to the door that opens our anger. Many times when we're angry, we don't take time to think about what drives us to act. That's when we can easily react in ways that are not worthy of a Christian.

Proverbs 14:17 says, "A quick-tempered person does foolish things, and the one who devises evil schemes is hated." This reminds us that getting angry easily can cause us to do crazy things, that is, under the control of anger we can do things that we wouldn't do under normal circumstances. On the contrary, later in verse 29, the person who is slow to get angry or who don't let their anger dominate them is considered to be of great understanding.

Many times, anger is caused because some situation didn't turn out the way we wanted or planned it, or at the right time we wanted it to happen. As Christians, we should let it be the Holy Spirit who dominates us and not our foolishness. "Whoever is patient has great understanding, but one who is quick-tempered displays folly" (Proverbs 14:29).

At the moment of feeling angry, the best we can do is let patience control us and know that the will of God will work in the midst of that circumstance. We must think about what God wants us to learn at that moment.

Up to this point, we can understand that anger itself is not the problem, but what we do because of it.

2. "Do not let the sun go down while you are still angry"

After understanding that the problem with anger is in the possible sinful reactions we have, Paul makes a second recommendation, that we don't let anger last a long time, "Do not let the sun go down while you are still angry" (Ephesians 4:26b). Anger that lasts for a long time causes discomfort in the person, which can even be evident in physical discomfort. Anger that is kept in also causes our heart to hold a grudge against the person or situation that we face, and little by little, this can undermine and affect all the areas of our lives. Furthermore, maintaining anger for a long time makes our minds harbor bad thoughts or ideas that in themselves are sin, and that can also lead us to sin by doing wrong against the person or situation that unleashed this emotion. The longer we're angry, the harder it will be to avoid giving in to sin.

3. "Do not give the devil a foothold."

This following phrase in Ephesians 4:27, "... and don't give the devil a foothold," gives us the main reason why we should be careful with anger. This emotion can cause us to sin by opening the door of our lives to evil. Paul exhorts the church to live a different life, to leave behind their former way of life. Anger is a fairly common emotion, but it can have very powerful effects. That is why we must be careful of this emotion.

In Colossians 3:10, we find an invitation "to put on the new self, which is being renewed in knowledge in the image of its Creator." Often we react with anger at what displeases us, but God expects that, since we understand that getting angry is opening a door to sin, we must put anger aside and put on humility, mercy and patience to be able to offer forgiveness to those against whom we have some displeasure (Colossians 3:12-13).

4. Is it right to be angry?

It's important that we understand when it's ok to get angry. In the Bible, there are several passages that speak of the anger of God and Jesus. Both John 2:13-17 and Isaiah 12:1 speak of God's anger. He becomes displeased with disobedience and becomes angry when His children don't live as He expects them to live. Isaiah 57:16 says, "I won't accuse them forever, nor will I always be angry, for then they would faint away because of me - the very people I have created." God's anger doesn't last forever since He loves us and expects to see changes in our lives. So as Christians, our anger must be provoked by those things or situations that offend God, that are opposed to the truth.

In the Bible, we find the example of the prophet Jonah, he was offended by sin and evil in the people of Nineveh. Apparently, his anger was for a just cause. God had sent him to announce the destruction of that people, but the mercy of God caused Nineveh to receive forgiveness. Jonah was not satisfied and became even more angry. It's at that moment that God questions his anger (Jonah 4:4) that although at first was well intentioned, ended up dominating Jonah, making him incapable of loving and forgiving the people of Nineveh.

We must be very careful with the way in which we justify our anger. Although it's true that God expects us to raise our voices to defend the good, nothing justifies that we stop forgiving or doing good to others. Ephesians 4:32 says, "Be kind and compassionate to one another, forgiving each other, just as in Christ God forgave you." We must not lose sight that our emotions must be controlled by the Holy Spirit and not by our personal desire to achieve some selfish goal.

Review/Application

Ask your students to share what is meant by "don't give the devil a foothold," and then discuss together what are the right reasons to get angry. Make sure they are clear on the fact that God expects us to get angry at the things that offend Him, but that we are also capable of showing love and kindness to those who offend us. Invite them to consider their reactions when they feel anger, and to be willing to change them if they discover that they are not pleasing to God.

Read John 2:13-17 and answer the following questions:
1. How do you think Jesus felt when he saw what was happening in the temple?
2. What do you think was the reason for Jesus to feel this way? (verse 17)
3. Read Ephesians 4:26-27 and write down what "do not give the devil a foothold" means to you.
4. How do you react when you are angry?
5. Considering the two passages you read, what do you think are right reasons to get angry?

Talk about how we can learn to monitor our state of mind. Ask them to make a commitment to stay vigilant during the week and come to class next week with a report of their experiences.

Unequal Yoke

Objective: That the students might get to know what the consequences of an unequally yoked relationship are.

To memorize: "Do not be yoked together with unbelievers. For what do righteousness and wickedness have in common? Or what fellowship can light have with darkness?" (2 Corinthians 6:14)

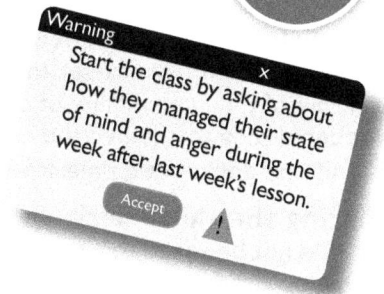

Warning

Start the class by asking about how they managed their state of mind and anger during the week after last week's lesson.

Accept

Connect | Navigate

Introductory activity (12-17 years)
- Materials: Prepare some slips of papers that have different names of animals (that make some sound that they can imitate such as: cow, chicken, frog, dog, etc.). Make two of each animal.
- Instructions: Give each student a slip of paper. They will read it in silence and then they must look for their fellow animal partner making only the sound of the animal.

  When they find their pair, they should stay together until everyone finds their partner.

  Reflect with them about creation. All creation was made with a purpose and with a system. Even among animals there was order about who they could relate to.

Introductory activity (18-23 years)
- Materials: Slips of paper written with the name of a city, make two of each (to start with)
- Instructions: Give each participant a paper with the name of a city (there will be two of each). All will look for their partner 'city' and talk about the meaning of the word 'yoke'. After a few seconds, the teacher will give out another slip of paper with the name of a city (this time there will be 4 of each), the 4 will come together and the dialogue will continue. Then, the same thing is done again but this time sips of paper with the same 8 cities are given out and once again they dialogue about the meaning of the word 'yoke'. Then the corresponding lesson can be given. If the group is small you can do it only twice.

The yoke concept that appears in this passage was used to unite two things or animals. In this verse it's being used metaphorically in relation to the union of two people.

Connect | Navigate

Deuteronomy 22:10 says, "Do not plow with an ox and a donkey yoked together." These animals are not of the same species, and they don't walk together with even steps. One of them will always be the heavier, and they don't have the same height. All of this would affect their trying to work together. They wouldn't be able to do work together successfully and it would probably end up in total chaos, tiring and risking the animals' health.

"Don't become partners with those who reject God. How can you make a partnership out of right and wrong? That's not partnership; that's war. Is light best friends with dark? Does Christ go strolling with the Devil? Do trust and mistrust hold hands? Who would think of setting up pagan idols in God's holy Temple? But that is exactly what we are, each of us a temple in whom God lives. God himself put it this way" (2 Corinthians 6:14, 15 MSG).

1. Unequal yoke in close friendships

John 17:15-16 says, "My prayer is not that you take them out of the world but that you protect them from the evil one. They are not of the world, even as I'm not of it." These verses clearly show us that we don't belong to this world, but we're in it. While we're in this world, we'll have to relate to the people who cohabit with us. It's part of the great commission, to go to the whole world to preach the gospel to every creature. That allows us to relate to different people in the commercial, family, and educational spheres, and to take advantage of these relationships to be witnesses and share the gospel so that they may believe in God.

But also, these verses clearly say that although we live in this world, we don't belong to it. The words of Jesus are clear in asking the Father to keep us from evil. Here is where we're warned about close relationships which may 'unequally yoke' us with our intimate friends. There is no problem in being friends with people who don't know the Lord, but definitely, we must reserve our friendships of trust to people who have their faith in Christ.

It's important to relate to different people and share some activities, but we should always keep in mind that if our faith is not compatible, we must be careful. For example, when a Christian has a problem and shares it with a friend who is not of his own faith, he will run the risk of receiving advice that goes against what the Bible and God want for him.

You must choose your friends very carefully; you must analyze if the friendship makes you a better son or daughter of God, or if, on the contrary, it's distancing you from Him. A true friendship will help you grow in your spiritual life. An 'unequal yoke', or to put it in another way, an unequal friendship, may slow down or halt the process of growth in your life, and very likely will lead you to move completely away from the Lord.

2. "Unequal yoke" with your boyfriend or girlfriend?

Although the context of the biblical passage of study doesn't specifically talk about courtship or marriage, the principle of the impossibility of communion between the believer and the unconverted is applicable. The yoke was the wooden device that joined the oxen while pulling the plow. In Deuteronomy, God told the Jews not to plow with one ox and one donkey at a time. It was an 'unequal yoke', painful for the animals and impractical for the owner.

Sharing the same faith

"Do not be yoked together with unbelievers. For what do righteousness and wickedness have in common? Or what fellowship can light have with darkness?" (2 Corinthians 6:14). We must not unite two different beliefs; that would lead to a spiritual, personal and marital failure, depending on two different opinions and points of view.

A relationship of courtship or marriage with people of other beliefs would have serious complications when deciding on their daily activities. One would have commitments in the church and the other, to different things. One would like to do something that for the other would be a breach of God's commandments and, in the specific case of marriage, which faith would the children follow?

In 1 Corinthians 7, the subject of marriage and the importance of this relationship are discussed. The apostle Paul also warns about the importance of marrying a person who shares the same faith as his or her partner. Paul warns that this difference can bring problems, but if they became Christians after being married, the situation is different, since they should always try to remain together. He says, "to the rest I say this (I, not the Lord): If any brother has a wife who is not a believer and she is willing to live with him, he must not divorce her. And if a woman has a husband who is not a believer and he is willing to live with her, she must not divorce him. For the unbelieving husband has been sanctified through his wife, and the unbelieving wife has been sanctified through her believing husband" (1 Corinthians 7:12-16).

We need to take into account that not only is it important for the other person to believe in God, but to share the same call to service for Him. Remember what the Word of God says in Amos 3:3 (MSG) "Do two people walk hand in hand if they aren't going to the same place?"

The Bible is specific in the comparison of light with darkness; they are total opposites, like wanting to mix water with oil! There will always be problems in a relationship of this kind. To establish a relationship of courtship, it's important to share the same faith, to share a similar level of emotional, physical and mental maturity with the other person.

Also, the students need to remember that it's important to analyze the opinions of their parents, pastors, church leaders and friends. Why? Because they will see things that these young people cannot see. Sometimes feelings interfere with reason and don't let us see aspects that others see.

Often, when we're in love, we lose objectivity, idealizing the other person. In the book, Don Quixote de la Mancha, Sancho says that when Don Quixote is in love, he looks through glasses that make copper look like gold, poverty look like wealth, and dusty tears like pearls. This is often true, since love blinds people, leading them to idealize their loved one.

This idealization causes many young people to see "signs" that their boyfriend or girlfriend is going to become a Christian like them. The sad thing is that they realize after years of marriage that it won't be easy, and they live lamenting having not heeded the warning of the "unequal yoke."

Let's look at some misleading phrases that people use to justify the unequal yoke:

*   It will happen ... he/she will become a Christian. I have faith.
*   We would suffer a lot if we ended the relationship. And God doesn't like to see us suffer.
*   It would be a bad testimony to break up with him/her.
*   He/She doesn't mind that I go to church.
*   My relationship with the Lord is personal. He/She doesn't have to share my faith.
*   At my age, there are no single believers. The Lord understands this.
*   My boyfriend/girlfriend is a better person than a lot of Christians I have met.
*   He/She has not been born again, but they believe in God.
*   He/She promised that when we get married, they will go with me to church.

Don't be fooled, don't justify the sentimental relationship you have; the Bible is clear - don't be unequally yoked with unbelievers.

Review/Application

Build an acrostic with the word UNEQUAL. They must write words or phrases related to the lesson.

Next, give them a few minutes to write down a list of their friends. Ask them to analyze during the week each of their relationships and determine if they are constructive or destructive for them.

All for Jesus

Objective: That the students learn that because of Christ, many times we'll be rejected and even persecuted, but God promises not to leave us.
To memorize: "Blessed are you when people insult you, persecute you and falsely say all kinds of evil against you because of me" (Matthew 5:11).

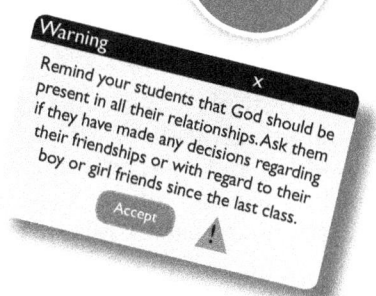

Warning
Remind your students that God should be present in all their relationships. Ask them if they have made any decisions regarding their friendships or with regard to their boy or girl friends since the last class.
Accept

Connect / Navigate

Introductory activity (12-17 years)

• Instructions: You will need one or two volunteers. The rest of the participants will form a circle, intertwining their arms tightly (elbow to elbow). The volunteer or volunteers must remain outside the circle, and when the order is given, they should try to convince or force the other participants to allow them to enter the circle. The boys and girls who form the circle will do everything possible to prevent the person or people who are outside from entering.

At the end of the game, ask the those who were on the outside how they felt when trying to enter the circle and saw that the other participants didn't allow them.

Then ask the rest of the group, if they have ever felt rejected by a group for one reason or other? Share answers before developing the topic.

Introductory activity (18-23 years)

• Instructions: The following list contains some phrases that the students could choose if they would be willing to risk being rejected or persecuted. Participants should sort the list by priority, using the values from 1 to 10, (higher scores for the situations for which they would definitely take the risk and lower ones for which they would not).

_____ Show my disagreement with my parents at having to clean my room
_____ Defend a family member
_____ Reject an invitation to drink alcohol
_____ Go to a football game with people my friends don't like.
_____ Defend my honor in front of the girl / boy I like
_____ Refrain from having extra marital sex
_____ Defend my Christian faith
_____ Help a friend who is being treated unfairly
_____ Fight against racial discrimination
_____ Rebelling against the way my girlfriend or boyfriend wants me to dress

Have them share the different ways they prioritized the phrases and why.

Connect / Navigate

Young people often accept the challenge of living the Christian life in their home, school or work. Without a doubt, they start out with the best intentions in the world, and with a commitment that we can describe as real. But then, something happens, something they didn't count on. They realize that maybe they were not ready to give up something, at least to the extent that they thought. They don't like to be rejected, they like to feel part of the group, and it seems that the only thing their new way of living has brought them is to be teased, rejected and even persecuted. These young people can feel discouraged, making them think that living the Christian life is impossible, and they may well ask themselves, "Is it worth it? Will I be the only one who suffers like this?"

1. The cost of following Jesus

When we read in the Gospels the way Jesus invited people to follow him, we realize that He was always very clear. He knew that around him there were people grateful for the miracles he had done among them, but He didn't want them to just follow him for the signs or the food they received. Neither did he want them following him simply so that they could escape from the punishment of hell. He wanted them to follow Him for who He Himself was. That is the great difference between Christianity and other religions: we follow one person, Jesus. That is what it means to be a Christian: a full and continuous relationship of love and obedience to Jesus.

Jesus makes it clear that having a full relationship with Him would mean that many would make fun of us, telling us that we're crazy, rejecting us, and that it could even mean giving up our lives (Luke 9:23). For the people of the time when Jesus expressed these words, the illustration of the cross was very clear; it meant suffering and death. This came to reinforce what Jesus said at the beginning of his ministry in the Sermon on the Mount in Matthew 5:11-12.

Does this mean that the Christian life is synonymous with suffering? No, on the contrary, if we read with care and as Jesus described it, it's synonymous with joy, happiness and peace, because even in the midst of suffering and rejection, our reward and hope are much greater. The most important thing that gives meaning to how we see our lives is that we're doing it for someone who is worthwhile to follow, someone who loves us so much that he gave his own life for us!

We have no doubt that rejection is a natural consequence of our decision to follow Jesus. When we lived far from God, our way of acting was according to the parameters or rules of a world, rebelling against the will of God. So, when we converted from that sinful life, we made a commitment to live according to God's will. For this reason, now our lifestyle may make many people around us uncomfortable since they don't live according to God's purpose. We ourselves become a mirror that confronts them and makes them see their reality. For that reason, many prefer to stand aside, insult us, mock us and do many other things in an attempt to escape from their reality and not to be exposed by light. Ask the students if they have received any kind of rejection or ridicule for being a Christian.

2. How to overcome rejection

After having spoken a little about the cost of following Jesus, we need to ask a question, "Should Christians be afraid of rejection?" I will try to answer this question, using the phrase 'denying oneself'. This requirement doesn't mean that we stop being human, with all that this implies. Our denial is not to satisfy our desires or needs in a selfish way, because now our desire is to be like Jesus. This means that we still have needs and desires, like any human being; but now we want and are committed to satisfying them within God's will. To socialize is a natural need. We're social beings by nature (Genesis 2:18) and for that reason, we like to be and feel part of a group. In a special way, adolescents and young people want to be accepted and appreciated by their peers. So many times, conflicts rise up between being accepted by the group, and confessing and living their faith in Christ. This may cause some frustration or fear for them. Many times, the fear that others won't accept them for who they are, for what they think or how they act, leads them to hide their relationship with Christ. Do you remember what Peter did when they asked him if he knew Jesus? He was afraid of being connected to Jesus! But hold on a moment. We ourselves have gone through that situation! To a lesser or greater degree, we all have that fear of rejection, and the only way to overcome it's to be aware that we have something greater than this fear.

Below are some tips that can help young people focus their minds and hearts correctly. Write on the whiteboard or sheets of paper these four tips so that the students can visualize and comment about putting each one into practice.

a. Recognize that even if friends or colleagues in school or work reject us for living a real and active relationship with Christ, we must remember that we're accepted and liked by someone much greater than them ... GOD (Acts 5:29). The approval of God is more important than that of men.

b. Be convinced that even if we're mocked, insulted and even receive physical abuse, none of that compares with the satisfaction of knowing that we have suffered for the love of Christ and the hope of an eternity with Him (Matthew 5:11-12). It's worth it being rejected for following Christ.

c. Have the conviction that God himself, through his Holy Spirit in us, is giving us the necessary courage, the opportune consolation, and the joy and peace that no one but God can give. Also, we're not alone. There are many other people who are part of our same team and are suffering because of Christ (1 Peter 5:9). God is with us and gives us courage to resist. There are many Christians like us who suffer for Christ.

d. By being radical in our relationship with Christ, we'll realize that not everyone will reject us. On the contrary, there will be many who won't only respect us, but will come to us because they know that we have something they need and that they may have been looking for for a long time. Something for which it's worth living and dying for! (Matthew 5:16) Many respect us and value us for daring to be different.

Being rejected is not easy to handle. However, despite the difficulty of following Jesus, the history of the church is full of people who gave themselves to Jesus, people who were willing to live and die for Him. These people didn't conform to the world in which they lived, but remained firm as they saw what is invisible (Hebrews 11 and 12). They were disciples who could shout at the top of their lungs that it was worth taking the risk; men and women who testified that having found Jesus and having made the decision to follow him was the best thing they could have made.

Once we come face to face with Jesus, there is no turning back. We cannot do it, we really don't want to do it. How can one leave a friendship relationship with someone who gave his own life for us and who is with us every moment! Once Jesus opens our heart and we begin to know the mystery of our relationship with Him, we must decide that there is no going back, despite being rejected. We can sum it in this sentence: It's good to follow Jesus!

Let's always live with this reality in our hearts and keep in mind the promise given by Jesus himself: "I have told you these things, so that in me you may have peace. In this world, you will have trouble. But take heart! I have overcome the world" (John 16:33).

Invite the group to reflect on the problems they face as a result of living their faith in Christ, whether at school, work or even in the family.

Review/Application

To get the most out of the time, divide the group into three teams. Each team will be assigned a passage. They must read the passage, determine what the situation/pressure was, how they handled it, and what the consequences of their decision was.

- Genesis 39 (Joseph fled from Potiphar's wife and went to jail.)
- Daniel 3 (Daniel's friends, Shadrach, Meshach and Abednego, didn't kneel before the golden statue and were thrown into the fiery furnace.)
- Acts 4:1-21 (John and Peter didn't shut up and went to jail).

Talk with the students about the rejection we can experience when we follow Christ. Challenge them to answer the questions and make a decision.

True Love

Objective: That the students learn about the concept of true love and its characteristics.
To memorize: "Whoever doesn't love doesn't know God, because God is love" (1 John 4:8).

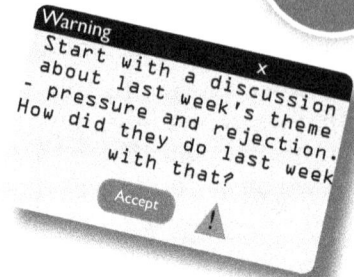

Warning
Start with a discussion about last week's theme – pressure and rejection. How did they do last week with that?

Accept

Connect | Navigate

Introductory activity (12-17 years)
- Materials: A handkerchief or scarf to blindfold the eyes and several objects of different shapes and sizes.
- Instructions: Ask one of your students to volunteer for this activity, bind their eyes up and ask them to identify the objects through touch, describing them and then trying to name them. Make sure that there are some objects that are easy to recognize and others that cannot be recognized because they are confusing (it could be some ceramic ornament or some kitchen utensil or some bit of office equipment that is not familiar to your students).

At the end, generate a discussion with your students about what made it easier for some objects to be identified and others not. Surely some comments will revolve around the idea that it's easier to recognize objects with which you are more familiar. Especially emphasize this idea. The better you know something (love in this case), the easier it will be to identify it in different circumstances.

Introductory activity (18-23 years)
- Instructions: Through this activity, try to know what ideas your students have about love.

Ask them to share what they think about the following phrases: "Love is blind" and "Love and having a cough cannot be hidden."

Your students' comments will be useful in helping you to understand how they value love, what love is and what it's not for them, and what they expect from someone they love.

Connect | Navigate

Talking about love can be somewhat complicated; society sells us new ideas but we need to be clear about God's original idea about love. Your students are constantly being bombarded by situations that equate love with sex, giving gifts or satisfying their own desires or whims or those of the person they love.

The Bible tells us that the only way we can know love is through God. Many of your students may be very clear about this idea, but others may be feeling frustrated that they are not receiving the love they want from their parents, their friends or their boy/girlfriend. Many of them have experienced rejection. Other students are likely to think they know what love is because they are enjoying their relationships with others.

1. What is love?

Answering this question is not a simple task; surely there are many notions that your students don't yet understand, but it's very important that you can provide them with a foundation for the criteria they will develop in their life regarding love. Remember that your life experience is different from theirs and also, you are sure of your walk with God.

If we go to the Scriptures, they tell us that "God is love." It's interesting to see that God doesn't have love or give love ... He is love. 1 John 4:8,16 says, "Whoever doesn't love doesn't know God, because God is love…And so we know and rely on the love God has for us. God is love. Whoever lives in love lives in God, and God in them."

Love is a decision. We decide to love or not love someone. Love doesn't depend on our mood or circumstances. We can see this more clearly when, for example, we get angry with our parents or our best friend but this doesn't determine whether we love this person or not. True love remains despite the misunderstandings and difficult circumstances. We can observe this in practical ways, for example, parents who work to give an education and provide for their children, a young woman who stays awake to help her friend study, a young man who respects his girlfriend at all times, etc. We cannot say that we love, and then do nothing for the person we love when he/she needs us or is unhappy. The greatest example of this we see is God who gave his son so that we can be saved and have eternal life according to John 3:16.

If we talk about God's sort of love, circumstances don't define love or at least they should not. A person can be happy, sad, angry and this doesn't determine the love he feels for others. A person can be busy, rested, relaxed or pressured and this shouldn't make him or her love someone more or less.

Be sure to make this point clear to your students; this will help them to be more attentive to how to identify love in our characters as something which goes beyond feelings, emotions or circumstances.

2. Characteristics of love

In I Corinthians 13, Paul says, "If I speak in the tongues of men or of angels, but don't have love, I'm only a resounding gong or a clanging cymbal. If I have the gift of prophecy and can fathom all mysteries and all knowledge, and if I have a faith that can move mountains, but don't have love, I'm nothing. If I give all I possess to the poor and give over my body to hardship that I may boast, but don't have love, I gain nothing. Love is patient, love is kind. It doesn't envy, it doesn't boast, it's not proud. It doesn't dishonor others, it's not self-seeking, it's not easily angered, it keeps no record of wrongs. Love doesn't delight in evil but rejoices with the truth. It always protects, always trusts, always hopes, always perseveres. Love never fails. But where there are prophecies, they will cease; where there are tongues, they will be stilled; where there is knowledge, it will pass away. For we know in part and we prophesy in part, but when completeness comes, what is in part disappears. When I was a child, I talked like a child, I thought like a child, I reasoned like a child. When I became a man, I put the ways of childhood behind me. For now, we see only a reflection as in a mirror; then we shall see face to face. Now I know in part; then I shall know fully, even as I'm fully known. And now these three remain: faith, hope and love. But the greatest of these is love."

Paul is speaking to the church as a body, and he defines what true love is. It's interesting to see the characteristics of this love. Paul clarifies that love is a verb of action.

Ask students to read I Corinthians 13 and write the characteristics that Paul mentions regarding love (long-suffering, kind, not envious or boastful, not puffed up, doesn't do anything wrong, doesn't seek his own, is not irritated, doesn't hold a grudge, doesn't enjoy injustice, enjoys the truth, suffers everything, believes it, waits for it and endures it, and the main one is that love never ceases to be).

The truth about love is well known, we have to show it. Couples talk about "the test of love"; commerce takes advantage of important dates telling us that we need to give a really expensive gift as a symbol of love. Although these ideas are not based on correct motives, the reality is that love can be demonstrated and in fact shouldn't be hidden.

When someone loves, there are characteristics in their lives that cannot be ignored. In the passage that we previously saw about love (I Corinthians 13), Paul encourged the Corinthians to consider love as the main motivation for doing things, and that beyond just performing "good actions," we should develop attitudes from within to support these actions.

Have your students look at each of the characteristics described in I Corinthians 13:4-8. They all require a commitment from the one who loves to perform them. This list represents direct actions in search of the well-being of the person who is loved; love is not for our own often selfish benefits. True love is not just 'feeling good' or obtaining personal pleasure. According to the apostle, love is seen in relation to the one we love and their well-being.

3. The Scope of Love

Surely all your students will agree that the greatest sign of love we have received is from God, sending Jesus into the world to die for us (John 3:16). It's very simple to think that whenever we want to find evidence of love, we turn to God. On the other hand, when we become Christians, we ourselves are are invited to demonstrate the love of God.

In John's first letter, we find an exhortation to love. John reminds us that showing love is the most real evidence that we're children of God and that we have a new life. "Dear friends, since God so loved us, we also ought to love one another. No one has ever seen God; but if we love one another, God lives in us and his love is made complete in us. This is how we know that we live in him and he in us: He has given us of his Spirit. And we have seen and testify that the Father has sent his Son to be the Savior of the world. If anyone acknowledges that Jesus is the Son of God, God lives in them and they in God. And so, we know and rely on the love God has for us. God is love. Whoever lives in love lives in God, and God in them. This is how love is made complete among us so that we'll have confidence on the day of judgment: In this world, we're like Jesus. There is no fear in love. But perfect love drives out fear, because fear has to do with punishment. The one who fears is not made perfect in love" (I John 4:11-18).

In I John 3:16-18, he reminds us that love should move us to do something for others. It's not just words but it requires actions ... we must love as Jesus did. Love is not an unpleasant sacrifice. If we live close to God, He is the one who pours out his love in us and allows us to show it to others. Also, in God's love, we can also find personal benefits, because it produces in us, security and trust (I John 4:17-18).

Review/Application

Have each student write their own version of I Corinthians 13 according to the realities of their context. They can do it from some verses that you choose or from the whole passage.

Ouch, it hurts!

Objective: That the students might understand that physical death is part of life, and also as Christians it's the step towards eternal life, so it is not necessary to see it as tragic and extremely painful event.
To memorize: Jesus said to her, "I'm the resurrection and the life. The one who believes in me will live, even though they die; and whoever lives by believing in me will never die. Do you believe this?" (John 11:25-26).

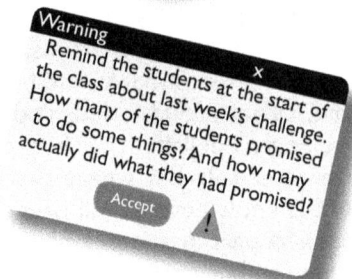

Warning
Remind the students at the start of the class about last week's challenge. How many of the students promised to do some things? And how many actually did what they had promised?
Accept

Connect | Navigate

Introductory activity (12-17 years)
- Materials: Whiteboard or large sheets of paper, markers, pens, pieces of paper for all.
- Instructions: Draw on the board a boat with its crew sailing in the sea. Explain that the crew is composed of a doctor, an engineer, an athlete, a thief, a drug addict, a Christian, a teacher, an alcoholic, a teenager, an older person, etc. (As a teacher, you have the freedom to make up the crew that would attract the attention of your group). The boat continues its course and suddenly the ship is shipwrecked. They manage to take out a small boat in which only two people can fit, one to drive it and another crew member. The question for the group is, which two participants should be saved, and why would you save them? They need to write the answer on their sheet of paper. Then allow them to express what they wrote. Try to reach a conclusion with the whole group.

This activity will help them to know what type of people they would leave to die and what motivates them to save others.

Introductory activity (18-23 years)
- Materials: Sheets of paper or cardboard, felt tip pens or colored pencils.
- Instructions: Ask everyone to draw a symbol about what makes them think about the subject of "death." After a few seconds, form small groups and give them time to interpret the symbols between them. Then ask each group to draw a symbol trying to collect elements from all their group members. Finally, each group will show their symbol or symbols and the others will try to interpret them.

This activity will allow you to know what concept they have about the subject of death, whether it's the traditional one or if they include something about what God says about death or how they relate to it.

We see in this passage how Jesus broadly explains to Martha the theme of eternal life. Jesus reminds her of the thought that physical death is the end of every human being, but God in his infinite mercy gives us eternal life.

However, everyone knows that before the death of a loved one a moment of pain has to be crossed. It's common to hear the advice, 'you have to work through your time of sorrow.' That is why our lesson will deal with the subject of mourning the loss of a loved one. Although it seems that when we face the death of a loved ones the world comes crashing down around us, God gives us this promises that the dead in Christ will rise to eternal life, (1 Thessalonians 4:16), but in those sad moments we seem to forget this.

Connect | Navigate

For young people, it's very rare to think about how to face the loss of a loved one, and about physical death itself. The writer Max Scheler says, "people today no longer live facing death, and it comes brutally before us as a wall with which we unexpectedly stumble into in the dark." The theme of death is a taboo, and also there are slogans like, 'live every day as if it were the last.' But what do Christians think when someone close to them dies?

1. How do Christians view death?
There are different psychological trends that offer therapeutic help to people who have had the experience of the death of loved ones so they can get through the period of mourning. In other words, they can be helped to accept that the person won't return and that they can live conscious of their loss, a void left by the loved one who died. So, it's important that they give themselves the opportunity to go through grief, because they are living the loss of someone who was appreciated and with whom they shared experiences and dreams. In this period of intense pain, the person is confronted with the fact that life is short. That can be painful, but it's part of the cycle of life. But these conclusions don't bring peace, because finally there is only a resignation to the inevitable, but not a serene acceptance of death.

Christians need to accept death because God gave us a great promise in the words of Jesus, "And if I go and prepare a place for you, I will come back and take you to be with me that you also may be where I am" (John 14:3). By faith, we believe in the resurrection of the dead, that Jesus Christ will return for his children and also that the bodies of the righteous as well as of the unjust will be risen from the dead and will receive a just judgment (Matthew 25:31-46). Physical death becomes the last step towards eternal life.

Before dying, people without Christ feel dejected because they have no hope. So, we have to ask ourselves the following question: Are we truly prepared to receive eternal life? Are our loved ones ready to face death? If the answer is positive we must affirm the Word of God that tells us, "Very truly I tell you, whoever obeys my word will never see death" (John 8:51).

2. What is grief?

We try to live to the fullest even though every year flies by; time swallows us up and we strive to experience and do many things before the time of our death arrives. This end is inescapable, although young people are not often conscious of this reality. Because the world thinks that death is equivalent to the end of each person's existence, there is suffering, crying and pain at each loss. So, we need to talk about grief. Some romantic writers talk about grief as "the daughter of death." They see it this way because it's the process that people have to experience, and with it there will be an emotional response to the loss of someone or something. But mourning the death of a loved one is one of the most harrowing experiences and causes the deepest and most lasting feelings because the loss is seen as irreversible. Although Christians don't see death as the end, separation from the one we love is always painful.

Many doctors and specialists talk about the six stages of grief. These don't necessarily always follow a set chronological process because they vary from one person to another person. The stages are the following:

a. Denial, which is a defense mechanism we employ in situations that are intolerable; People use this as a way out. They don't accept what has happened. That say 'it cannot be,' 'I cannot believe it.'

b. Anger - Often the questions are asked, "why did he have to die?", "Why now?" etc. Such questions have no answers, and in the face of such powerlessness, the person sees his surroundings in an aggressive and impatient manner.

c. Making a pact or negotiation is the attempt, often unproductive, to try to stop grieving, feeling, or crying, or to postpone the traumatic event, that is, to put limits on pain, perhaps with specific times to cry. "I won't cry anymore," "I won't think about it anymore," etc.

d. Depression, known as a deep sadness, which it's very difficult to overcome, and brings physical consequences, loss of appetite, sleep and behavioral disorders or pain; the mourner is completely overcome by sadness.

e. Acceptance, when the person finally admits that the loved one is not going to return or won't recover.

f. Hope is the security that they can go ahead and manage their lives, overcoming their sorrow.

3. How should Christians grieve?

The main time that we're aware that we're going to die someday is when someone else dies. It's at that moment when we realize that death is a part of life, that sooner or later we'll have to die too. The question is, how will we face the death of a loved one? As Christians, we have the option to grieve. But we must walk through this world very aware that "If we live, we live for the Lord; and if we die, we die for the Lord. So, whether we live or die, we belong to the Lord" (Romans 14:8). Thus, physical death becomes a means of entering the eternal presence of God. Therefore, mourning becomes for us the acceptance of the departure of our loved ones who have gone to the Lord's presence.

Until Jesus comes back, his church must continue proclaiming the gospel and must obey our divine Master's teachings by living a holy life. We must share the gospel with our loved ones, and if they are ready, we can say with the psalmist, "Precious in the sight of the LORD is the death of his faithful servants" (Psalm 116:15). Does God see with pleasure the physical death of our loved ones? Yes, for if they are his saints, he will be waiting for them to enjoy eternity with Him.

Christians and non-Christians must live through the grief for those we love. But if our loved ones are in Christ, we have an extra hope, which is to know that they are not just disappearing, but passing into the presence of our beloved God. Out of love for the lost, we need to lead them to Jesus' feet, so they won't suffer the true death: which is spiritual death, and is irreparable.

As young Christians, you are called to face physical death with integrity because you have the Comforter who reminds you and guides you to all truth. Of course, this doesn't mean that you shouldn't mourn or grieve. Tears were placed by God to express feelings and vent our anguish. John 11:35 tells us that Jesus wept at the death of his friend Lazarus.

We're called to share the gospel so that others can have that assurance of salvation when they face death. We should live thinking about what James 5:19-20 urges us to do: "My brothers and sisters, if one of you should wander from the truth and someone should bring that person back, remember this: Whoever turns a sinner from the error of their way will save them from death and cover over a multitude of sins." So when we have to, we'll face mourning and grief with peace and calmness that our loved one will soon be in the presence of God. And if the death of someone else confronts us with our own death, let's know joyfully that we'll follow a wonderful destiny: eternal life and glory!

Review/Application

Individually or as a class, have your students list out and briefly explain the 6 stages of grief.

Share a few moments about the importance of being prepared to face death. Challenge your students to memorize the six steps of grieving.

Option or Command?

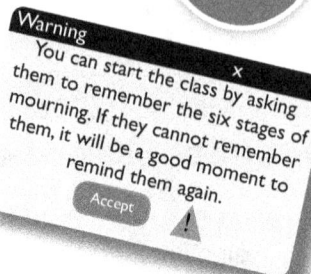

Zeida Lynch • Argentina

Lesson 44

Warning
You can start the class by asking them to remember the six stages of mourning. If they cannot remember them, it will be a good moment to remind them again.

Accept

Objective: That the students can understand that forgiveness is not an option, it's a mandate from the Lord.
To memorize: "Forgive us our sins, for we also forgive everyone who sins against us" (Luke 11:4a).

Connect › Navigate

Introductory activity (12-17 years)
- Instructions: Ask the students to act out the biblical passage found in Matthew 18:23-35. The teacher will encourage the students to decide who will be participating. The characters are: Jesus, the king, the first debtor, the second debtor, the friends, the officials. Allow your students to use their imagination and creativity to recreate this biblical passage. Then start the lesson.

Introductory activity (18-23 years)
- Instructions: Divide the class into groups and ask them to read the passage found in Matthew 18:23-35. Then have them think of a contemporary story that resembles the one Jesus told and ask them to share it with the group.

  This will help you see how they view the issue of forgiveness in their daily lives.

Many times, the bitterness and hatred that people have start with small problems that were not solved in time. When we exercise forgiveness on a constant basis, we prevent small wounds from growing and turning into diseases that can kill us. Jesus was very clear in teaching us about the importance of forgiving those who offend us. For young people, it's a very delicate area because they are discovering new ways of relating to their parents, siblings, relatives, friends, etc. And many times, they are hurting but they don't dare speak about it, and they don't practice asking for forgiveness or forgiving others.

Connect Navigate ›

Forgiveness is a subject to which Jesus paid special attention. But why do we need to forgive? Forgiveness is necessary in order to restore a broken relationship. When we intentionally or unintentionally do something that offends our neighbor, the relationship is affected, trust is lost and friendship is often lost. It's at that point that we need to forgive or ask for forgiveness. God commands us to forgive (Matthew 6:14-15) and be at peace with all (Hebrews 12:14).

Where does forgiveness originate? Forgiveness has its origin in the redeeming love of God for humanity. When Adam and Eve broke the relationship that existed with God because of disobedience, God didn't leave them in the same situation. Along with the punishment there was a promise of restoration and redemption. We can say that forgiveness is born out of the merciful heart of God. He has always been willing to reestablish his relationship with humanity. Christ came and gave his life for that purpose. He sent his Holy Spirit so that we can enjoy that holy relationship with Him.

1. God and forgiveness

In Matthew 18:23-27, Jesus related the following parable: "Therefore, the kingdom of heaven is like a king who wanted to settle accounts with his servants. As he began the settlement, a man who owed him ten thousand bags of gold was brought to him. Since he was not able to pay, the master ordered that he and his wife and his children and all that he had be sold to repay the debt. At this the servant fell on his knees before him. 'Be patient with me,' he begged, 'and I will pay back everything.' The servant's master took pity on him, canceled the debt and let him go."

The king called his servants to come to him to settle their accounts with him. In the same way, God calls us today to be accountable to Him. Have your students experienced God's forgiveness in their lives? It's interesting to note that God is the one who calls his servants to account. He now calls us all to be accountable to Him.

William Barclay's Commentary on Matthew says that the debt that this servant had "would be superior to the budget of a province of the time. The total income of the province that included Idumea, Judea and Samaria wouldn't have been any more than 600 talents and this man owed 10,0000 talents" (p. 227). That debt couldn't be paid. In the same way, there is no way we can settle accounts with God. The offenses that we have committed against Him because of our sin are unpayable. There is no big or small sin, white, red or green sin. Nor is there the possibility of being exempt from the nature of sin. We have all sinned and we are far from the glory of God.

What would be the punishment for not paying the debt? The punishment for not paying the debt was the loss of his family and all his assets. That left the servant in a worse situation. The punishment that humanity deserves for sin is eternal death. Not only physical death, but eternal separation from God.

What was the king's attitude? The king's attitude was based on mercy ... he forgave him and let him go. Not only did he forgive the debt, but he also spared him from punishment.

In the same way that the king showed mercy and forgave the servant, God in his infinite mercy forgives us through Christ. When he calls us to judgment, our debt to God is unpayable. There is nothing that we can do to make us deserve God's forgiveness. The Bible tells us that the wages of sin is death. However, God in his infinite mercy forgives us and frees us from punishment, because Christ already paid the price for our sins on the cross. His forgiveness is not based on our actions. His forgiveness is free and restorative.

Ask the students if they have experienced God's forgiveness in their lives. Lead them in a time of prayer and invite them to renew their commitment to God. If some have not accepted Jesus as their Savior, this is the time to invite them to do so. At the same time, give the opportunity to others who for some reason have moved away from the Lord and need to come back to Him.

2. Forgiveness and Us

In Matthew 18:28-33 we read, "But when that servant went out, he found one of his fellow servants who owed him a hundred silver coins. He grabbed him and began to choke him. 'Pay back what you owe me!' he demanded. His fellow servant fell to his knees and begged him, 'Be patient with me, and I will pay it back.' But he refused. Instead, he went off and had the man thrown into prison until he could pay the debt. When the other servants saw what had happened, they were outraged and went and told their master everything that had happened. Then the master called the servant in. 'You wicked servant,' he said. 'I canceled all that debt of yours because you begged me to. Shouldn't you have had mercy on your fellow servant just as I had on you?'"

The servant who had been forgiven found a friend who had a debt to him.

a. The passage tells us that when he left his meeting with the king, he looked for a friend who owed him money.

b. This debt was 100 denarii, which was not any way near to the amount of debt he had with the king.

c. The attitude towards his friend was the opposite of that which the king had showed him. He threw his friend in jail.

d. The king was immediately notified of what had happened.

e. The king had hoped that the servant's attitude would had been one of mercy towards his fellow servants.

God expects us, especially those who have been forgiven by Him, to act in the same way to those who offend us. The forgiveness that God requires of us is more than just saying it with words. It's an attitude that must spring from a merciful heart. We get a compassionate merciful heart when we let Christ reign fully in our hearts. To forgive our neighbor is to do what the king did, pay the debt, let the person go free and not to hold it against them anymore.

Maybe we won't forget what they have done to us, but we can remember it without causing us pain and without feeling badly against the other person. When that happens, we'll have forgiven. For young people, it's very common to become disillusioned with parents, and this affects their relationship with them.

Guide them to seek God's help to forgive. Highlight the fact that the king in the biblical story demands mercy from the servant to his friend. In the same way, God asks us to be merciful to those who have offended us. It's not a matter of who was or is right, or who was or is at fault, it's a question of extending mercy to that person and obeying what God asks of us.

3. Consequences of not forgiving

Matthew 18:34-35 continues, "In anger his master handed him over to the jailers to be tortured until he should pay back all he owed. 'This is how my heavenly Father will treat each of you unless you forgive your brother or sister from your heart.'"

He tells us that the punishment for the first servant was fatal. He was sent to prison until he paid all his debt. As we saw in the beginning, that was impossible because the debt was very, very large. That servant suffered eternal punishment.

Jesus finishes with the conclusion that the same will happen to us if we don't forgive. Forgiveness is not just a matter of choice or decision, it's a very clear commandment from Jesus. But at the same time, only He can help us fulfill it. Forgiveness is the product of our relationship with Him. Many times, our Christian life is impeded from advancing because of this issue of forgiveness.

Review/Application

Have your students write their ideas about the following questions and share them with the group.

1. What does Jesus say about forgiveness in Matthew 6:12? (We must forgive so that God will forgive us.)

2. What will happen if we think that something they did to us is unforgivable and we don't forgive according to Matthew 6:15? (If we don't forgive those who offend us, God won't forgive us.)

3. Do you think that the magnitude of the offenses we receive are greater than those we do against God? (No)

4. According to Jesus in Matthew 18:21-22, how many times must you forgive offenses? (Every time I get offended, I must forgive.)

Let them express themselves freely about this topic in a group discussion.

Then give cards to your students and ask them to write names of people who have offended them and who they have not yet forgiven. Encourage your students to examine their own lives and identify people they need to forgive and ask for forgiveness.

Guide them to meditate for a moment on the type of offenses they have received. Indicate that these cards are private. Have a special moment of prayer asking for God's help for their lives in this area.

Then ask your students to take time to pray and be able to forgive the people who have offended them, and then rip up the cards as a sign that they will endeavor to forgive them with the help of God. If they have a chance, tell them that it would be good if they could also go to these people and ask for their personal forgiveness.

Fear the Enemy within

Objective: That the students learn that fear is the opposite of faith and that it limits us in trying to achieve our goals.
To memorize: "Peace I leave with you; my peace I give you. I don't give to you as the world gives. Do not let your hearts be troubled and don't be afraid" (John 14:27).

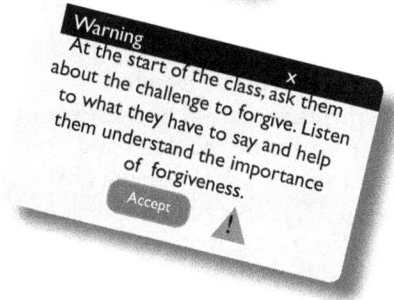

Warning
At the start of the class, ask them about the challenge to forgive. Listen to what they have to say and help them understand the importance of forgiveness.
Accept

Connect / Navigate

Introductory activity (12-17 years)
- Instructions: Ask each student what things they would do or not do out of fear? Listen carefully to each of the things they mention, and then point out how some situations that scare us are a warning, preventing us from danger, and on other occasions fear stops us from achieving something good. For example, ask them if they remember being told by their mothers 'Don't play with fire' and they disobeyed and burned themselves. They probably learned their lesson and were afraid to touch fire again? That kind of fear is a normal fear that protects us from danger. Emphasize that the sort of fear which this class is about is the fear that doesn't let us move towards a goal because we're afraid of failing.

Introductory activity (18-23 years)
- Instructions: Ask your students to share situations in which they have felt fear. Let them share their experiences After three or four stories, help your students to see how fear can prevent us from taking certain actions, that sometimes we're saved from harm, also how in some cases, fear is an obstacle to achieving a goal. Let them see also that sometimes, one goes through situations that must be faced in spite of being afraid.

Connect / Navigate

Although fear is a natural human emotion resulting from a perceived threat which puts us of the defensive, Jesus encouraged his disciples to not allow fear to dominate their hearts. What they were going to face was going to be difficult, but Jesus knew that if they allowed fear to paralyze them, they wouldn't be able to accomplish the task. Jesus offered his disciples His peace as a resource to ensure that their hearts wouldn't be governed by fear. When Jesus commissions us, he promises that he will be with us. "Therefore, go and make disciples of all nations, baptizing them in the name of the Father and of the Son and of the Holy Spirit, and teaching them to obey everything I have commanded you. And surely, I'm with you always, to the very end of the age" (Matthew 28:19-20).

1. What is fear?

"Adam answered, 'I heard you in the garden, and I was afraid because I was naked; so, I hid.'" (Genesis 3:10). Fear is an emotion provoked normally by the presence or expectation of a threat. Usually, fear causes us to defend ourselves to avoid danger.

The first time the Bible tells us about fear is in the book of Genesis after Adam and Eve disobeyed God. According to the definition of fear as a normal reaction to circumstances, Adam was afraid of what could happen to him and opted to defend himself, hiding from God. It's interesting to consider the relationship that exists between sin and feeling afraid. Up until that moment Adam and Eve had enjoyed a perfect relationship of trust with God; their disobedience made them experience a new sensation - fear. God's plan is that we should be free from fear.

In many cases, fear prevents us from achieving our goals, and becomes an enemy within us that doesn't allow us to develop faith, directly attacking our trust in God. God has a purpose for each of us; if we want to be faithful disciples, we need to face fear and act with courage in doing his will.

2. Jesus invites us to not be afraid

Jesus knew that his disciples would have to live through difficult situations which could directly affect their faith by making them fearful. In John 14, Jesus offers us an alternative to a fearful heart.

a. Believe in Jesus
Jesus said, "Don't let your hearts be troubled. You believe in God; believe also in me… And I will ask the Father, and he will give you another advocate to help you and be with you forever" (John 14:1,16).

As Christians, the first step is to believe in God (v. 1). Jesus invited his disciples to believe in Him, and in this way, receive the help they would need. Jesus never put his disciples' feelings to one side; he knew that they received great support through his presence, but he also knew that He would soon have to leave.

We can understand an important principle from Jesus' invitation not to be afraid: When God asks us to do something, he also equips us to achieve it. Jesus wanted his disciples to keep their commitment to him; he knew that what they would have to face wouldn't be easy, and knowing their hearts, he promised them that he wouldn't leave them alone (v.16).

b. Receive His peace

Jesus promised them, "Peace I leave with you; my peace I give you. I don't give to you as the world gives. Don't let your hearts be troubled and don't be afraid" (John 14:27).

When we feel fear, we change, we cannot think clearly and our impulses react, making us take unnecessary risks. In verse 27, Jesus offers a valuable gift to his disciples as an antidote against fear: His peace.

The peace that Jesus offers is meant to guard our hearts from fear. Feeling calm allows us to not stray from our purposes. If we want to do God's will, we'll have to face many difficult situations, but Jesus offers us His peace to support us in those circumstances. A heart troubled by fear focuses on what ails it and not on the goal it wants to achieve.

c. How to overcome fear

Paul told Timothy, "For the Spirit God gave us doesn't make us timid, but gives us power, love and self-discipline" (2 Timothy 1:7). The best way to overcome fear is by confronting it with the truth and the promises that God has for us in His Word.

After Jesus' death, the disciples' hearts were hurt by their loss. John tells us how afraid the disciples were: they feared the Jews and locked themselves in the upper room. "On the evening of that first day of the week, when the disciples were together, with the doors locked for fear of the Jewish leaders, Jesus came and stood among them and said, 'Peace be with you!'" (John 20:19). Jesus appeared before them, and seeing that they had forgotten what he had told them, he reminded them saying, 'Peace be with you.' Seeing Jesus again was a great relief for the disciples and a reason for great rejoicing. Once the disciples abandoned fear, Jesus was ready to send them out to do God's will. His commission included the promise of the Holy Spirit who would give them the power they needed to face any circumstance as they carried out their task for God (John 20:22-23).

Throughout history and even today, Jesus' disciples have had to face adversities in order to fulfill God's call on their lives. For the first disciples, the path was not simple; many of them gave their lives for their faith in God and were willing to sacrifice many things to defend their convictions. Without doubt, this attitude required putting fear aside. The key to those heroes of the faith was to believe in the promises that the Lord Jesus had given them. These promises removed all fear and injected courage into their lives, helping them face every circumstance. Today too, we must believe in the promises of our God.

In his second letter to Timothy, Paul reminds us that God has not given us a spirit of cowardice that prevents us from fulfilling his mandate. On the contrary, each time we feel fear beginning to invade our hearts, we're invited to overcome it with the spirit of power, love and self-control (2 Timothy 1:7). As long as there is sin in our lives, we'll experience the opposite of what Paul tells us. Instead of power, there will be weakness due to fear and cowardice. Instead of love, there will be resentment, which is also a product of fear. And instead of self-control, there will be a lack of control of our emotions and actions. This will lead us to be enslaved by our fears and will prevent us from fulfilling our purpose in God. But if we are in Christ, "in all these things we're more than conquerors through him who loved us" (Romans 8:37).

Review/Application

Fear is an enemy of faith that prevents us from resting in God. The peace that Jesus offers us is our best ally for overcoming fear.

Take time to identify your fears by completing the following sentences:

1. I'm afraid of _____

2. I feel scared when _____

3. It scares me when I think of _____

In 2 Timothy 1:7, it says that God has given us a spirit of power, love and self-control. Read the following verses and relate them to each of your previous answers and discover how power, love and self-control help you overcome your fears:

- 2 Corinthians 12:9
- 1 John 4:18

End by taking a few minutes to make a list of the fears that each person in the class has and ask the students to make a commitment to face them according to the Bible.

Created for a Purpose

Sara Cetino • Guatemala

Objective: That the students can understand that God created us with a purpose.

To memorize: "The Lord will work out his plans for my life—for your loving-kindness, Lord, continues forever. Don't abandon me—for you made me" (Psalm 138:8, Living Bible version).

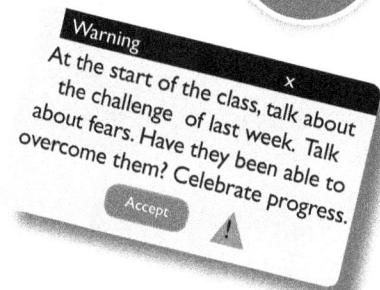

Warning
At the start of the class, talk about the challenge of last week. Talk about fears. Have they been able to overcome them? Celebrate progress.

Accept

Connect | Navigate

Introductory activity (12-17 years)

- Instructions: Students will be asked to answer the following questions:
  1. Do you work or study?
  2. Do you practice any sport?
  3. What would you like to be doing in 10 years?
  4. What personal dream would you like to achieve?

  Then ask each student, or some of them, if the group is too large, to share their answers in front of the class. Each time a student answers a question asked by the teacher, the rest of the students must ask follow up question to their answers. For example, for the question 'do you work or study?' if the student answers that they study, they can ask: 'What do you study?' 'Do you enjoy studying?' 'Is what you are studying for going to help you later on in life?' etc. The objective is to verify that the person is convinced that what he/she is doing is going to help them achieve what they what in life.

Introductory activity (18-23 years)

- Materials: Cards and pencils.
- Instructions: The teacher will ask the students to answer the following questions:
  1. What are your plans for this year?
  2. What are your plans for the next 3 years?
  3. What are your plans for the next 5 years?
  4. What are your plans for the next 10 years?

  Encourage everyone to respond. After having answered the questions, each (or some if the group is very large) should explain their response. The teacher should try to obtain as much information as possible to find out if the students have a life purpose.

The Bible states that we are God's creation. In the book of Genesis, we read how God was preparing the 'stage' for his most important creation: mankind. God had a purpose when he created us. Ask your students if they know the purpose for which they were created.

Connect | Navigate

Why did God create us? Many people think that we were created to fill the world with important people who could carry out specific tasks; just as Paul was created to take the gospel to the Gentiles; or Gandhi to bring freedom to the Indian nation. Others think that we were created to contribute to the development of society or to the world. For example, Thomas Edison was created to invent the light bulb, and thanks to him we can have light in our homes. Others think that we were created to reproduce, to procreate children, to love them, to take care of them and to establish a family.

1. We are God's creation

What if we don't do important tasks like those described above, or if we don't get married or have children. Have we failed in achieving the purpose for which we're here on earth? So, we must come back to the question, "Why did God create us?" Why would God bother to create someone who has not been able to go to school, or someone who has not achieved anything special, or contributed to society in a remarkable way? The word "purpose" means: the reason for which something is done or created or for which something exists. When we say that we are God's creation, we mean that God intended to create us. He didn't create us by accident.

Chapters 1 and 2 of Genesis narrate the creation of the world and all that dwells in it. Mankind was the wonderful and culminating work of God. Genesis 1:27 tells us that both man and woman were created by God.

From then on, we understand from the Bible that we are all God's creation, formed by Him (Psalm 139:15-16). There is no reason to believe that we were born by accident. Our birth was not by chance, or carelessness or a miscalculation. We're part of God's plan, and he has a purpose for our life. "The Lord will work out his plans for my life—for your loving-kindness, Lord, continues forever. Don't abandon me—for you made me" (Psalm 138:8, TLB).

2. Created to have communion with God

God created us with the purpose of having communion with Him, of having a relationship with Him, of sharing all that we are with Him. "What were we created for?" We were created to have communion with God and to live in a very intimate relationship with Him, to be like Him. We were created with that main purpose. If you achieve many things in this life, that is wonderful, but that is not the main reason for your existence. If you help many people, good! But you were not created just for that. If you invent something that will benefit society, Excellent! But you were not created primarily for that.

God wants us to live in communion with him. His desire is that we have His salvation, live according to his commandments, and maintain an intimate communion with him. "The LORD confides in those who fear him; he makes his covenant known to them." (Psalm 25:14, see also Proverbs 3:32b, James 4:8)

3. Created for a purpose

In Ephesians 1:3-6, we can see that God created us to praise Him. That is the reason for our existence. We no longer have to ask "Why did God create us?" We were created to bring glory to God, to praise God.

In Romans 8:28 we read, "And we know that in all things God works for the good of those who love him, who have been called according to his purpose." What is that purpose? He wants us to become like Jesus. God allows things to happen in our lives to fulfill that purpose.

Apart from the general purpose, God created each person with a specific purpose in this life. God has given us different talents and abilities. The important thing is not only knowing that we can fulfill a purpose, but being clear that God didn't create us by chance. God created us for a reason and in our struggle to achieve it, He will take care of us and won't forsake us.

Our life goes through several cycles. We start in childhood and little by little, we have to make decisions about our future. We have to face questions like "What will I study?" "Where will I work?" "Who will I marry?" (among others). In each of these questions, we must seek God's will to fulfill his purpose for our life. Whatever we do, we must be sure that the options we choose will help us to do what God wants us to.

Review/Application

Have the students answer the following questions individually or in small groups, and then discuss as a class.

1. How do you feel when you read Isaiah 46:3-4?
2. For what does Ephesians 1:4-5 say we were created? (Saints, without blemish to be children of God.)
3. In your personal life, do you think you are fulfilling the purpose for which God created you? If your answer is negative, what should you do to start doing that? If your answer is positive, thank God and ask him to help you to continue fulfilling his purpose for your life.

Talk about our purpose. End by praying and thanking God for the particular purpose He has created each one of us with.

24 Hours

Objective: That the students can understands that being a Christian means living our Christian lives through all 24 hours and not only when it suits us or when we go to church.

To memorize: "Therefore, I urge you, brothers and sisters, in view of God's mercy, to offer your bodies as a living sacrifice, holy and pleasing to God—this is your true and proper worship Do not conform to the pattern of this world, but be transformed by the renewing of your mind. Then you will be able to test and approve what God's will is— his good, pleasing and perfect will" (Romans 12:1-2).

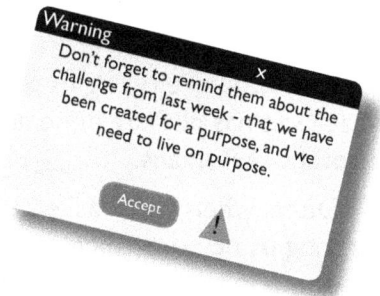

Warning
Don't forget to remind them about the challenge from last week - that we have been created for a purpose, and we need to live on purpose.

Accept

Connect | Navigate

Introductory activity (12-17 years)

- Materials: Balloons filled with air (approximately three times the number of students in your class).
- Instructions: Ask your students to form a circle (standing and looking in), leaving an empty space in the middle. Tell your students that the task is to keep the balloons that are entering the circle up in the air. Little by little, you can put more balloons into the circle and watch the students face the difficulty of keeping them all up in the air. Remind them that they can only use their hands for this exercise.

  When they have finished, guide your students in a small discussion about how they invested all their energy, attention, and perseverance in this task. Compare this process with being a full-time Christian, keeping up our devotion, attention and energy in being faithful to God. Encourage them in the process, letting them know it's worth it.

Introductory activity (18-23 years)

- Materials: Three plastic bags, three cups of flour, a little soil. Fill the three see-through plastic bags with a cup of flour in each one. One bag must also have two tablespoons of earth with the flour, another must have only a pinch of dirt mixed with the flour (you must make sure that it's enough so that the students notice that there is some earth in the flour, and it must be clearly less quantity than in the first pouch) and another bag must have pure flour.

- Instructions: At the beginning of the class, introduce the students to the idea of cooking a cake for a very special birthday, and ask them about the ingredients needed to make a cake. Tell them that today you brought the flour to class, and you can show them the plastic bag containing the flour with lots of dirt and the bag containing flour with a little bit of earth. You must make sure that no student has yet seen the bag with pure flour. Ask them which plastic bag they would prefer to make a cake with. Probably they will choose the one with the least earth. At that moment, you can remind them that as C.S Lewis says, "the devil does the same with us. He trusts that we prefer one sin over another one, choosing the 'best sin'. However, God expects us not to accept either sin and accept what He has for us, a true pure life" (adapted from Mere Christianity). Now is the time to show the bag of pure flour and tell them "This is the flour to make a good cake; it will make a delicious cake and won't hurt anybody."

Nowadays, people have many options to choose from: in fast food places, in computer stores and video games, as well as in clothing and shoes stores; not to mention the makeup boutiques! Even in the spiritual area we have many different options such as messages on the television, radio, variety of churches and preachers. For this reason, it's important that as young Christians you know what God's call is for your lives, and thus be able to concentrate on it without distractions. God's call to us covers our entire life, and he asks us to consecrate ourselves completely to Him, that is, to be full-time Christians!

Connect | Navigate

One of God's greatest desire is to have a personal and intimate relationship with us. When considering this fact, we could ask ourselves, "Where do we begin with such a large task?"

The truth is that God Himself put this process in motion, and He began to draw our attention and prepare everything so that we could have a relationship with Him. This truth reminds us that God is willing to do everything necessary to be able to have a relationship with us; in fact, He has already done it.

1. The mercies of God

In Romans 12:1, the apostle Paul begins by saying, "in view of the mercies of God." One meaning of the word "mercy" is "not giving someone the punishment he or she deserves." From the very beginning of this passage, Paul reminds us that we are sinners, and that the result of sin is death. We deserve death. However, God, because of his mercy, doesn't want us to die eternally, which we deserve, so he sent his son Jesus to die for our sins.

That is, before telling us or asking us for anything else, the apostle Paul clarifies how the situation was and what God has already done about it. The mercies of God are named more specifically in the eleven earlier chapters of Romans.

Often, when we're asked to do something, we say to ourselves, "Why should I obey?" In this case, God is asking us do something, and the reason why we should obey is because of all He has done for us by giving His only son to die on the cross for us. So now, God is asking us for something based on what He has already done for us. He speaks to us with words and also with his example. We can trust Him!

2. The call of God

In the first part of Romans 12:1, we read that Paul begs us, urges us, calls us to do something. The verb "urge" means earnestly or persistently persuading someone to do something. Paul's request is amazing. He asks us to "offer our bodies as a living sacrifice, holy and pleasing to God." Just as Jesus Christ presented Himself as a sacrifice for our salvation, now God asks us to give ourselves completely to Him. In the case of Jesus, the sacrifice involved physical death. For us, Paul explains that we must be a sacrifice, but a living one. At first glance, it seems somewhat contradictory since the sacrifices in Old Testament times required death and the shedding of blood. In the new covenant, the blood of Jesus was the sacrifice for all; God doesn't require our blood. God now wants us to sacrifice our own desires and plans and follow the desires, plans, and desires of His heart.

Secondly, the apostle Paul also asks us to present our bodies as a holy sacrifice. In the sacrifices of the Old Testament, it was of the utmost importance that the animal presented for the sacrifice had no defect, because God deserved the best. In the new covenant, God has sacrificed the best, his son Jesus (John 3:16). We must deliver today our best ... our holy lives ... for God's service.

Finally, as we read at the end of Romans 12:1, this kind of sacrifice will be truly pleasing to God.

In Romans 12:2, Paul explains to us that in order to be able to present our bodies as a living and holy sacrifice to God, we must fight against the patterns of this world. These worldly trends around us don't take God into consideration, much less talk about a life of "self-sacrifice." Paul wisely describes how the process should be. He says, "Do not conform to the pattern of this world, but be transformed by the renewing of your mind." In this verse, Paul warns us that in order to fulfill God's call for our lives, we'll have to "go against the grain" by being different from others, and being transformed (which literally means "changing our form"), in order to adopt God's way.

What would be some things that we should change so as not to conform to the world? Is our behavior always the same? How do we behave at school or university, or at work? If Jesus could be with us during 24 hours, would we always be the same? Do we wear the same clothes during the week that we wear when we go to church? Do we always use the same vocabulary and the same expressions?

(Allow students to respond, don't judge them, and let them express themselves. This will help them get to know themselves better and help them to consecrate themselves to the Lord. God will speak to them through the lesson.)

3. Our complete surrender to God

It's interesting to note that both verses mention words related to the mind or the intellect. Paul talks about our "true and proper worship" and the renewal of our "minds." It's important to understand that what we see and hear is very intimately related to what we think, and then with what we feel and do. That is why we must be careful with what we see, hear, read; what is filling our mind. God calls us to give everything to Him, everything we see and hear, in church, at home, at school, when we're with our friends and when we're alone. What do the following passages tell us about this subject: Ephesians 4:29; 5:1-8; Philippians 4:8; Colossians 3:16-17? (Distribute these passages among the students and have them explain how their passage applies to our lives.) God's call for our lives is radical. God calls us to be full-time Christians, that is, to be truly changed from the inside out.

Ralph Earle describes the Christian's call in three aspects. He says that the Christian call is a call to consecration – "offer your bodies," a call to separation – "do not conform" and, finally a calling to radical change – "be transformed" (Beacon Bible Commentary, Vol. viii, p. 258). A call of such magnitude encompasses everything we are, no matter where we are, who we're with, or what time it is. We must understand and appreciate that God's call on our lives is a full-time calling, and it requires all our effort.

4. God's Provision

After studying the wonderful call that God presents to our lives, we can feel weak and begin to think about how difficult it's and how hard it might be to be able to make this call our own. It's true, in our own strength, it's impossible to live for God full time! However, something we should always remember is that God never leaves us alone. He has made provisions to help us be able to answer this call. In Romans 12:2b, Paul says, "but be transformed by the renewing of your mind. Then you will be able to test and approve what God's will is—his good, pleasing and perfect will." The proof then, is in the doing. Accepting being a full-time Christian implies accepting God's will for our lives unconditionally. But to accept it, we must understand, as Paul asserts, that this will is pleasant and perfect. Each step taken according to the call or will of God reveals to us that God intends that we get closer to Him because He loves us. For this reason, we understand that God has made provisions, and that we're not alone along this journey.

Review/Application

Have each student answer the questions below.

a. Name some of God's mercies about your life. They can be from the past or the present.

b. What things have you put aside to respond affirmatively to God's call?

c. If you were to consecrate your life to God today, what things should you put before God?

Remember that it's good to think and consider the ways in which God is working in our lives. That won't only help us take breaths in times of trouble, but it will also help us have a correct attitude of thanksgiving to God. It's a privilege when God works in our lives! Don't overlook it! Tell him to continue working on you, and put before the Lord the things you mentioned in point c above.

Think of a camp with a group of young people. When they reach the campground, they decide to climb a mountain several hundred meters high during the heat of the afternoon. When they reach the top, everyone is very thirsty and needs to drink fresh water. Soon they realize that nobody remembered to bring bottles of water. How hard the trip back down is going to be! Later, when it's time to go to bed, the group begins to look for the tents, and they realize that they forgot to pack them, and that there are no blankets either! How long that cold night will be for all the campers!

The good news is that with God, we can rest easy. He has provided us with everything necessary for the journey of being full-time Christians. Remember that the Holy Spirit is at your side, to remind you, show you, and help you follow the "will of God, which is pleasant and perfect."

Talk to the class about God's call to be full-time Christians. Have them commit to analyzing themselves in each area of their lives during the next week. End the class with prayer.

Citizen of Heaven

Warning
Ask for some volunteers to share their experiences of being full-time Christians during the past week.
Accept

Objective: That the students realize that as Christians, we are citizens of heaven, and that we must store up treasures for heaven and not for earth.
To memorize: "For where your treasure is, there your heart will be also." (Matthew 6:21)

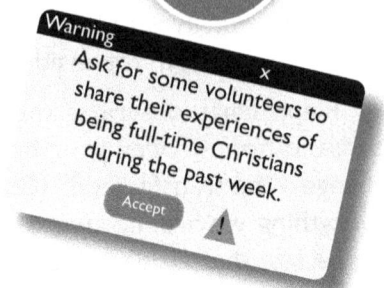

Connect | Navigate

Introductory activity (12-17 years)
- Instructions: Ask the students to list 10 essential things that make people happy. The teacher will write them down on the whiteboard or a large sheet of paper.

  Then you should try to put them in situations where they realize that the things they chose can be destroyed and are not eternal. For example, if they chose 'having a car' you could ask them: "What would happen if the car was stolen?" "Would that be the end of happiness?"

Introductory activity (18-23 years)
- Instructions: Draw a large pyramid on the whiteboard or on a large sheet of paper. Ask the students to fill in the pyramid priorities (for example, house, family, etc.). At the top, they need to put what is most important to them and then go down in priorities until they reach the bottom with the lowest ones. They can share and you can write them in the pyramid in the order they express.

At the beginning of the class, ask what things are high priority in their lives? Matthew says that what we consider to be our treasures is where we invest the most of our time and effort. Ask them if they have thought about this before.

Connect | Navigate

Do you have a piggybank (or something else you save money in) in your house? How often do you put money in it? I know of some people who at the end of the day, put all the change they have in their pockets into a piggy bank. It may not be a lot of money, but when you add something to it every day, it's amazing how quickly the account grows.

Whether we use a piggybank or a savings account in the bank, it's a good idea to have a savings plan for unexpected emergencies or when we want to do something special; but we must be careful that the treasure we're creating doesn't become the most important thing in our lives. Jesus warned us about this when he taught his followers about money. He told them that they shouldn't worry so much about collecting treasures on earth, but that they should concentrate on collecting treasures in heaven. Read Matthew 6:19-21.

1. Treasures on earth

Treasures on earth don't last.

Moths destroy our clothes. Among the material riches mentioned in the Bible, clothing is often mentioned. After losing the battle in Ai, Achan had to admit that he had disobeyed God by hiding "a beautiful robe from Babylonia, two hundred shekels of silver and a bar of gold weighing fifty shekels." He and his family were punished by being stoned to the death (Joshua 7:21-26).

After Naaman was healed by God through Elisha, the proposed gift was "a talent of silver and two sets of clothing" (2 Kings 5:22). God compares the enemies of Zion saying, "For the moth will eat them up like a garment; the worm will devour them like wool. But my righteousness will last forever, my salvation through all generations" (Isaiah 51:8). God is above all the transient things of this world. James writes about the rich: "Your wealth has rotted, and moths have eaten your clothes" (James 5:2).

So why bother having a lot of clothes if it's a treasure that will eventually rot or bore us.

- Rust corrupts (destroys). All metal products (cars, electrical appliances, machinery) eventually break down, wear out or become moldy, rusted and ruined. Today many people install security alarm systems in their cars, and the thieves have fun stealing these alarm systems to sell them (along with the car, or separately) to others. It's good to lock the car and it's good to keep our homes and businesses secure with good locks on the doors and bars on the windows. But is it really possible to keep all our earthly possessions secure?

- Rats, mice and termites. You can add a long list of other "destroyers" to what Jesus is saying: such as earthquakes, floods, fires, and storms which destroy properties that are worth millions. Rats and mice destroy the grain. Termites are a hundred times more destructive than fires and storms, because in a short time they destroy almost new wooden houses. It seems that for this insect, every species of wood is very tasty and they eat them with an insatiable appetite.

- Bankruptcies. Many institutions have fallen into bankruptcy. How many people lose their savings in this way! And of course, many companies go bankrupt, and the consequences are disastrous for the rich (they lose their investment) and for the poor (they lose their jobs). Fraud and corruption are a major cause of bankruptcies.

There are many other destructive forces apart from what we have mentioned here. The conclusion of all this is that the treasures of earth don't last; they are very transient. How intelligent is it, then, to dedicate our lives to accumulate things of such short duration? In addition, even if possessions are kept for a hundred years or more, "What good will it be for someone to gain the whole world, yet forfeit their soul? Or what can anyone give in exchange for their soul?" (Matthew 16:26).

When we die, what happens? We have to leave it all to someone else. The preacher in Ecclesiastes tell us, "So I hated life, because the work that is done under the sun was grievous to me. All of it's meaningless, a chasing after the wind. I hated all the things I had toiled for under the sun, because I must leave them to the one who comes after me. And who knows whether that person will be wise or foolish? Yet they will have control over all the fruit of my toil into which I have poured my effort and skill under the sun... For a person may labor with wisdom, knowledge and skill, and then they must leave all they own to another who has not toiled for it. This too is meaningless and a great misfortune. What do people get for all the toil and anxious striving with which they labor under the sun?" (2:17-22).

2. Treasures in heaven

Ask the students, "What are the treasures in heaven?" "How do we create treasures in heaven?" Jesus taught that one of the ways is to give money to the poor. Ask them, "Can you think of some other ways we can create treasures in heaven?" We can create treasures in heaven when we do things to help others. Things like visiting the sick, feeding the hungry, comforting those who are sad, praying for one another, working in a shelter for those who don't have a home, being friendly to someone who feels lonely, forgiving someone who has hurt us, asking for forgiveness when we have hurt someone, etc.

These things are what we can do here and they will be stored as the "treasures in heaven" of which Jesus spoke. They may not seem like much, but if we do something for someone every day, and we do it with love and without expecting something back, very soon our treasures will be adding up in heaven. In 2 Corinthians 5:1, we read, "For we know that if the earthly tent we live in is destroyed, we have a building from God, an eternal house in heaven, not built by human hands." The Bible teaches us that the things or treasures that we accumulate on earth can suffer deterioration or be completely ruined, while the treasures that we accumulate in heaven are eternal and indestructible.

We can know if we're working for earthly purposes or for heavenly ones by simply observing how we use time, what we talk about, how we use resources (to serve God (Proverbs 3:9) or to accumulate more things

(Luke 12:18), etc.)What encourage us ... the things of God ... or the business of accumulating more stuff? How many Christians are bored in church services, but when talking about their work and their businesses, they are very animated! (God is seeing this). Where are our hearts? It's not difficult to know. Paul says, "But if we have food and clothing, we'll be content with that" (1 Timothy 6:8).

How many of our fellow Christians are truly happy with only the basics of life? Paul wrote to Timothy, "For the love of money is a root of all kinds of evil. Some people, eager for money, have wandered from the faith and pierced themselves with many griefs" (1 Timothy 6:10). The love of money has motivated men and women to commit every sin in the world. This thought is alarming! We must wake up and become aware of the danger in wanting to accumulate material goods, simply for the sake of doing so.

3. Eternal Riches

What is the remedy? Paul advises, "Command those who are rich in this present world not to be arrogant nor to put their hope in wealth, which is so uncertain, but to put their hope in God, who richly provides us with everything for our enjoyment" (1 Timothy 6:17). Job said, "If I have put my trust in gold or said to pure gold, 'You are my security,' if I have rejoiced over my great wealth, the fortune my hands had gained ... then these also would be sins to be judged, for I would have been unfaithful to God on high" (Job 31:24-35 y 29). Psalm 52:7 says, "Here now is the man who didn't make God his stronghold but trusted in his great wealth and grew strong by destroying others!" Psalm 62:10b expresses, "though your riches increase, don't set your heart on them." When the rich young man went away sad because he had so much wealth, Jesus said, "Children, how hard it's to enter the kingdom of God!" (Mark 10:24b).

The heart is bound to its treasure, and it cannot be in two places. If the treasures are on earth, the heart will be here; If the treasures are in heaven, the heart will be there. We should be generous with our giving, (Luke 6:30, 34, 35, 38). Let's always remember that God says, "The silver is mine and the gold is mine" (Hag. 2:8). We should always serve God with "our" material goods, because they are really from Him (Proverbs 3:9, 1 Chronicles 29:14) and if God gives us in abundance, it's so that we can give in abundance to those who don't have much. We're only stewards! Never lose the blessing of sharing with someone who doesn't have much; giving is the best treasure we can have.

Review/Application

The students will be presented with the following biblical quotations. They need to read them and find in them the treasures that we can accumulate in heaven and what we need to do:

1. 1 Timothy 6:17,18 (hope in God, good deeds and giving)
2. Acts 2:44-45 (distribute according to the need of each one)
3. Acts 4:32-37 (share, give our testimony, distribute according to the needs)
4. 1 Corinthians 16:1-2 (give offerings)
5. Matthew 25:35-40 (give food, lodging, clothing and water to the needy, visit the sick and those in jail)
6. Galatians 2:10 (help the poor)
7. Galatians 6:10 (doing good)
8. James 1:27 (visit the orphans, widows and keep themselves without blemish)
9. Philippians 4:14-18 (give to those who are in tribulation)
10. 2 Corinthians 8:2-3 (be generous)

Ask them to commit themselves to looking at their actions during the week, and beginning to put away treasures in heaven.

Weak but Strong

Objective: That the students become aware that we all have strengths and weaknesses; and God can use them.

To memorize: "But he said to me, 'My grace is sufficient for you, for my power is made perfect in weakness.' Therefore, I will boast all the more gladly about my weaknesses, so that Christ's power may rest on me" (2 Cor. 12:9).

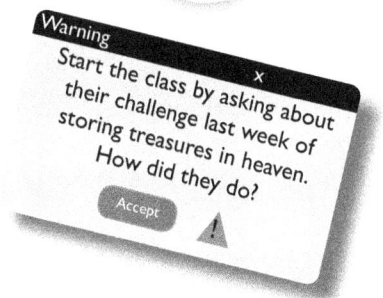

Warning
Start the class by asking about their challenge last week of storing treasures in heaven. How did they do?

Accept

Connect | Navigate

Introductory activity (12-17 years)

- Materials: A ball of yarn.
- Instructions: This activity consists of throwing the ball of yarn around to form a spider's web, but each participant to whom the wool is thrown must indicate a weakness that they possess (timid, too serious, silent, impulsive, etc.), and then throw the yarn ball to someone else. Everyone must participate.

  At the end, repeat the memory verse together several times while thinking about the weaknesses that have been expressed. "But he said to me, 'My grace is sufficient for you, for my power is made perfect in weakness.' Therefore, I will boast all the more gladly about my weaknesses, so that Christ's power may rest on me" (2 Corinthians 12:9).

Introductory activity (18-23 years)

- Instructions: Ask two volunteers to leave the room. Those who stay must each express a strength and a weakness. Then they will sit in a circle and choose a person to act out the strengths and weaknesses of the group. One of the volunteers will enter the classroom and guess what is the strength or weakness that is being acted out, and who it refers to. After the volunteer is successful, another person will act out a different weakness for the volunteer to guess. After he has guessed two or three, the other volunteer will enter and guess while others act out additional weaknesses.)

  Strengths are defense mechanisms to protect against enemies; to face or resist difficult situations. It's the courage to endure adversity and resist dangers. Some synonyms are: resistance, vigor, energy, firmness, character, rectitude, strength.

  Weakness is the lack of physical, mental, or emotional strength to withstand difficult situations. Some synonyms of weakness are: lacking strength, fragility, frailty.

Connect | Navigate

We're all different from one another because we have different personalities, characters, abilities and gifts. What is easy for some can be difficult for others. In a class room or in a family, there are differences not only because of gender (male or female), but because some are good at facing pressure and others are not; some are courageous in dangerous situations and others are not, but all are important.

Some people are strong at making friends easily, for example, while others are not and feel frustrated or disappointed and their self-esteem starts to suffer. We should be realists and not focus on ideals. When we're aware of our strengths and weaknesses, our self-esteem will be more balanced because we value what we know we do well and accept what we cannot do well.

1. Our strengths

Paul calls on the Corinthians to reflect on the position of those whom God has chosen to demonstrate the nature of God's wisdom. The elite of the first century, the leaders in the cities, were described as wise, well born and influential in politics. But God didn't call the elite to teach wisdom. He chose the foolish instead of the wise, the weak rather than the powerful, the no-bodies of secular society rather than those who considered themselves important. "For the foolishness of God is wiser than human wisdom, and the weakness of God is stronger than human strength. Brothers and sisters, think of what you were when you were called. Not many of you were wise by human standards; not many were influential; not many were of noble birth. But

God chose the foolish things of the world to shame the wise; God chose the weak things of the world to shame the strong. God chose the lowly things of this world and the despised things—and the things that are not—to nullify the things that are, so that no one may boast before him" (I Corinthians 1:25-29).

There is no place for boasting based on the secular standing or supposed strengths (v.29). All this is the work of divine favor. The only thing necessary is to be found in Christ Jesus, as Paul has emphasized in his words of thanks. "I always thank my God for you because of his grace given you in Christ Jesus. For in him you have been enriched in every way—with all kinds of speech and with all knowledge— God thus confirming our testimony about Christ among you. Therefore, you don't lack any spiritual gift as you eagerly wait for our Lord Jesus Christ to be revealed. He will also keep you firm to the end, so that you will be blameless on the day of our Lord Jesus Christ" (I Corinthians 1:4-8).

For Paul and for all believers in Christ, wisdom, justification, sanctification and redemption are found in Christ. The prophet Jeremiah said, "But let the one who boasts boast about this: that they have the understanding to know me, that I'm the Lord, who exercises kindness, justice and righteousness on earth, for in these I delight, declares the Lord" (Jeremiah 9:24). The prophet spoke against the elite of his time, since neither the wise, nor the powerful, nor the nobility should glory in themselves but only in the Lord.

A paradoxical text mentions the strength of the weak. God confuses and makes the strong fail. God is the efficient cause of our existence in Christ Jesus. This passage is not saying that it's bad to have strengths, or to be good at something. What this passage is saying is that we must not forget that our strength comes from God who is "…our refuge and strength, an ever-present help in trouble" (Psalm 46:1). The strengths we have must be taken care of, but we must not forget that it's in weaknesses that we find strength from on high.

2. Our weaknesses

In 2 Corinthians 12:1-5, Paul shares some special moments of revelation that he had been given by the Lord. However he ends by saying, "I won't boast about myself, except about my weaknesses." Paul in this passage is defending himself against the criticisms of the Corinthians. Although he had been "caught up to paradise and heard inexpressible things" (v.4), experiences which he could truly boast about, he prefers to underline his weakness.

He shares with them what must have been a physical weakness, his "thorn in the flesh" (v.8) which he had been given in order to keep him from becoming conceited (v.7).

Paul discovered that when he was weak, he was truly strong. In the midst of weakness and frustration, after pleading three times that God would take this 'thorn' away (v.9), he discovered the great promise of the Lord: "My grace is sufficient for you, for my power is made perfect in weakness" (v.19a). Paul concludes, "Therefore I will boast all the more gladly about my weaknesses, so that Christ's power may rest on me. That is why, for Christ's sake, I delight in weaknesses, in insults, in hardships, in persecutions, in difficulties. For when I'm weak, then I'm strong" (2 Corinthians 12:9b-10).

Paul's purpose in speaking in this way was to help his readers understand more about human weakness and the power of God. Weakness always has an implicit potential power. Our apparent weakness is just an opportunity for receiving His immense power. When we feel weak, we can trust more in the Lord and in what He can do through us by not trusting so much in our ability, but rather in what God can do through us. Although we may see ourselves as weak, the Lord's power is available to us.

Review/Application

Ask your students to answer the following questions:

1. Write down three of your weaknesses and three strengths.

2. How do you think your weaknesses can be turned into strengths?

Ask your students to choose one of their weaknesses and work to strengthen it this week, and then share their experience with the group during the next class.

Approval or disapproval

Objective: That the students will seeks the will of God and follow Him.
To memorize: "I desire to do your will, my God; your law is within my heart." (Psalm 40:8)

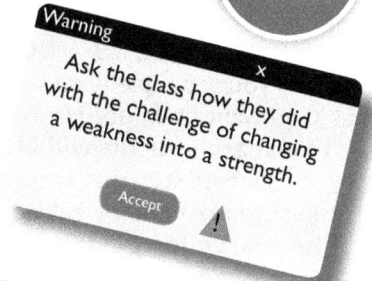

Warning
Ask the class how they did with the challenge of changing a weakness into a strength.
Accept

Connect | Navigate

Introductory activity (12-17 years)
- Instructions: Divide the class into two groups. Ask each group to read the story that is told in 1 Samuel 15:1-23. Afterward, ask them to adapt the story to a current situation. Conclude by saying that when we know clearly what God's will is, anything we do to change it because we think we can do it better, is foolishness and rebellion and can bring sad consequences for the rest of our lives.

Introductory activity (18-23 years)
- Instructions: Divide the class into two or three groups. Ask each group to make a list of the principles, strategies or general resources they have access to in order to know God's will for them. After a few minutes, allow the two groups to share their list. Then start the lesson and address the things they mentioned during the lesson.

We don't always find in the Bible the answers to our questions about what God wants us to do. Let's look at some examples:
- Should I accept this new job or not?
- I'm deeply attracted to someone and we both believe we're in love. Is it God's will that we start a special relationship?
- I have a very tense situation in the church with the pastor, a leader or another member. Should I look for another church?
- How does the Lord want me to prepare to serve Him better?
- I have non-Christian friends who I know and with whom I have a good time. Are these friendships advisable?

If we want to find out the will of God for a specific issue, we won't find what He wants by resorting to talismans or oracles, but rather through spiritual perception and sensitivity that we develop as we grow in our relationship with God.

Connect | Navigate

In the Christian life, God's approval or disapproval depends on our knowing God and fulfilling His will. Jesus is an example of this. He was totally obedient to the will of the Father, and he compared that obedience to God's will with something as vital as food for the body (John 4:32-34).

In the Bible, we find many examples of men and women who didn't follow the will of God and had to suffer sad consequences. But we also find David who, as the memory verse reminds us, desired to do God's will, and Paul who describes in Romans 12:2 the will of God as "pleasant and perfect."

1. God's will for all men
Throughout Scripture we find three things that are what God desires for everyone in the world:

a. **Salvation:**
God desires all men to be saved! In John 3:16, he says that he loved us so much that he sent his son so that everyone who believes in him may be saved. God's will, first of all, is that we have a relationship with him through his son, Jesus Christ. "This is good, and pleases God our Savior, who wants all people to be saved and to come to a knowledge of the truth" (1 Timothy 2:3-4).

b. **Sanctification:**
God desires for everyone to be holy! 1 Thessalonians 4:3a says, "It is God's will that you should be sanctified..." We'll achieve this through his Spirit that guides us to the truth. "But when he, the Spirit of truth, comes, he will guide you into all the truth" (John 16:13).

c. **Service and worship:**
God desires everyone to serve and worship Him. God has given us gifts and abilities to use in his service. God

always equips us to do what He calls us to do. God's ultimate purpose for all of us is for us to bring Him glory (1 Corinthians 10:31), and for the gospel and the kingdom of God to expand (Matthew 28:19-20 and Philippians 1:12). On the other hand, God also wants to worship him by living lives that honor his name. He wants to be worshiped in Spirit and in truth (John 4:24).

2. God's will for us

Many young people want to do God's will, but fail because they don't know what God's will is for their lives. What does God want us to do? How can we know his will? We'll look at some tools that we have at our disposal:

a. The search for his will in prayer

The first step that should be taken in seeking God's will is to pray every day and whenever there is an opportunity to ask God for guidance and direction to do His will (Ephesians 1:17-18, Colossians 1:9-10).

b. The search for guidance in the Word

Sometimes the Scripture is very clear, but sometimes it may not be. However, when we consider the whole message of the Bible, it will always give us light when making our decisions.

Before his conversion, Augustine was not living as he should. He writes in his Confessions that he heard a voice saying "Take and read." In that moment, he opened up his New Testament at random and his eyes were fixed on the text of Romans 13:12-14, which was the verse that led to his conversion.

There is another story that is told of a believer with a serious problem who tried to find the will of God by opening at random the New Testament, like Augustine did. The text that leaped up from the pages referred to the passage where it says that Judas went and hung himself (Matthew 27:5). Since he didn't like that verse, he closed the Bible and opened it again with his finger pointing to the passage that says "go and do the same" (Luke 10:37b). Dissatisfied, he tried one more time. The text he read on the third attempt was, "Whatever you are going to do, do it soon" (John 13:27). But seriously, we cannot trust the message taken from a single verse at random, or open the Word of God at random after having prayed. We must read the Scriptures every day, seeking the Lord to guide us and show us his will. We must take time and seek his direction with seriousness and patience (Philippians 2:16, Colossians 3:16a).

c. Search for the counsel of holy men and women that God has placed in our lives

Proverbs 1:5 says, "Let the wise listen and add to their learning, and let the discerning get guidance" (See too Proverbs 8:33). Many important wise decisions of various biblical characters were made because of wise counselors (Esther and Mordecai, Esther 2:19-20).

d. Trust that God will do his will in our lives

"Trust in the Lord with all your heart and lean not on your own understanding; in all your ways submit to him, and he will make your paths straight (Proverbs 3:5-6). Paul said to the Christians in Philippi, " Being confident of this, that he who began a good work in you will carry it on to completion until the day of Christ Jesus" (Phil. 1:6).

e. The Bible says there is a peace that comes when we please God with our lives

When we need to decide between two alternatives that we have been praying about, sometimes one of the options will give us more peace (Philippians 4:6-7). That option is probably God's will. "The fruit of that righteousness will be peace; its effect will be quietness and confidence forever" (Isaiah 32:17).

We can be sure of one thing: "The Lord makes firm the steps of the one who delights in him; though he may stumble, he won't fall, for the Lord upholds him with his hand" (Psalm 37:23-24).

Review/Application

Have each student answer the following questions, and then discuss as a class.
1. What are the questions you would like to ask God about his will for your life?
2. In what ways have you tried to find an answer?
3. What resources or strategies do you use to know the will of God for you?

The Treasure Hunt

Together with the students, discover through the Word of God what are the tools that are proposed for us "to know His will for our life."
- Colossians 1:9 (pray)
- Philippians 2:16 (the Word)
- Psalm 16:7 (advice)
- Proverbs 3:5 (trust)

If they have not yet memorized the Bible memory verse, take some time to do it. Have them answer the questions and commit to seek the will of God according to the Bible.

Let's dream

Warning
Ask your class how they have been doing during the week in their desire to find God's will in what they do.
Accept

Objective: To challenge students to have dreams and goals, but within God's purpose for their lives.
To memorize: "Take delight in the Lord, and he will give you the desires of your heart" (Psalm 37:4).

Connect | Navigate

Introductory activity (12-17 years)
- Materials: Prior to class, write on slips of paper the names of different professions and jobs (bricklayer, carpenter, doctor, teacher, etc.).
- Instructions: At the beginning of the class, stick a piece of paper on the back of each participant with adhesive tape, so that they cannot see what is written. The goal of each participant will be to discover which job is written on the piece of paper on their backs, by asking the others about the possible activities they do. The limitation is that participants can only respond with a 'yes' or a 'no.' For example: "Do I work in an open place?" "Yes."

   It will end when each participant discovers what is their profession or occupation. Then ask them how they feel about the job they have. Maybe someone is dreaming of being what their paper says.

Introductory activity (18-23 years)
- Materials: Prior to class, write the names of different professions and jobs on pieces of paper (bricklayer, carpenter, doctor, teacher, etc.).
- Instructions: At the beginning of the class, give each participant a piece of paper and ask them to think of some reason why they think their 'role' is the most important in society. Ask them to be as creative and fun as possible as they will share it with the rest of the class.

   This will be a good time to laugh and comment that there is not necessarily a profession or job more worthy or superior than others, as long as we allow God's purpose in our lives to be fulfilled.

Connect | Navigate

When we were children, dreams flooded our mind. We imagined ourselves doing amazing things, living in fantastic places, and above all things, happy for who we were and what we did. I'm sure that many of us are happy now and are satisfied, although perhaps our lives are a little different from what we imagined when we were children. However, we can also find people who live with dissatisfaction because they gave up their childhood or adolescent dreams, or even worse, they gave up their right to dream.

The Bible is clear in telling us that if we delight in the will of God and entrust our wishes and requests to Him, those dreams of our hearts will be granted. We find many examples throughout the Bible, such as Joseph, Daniel, David, Abraham, and the list could go on; but for purposes of this lesson, we'll take a look at the life of Nehemiah.

1. Don't cut your wings!
Nehemiah is a good example of what it means to have dreams and goals, and of course to work to achieve those goals. Although we don't find in the Bible that Nehemiah dreamed of rebuilding the walls and the city of Jerusalem as a child. However, we do find elements that make us see that in his heart he waited to return and do something to help his nation. It was precisely this desire that caused him to have a burden on his heart when he received the news about the condition of the city of Jerusalem (Nehemiah 1:3-5).

We don't know exactly how long Nehemiah had kept in his heart the dream of helping his country, but it's a fact that his heart was aligned with the will of God. For that reason, he interceded for his country, was patient and didn't lose hope.

Living according to God's will makes us 100% focused on what He wants. At the same time, that makes us give 100% to what we're doing at that moment, because we consider it as part of the plan to fulfill our dreams (although at times it seems that there is no relation). In addition, living in the center of God's will gives us the assurance that our dreams won't be selfish but, on the contrary, a blessing to other people.

In the case of Nehemiah, the fact that King Artaxerxes held him in high esteem (2:1,2,5) shows us that Nehemiah was a responsible worker, he was the king's cupbearer (2:1). This made it possible for Nehemiah to obtain a favorable response when he asked permission to travel to Jerusalem (2:4-6). In some way, being a cupbearer was key to Nehemiah's access to the king, and his responsible work allowed him to be ready when the time came to take the next step.

2. Fight for your dreams

There are many people who have given up their dreams because they considered them too difficult and have not wanted to pay the price. Some start the adventure and stay on the road, while others simply decide not to try. The reasons? There are many, but perhaps the most relevant are: lack of planning, little or no motivation, an environment that doesn't encourage their ability to dream, and most importantly, not putting their dreams into God's hands. The consequences? Dissatisfaction, bitterness, inconsistency in work, low self-esteem, relationship problems with people, etc.

God gave a dream to Nehemiah, but Nehemiah had to make an effort. The same happened to Joshua and his mission to take the people of Israel into the promised land (Joshua 1:9). Now in the case of rebuilding the city, Nehemiah knew it was worth it, even though he knew that the task wouldn't be easy.

The book of Nehemiah teaches what it means to fight for our dreams:

a. We must take risks. Nehemiah had to speak to the king of Persia and ask permission to travel to Jerusalem. Furthermore, Nehemiah didn't know exactly what the city was like, for he had never seen it. Neither did he know the people who lived in Jerusalem, or know their state of mind; but one thing was for sure, he trusted in the Lord!

b. It's necessary to leave our comfort zone. A 100-km journey starts with the first step. The road to rebuild the walls began with the decision to leave the palace and start the adventure. Many times, we plan and we get excited, visualizing the future, but what happens next? Are we willing to leave behind what hinders us and take with us what we need for the trip? Nehemiah did it (2:11-3:1).

c. We'll find opposition (Nehemiah 2:10; 4:1; 6:1-4). This is a fact. In every project, there will be people who will try to make the path difficult for us, but let's not lose sight of the fact that it's God who has promised to help us. So, if we cannot avoid finding people who will make life difficult for us, a good decision is to go around and look for people who will make life easy for us; that is, people who share our dreams, who believe in us, who listen to us, who love us, and who themselves have also fought or are fighting to achieve their dreams and know what it takes.

d. It requires sacrifice and preparation. It's important to take the initiative in every way. Nehemiah was very clear about that. If the walls were to be built, Nehemiah had to set the example, even with personal sacrifice. He decided not to receive a salary for the work he was doing (5:14-19). Many times, we'll have to deprive ourselves of something, either in a definitive way or only temporarily, because we know that there is something later on that is worthwhile. In the same way, it was necessary for Nehemiah to make a plan and prepare for the construction of the wall, including strategies in case of an enemy attack (4:9-13).

e. It will take time. Nehemiah knew that the great dream wouldn't be realized overnight. For that reason, he decided to be patient and to persevere. One tip about how to be patient and at the same time stay motivated is to start with small goals that help us see that we're moving forward...that we're making progress toward the final objective.

We can talk for hours about dreams and goals, but if we just get excited and then sit around avoiding making the right decisions, and forget to set and start moving towards the goals we want to meet, this can get in our way. First of all, we need to decide what we want to be tomorrow, giving our lives in complete obedience to God.

He not only puts dreams in our hearts, but also gives us gifts, skills, abilities, enthusiasm, people around us that motivate us, and many other things so that we can walk with faith, patience and determination in search of those dreams. What is the key? To delight in doing His will!

Review/Application

Have each student answer the following questions, and then discuss as a class.

Fight for your dreams

1. Name some characters in the Bible who fought for their dreams:
2. In what way would you describe Nehemiah?
3. What do you think was the reason why he fulfilled the goal of rebuilding the walls of Jerusalem?
4. When I was 5 years old, what I most wanted in life was to be:
5. Currently my goal in life is:
6. When comparing my dreams as a child and now as a young person, I realize that the main reasons why my dreams changed / were kept were:
7. People believe that I'm good at:
8. I think I'm good at:
9. I'm currently doing the following to achieve my dream:
10. When I reach my dream, I'm sure that I will be a blessing to other people in the following way:

Motivate your students to write down their biggest dream. Encourage them to make the commitment to ask for people's help in accomplish their dreams. Finish class by praying for the Lord to guide your students in reaching their God-given dreams.

Responsible pilgrims

Objective: To understand that although we're citizens of heaven and pilgrims on this earth, we have responsibilities while living on earth.
To memorize: "All these people were still living by faith when they died. They didn't receive the things promised; they only saw them and welcomed them from a distance, admitting that they were foreigners and strangers on earth" (Hebrews 11:13).

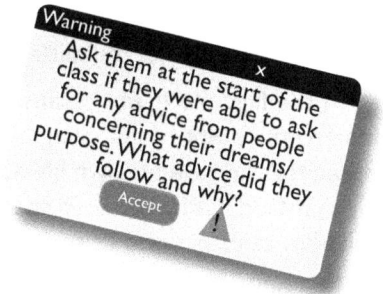

Warning
Ask them at the start of the class if they were able to ask for any advice from people concerning their dreams/purpose. What advice did they follow and why?
Accept

Connect | Navigate

Introductory activity (12-17 years)
- Instructions: Ask one of the students to leave the classroom. In the meantime, ask the rest of the young people to sit in a circle, and choose someone to start making a rhythm with their hands (he will be the "extra terrestrial"), either clapping or any other rhythm. The rest of the participants must always imitate the pace that the "extra terrestrial" performs. Periodically change the pace.

Once the instructions are clear, and the whole group is following the rhythm, the student who was outside will come in with the mission of discovering the extra terrestrial. They will have up to three opportunities to guess who it is. You can choose some else to go out of the room and do the activity again with a different "extra terrestrial" if you want.

At the end of the activity, comment that Christians often feel like "extra terrestrials" or aliens, sometimes even hiding to avoid being discovered. But in today's lesson, we'll see that as Christians, we belong to the kingdom of God and have a great responsibility to fulfill while we live in this world.

Introductory activity (18-23 years)
- Materials: Paper and a pencil for all participants
- Instructions: Ask the young people to make a list of five things that make them different or unique from each other and from other people. After about 2 or 3 minutes, ask them to share what they wrote.

The next task is to make a list of 3 characteristics that distinguish Christians from those who are not. Ask them to share what they wrote, and then make the transition to the topic, explaining that in some ways, being a Christian means that we're different than many people. Of course, this recognition is not with the intention of belittling someone, but recognizing that God has placed a special seal on us for a particular purpose that we must fulfill on earth.

Connect | Navigate

Ask them if they remember the movie E.T.? Maybe the very young don't even know that the movie existed. But if they don't know who the "extra terrestrial" (alien) or E.T. was, you could describe him as a strange being in a strange land. In the movie, E.T. spoke a different language, he had different rules and customs, simply ... he was not a part of the place where he had arrived.

1. Citizens of another Kingdom

Somehow, Christians are extraterrestrials in this world. This is what Jesus said in John 17:14-16, "they are in the world but they are not of the world." Also in Hebrews 11:13, we find another description about Christians; It says that we are foreigners or pilgrims in this world. For this reason, many of the principles and values of the world are foreign to us. As disciples of Christ, we're continually confronted with culture, because we have different values, different priorities, a different language, and many other things. We're citizens of another kingdom, and we hope to reach the place where we belong in order to fully enjoy the King who called us to be part of his kingdom.

It's not easy to live like a foreigner in school, with friends, at work, in the family. Many times, we can feel alone. In this situation, you can give them some advice. They shouldn't lose sight that they are not alone. God has promised to be with us at all times. He not only promised to be with us while we lift our hands and sing on Sunday morning. God also promised to be with us when our school friends invite us to do something we know is not according to God's will, and that sooner or later will hurt us. God promised to be with us when no one sees us, and the temptation to see, touch, wish, or do something wrong comes into our life and makes our faith wobble. Of course, God is also with us in the plans we want to make, giving us wisdom and encouraging us to keep going.

2. A great responsibility

It's clear that we're foreigners in this world and that our citizenship is in heaven. However, as we reach for our final destination, we have a great responsibility in this world. In this lesson, we'll read some passages that will show us at least 3 specific responsibilities.

In the first place, Philippians 2:3-12 exhorts us to follow Jesus' example. He loved the world that he created. He came to the point of humbling himself and becoming truly human. But he went further; he humbled himself to such a degree that he gave his own life as a ransom for us. We have the responsibility and privilege to love people in the same way that God has loved us; to share the news that Jesus came so that those who still don't enjoy a personal relationship with Him can start one as soon as possible.

Secondly, we have the responsibility to help other pilgrims like us who are passing through this world. Galatians 6:9-10 tells us to do good to everyone, but mostly to the family of faith. For those of us who are pilgrims, there is a lot of pressure to persuade us to renounce our citizenship in heaven. For this reason, it's vital that we love and support the other pilgrims, who together with us are convinced that it's worthwhile to follow Jesus. Let's befriend and encourage and help our brothers and sisters in Christ, so that together we can persevere in this adventure and joyfully reach the goal.

In third place, we're responsible for the rest of our king's creation. When God created us, he told us to take care of and govern the earth (Genesis 1:28). That was part of the role or responsibility of mankind when people were first created. As Christians, we know that this is the original design of God. We must take it on as part of our responsibility. The Bible tells us that creation itself, including nature and the animals that surround us, is crying out to be restored (Romans 8:21-23). As citizens of the kingdom of God, we have the mission to be good stewards of God's creation, caring for and conserving the environment that surrounds us.

3. To finish up

Being a Christian doesn't mean staying away from others. There is nothing wrong with getting along with friends from school and work. On the contrary, we must try to relate with all of them and help them with their needs. But we must never lose sight of the fact that we belong to the kingdom of God. He asks us to make wise decisions and live according to his will. He himself helps us make this possible, and through our example, we invite others to follow him and love him.

Review/Application

A. Citizens of another Kingdom

- Have you ever felt like an "extraterrestrial" compared to people who are not Christian? Why?
- Rewrite John 17:14 in your own words.

B. A great responsibility

- According to Philippians 2:3-11, what was Jesus' attitude? (I don't consider being equal to God as something to cling to ...)

List the main responsibilities that we have as citizens of the kingdom of God: (Philippians 2:3-11, Genesis 1:28, Galatians 6:9-10, etc.)

1. _____

2. _____

3. _____

4. _____

5. _____

Encourage them to write down real things that each student can do. Pray asking God for His help to carry out their commitments.

www.ingramcontent.com/pod-product-compliance
Lightning Source LLC
Chambersburg PA
CBHW081541040426
42448CB00015B/3178